Issues and Responses:
Land Use Planning

in Eastern and Southern Africa

Issues and Responses:
Land Use Planning

in Eastern and Southern Africa

Wayne Caldwell, editor

Published by:
Weaver Press, P O Box A1922, Avondale, Harare, Zimbabwe

Cover design: Danes Design, Harare

Layout: Fontline Electronic Publishing, Harare

Printed in Zimbabwe by Mazongororo Paper Converters.

ISBN 0 7974 2016 9

Environmental Capacity Enhancement Project

Environmental Roundtable Series

John Devlin, series editor

TABLE OF CONTENTS

SERIES PREFACE

The Environmental Capacity Enhancement Project (ECEP) has sought over the past four years to contribute to improved regional environmental management in Eastern and Southern Africa. The project has involved participants from 13 countries (Angola, Botswana, Kenya, Lesotho, Malawi, Mozambique, Namibia, South Africa, Swaziland, Tanzania, Uganda, Zambia, Zimbabwe) and has concentrated upon six environmental areas: eco-tourism, ecological agriculture, land use planning, small scale mining, waste management and watershed management. The project has not sought to develop a narrow set of regional environmental experts. Rather it has sought to bring together development practitioners, activists, analysts, researchers and policy-makers so that all could become familiar with the policy options and technology choices available to respond to the complex range of environmental problems shared across the region.

The regional training courses, the collaborative research projects, and the professional exchanges supported by ECEP have created multistakeholder venues where representatives from governmental and non-governmental institutions, the private sector and academic institutions could build linkages for mutual support and on-going information exchange. During its four years of operation ECEP has graduated 180 from its training courses and funded 53 collaborative research projects involving 125 principal researchers. It has also supported 35 professional enhancement attachments of which 27 have involved exchanges between different countries. Having brought environmental practitioners together ECEP then sought to establish the conditions for continued networking among them so that the regional and multistakeholder perspective would be maintained over the long term. Six networks of researchers and practitioners have been created. And all have had an opportunity to meet during the networking conference held in Harare from May 13-15, 1998 to exchange papers, discuss their future organizational efforts and evaluate what had been achieved to date.

The final outputs of the project are the five volumes of collected papers comprising the Environmental Roundtable Series. These five volumes represent the best of documents and reports that have been produced by ECEP participants. They will serve not only as valuable collections for environmental policy makers, environmental educators and environmental activists but also as catalysts for future initiatives dedicated to building an effective environmental management culture in the region. The preparation of this series has been made possible by two important groups. First, the Canadian International Development Agency, which has generously funded ECEP over the past four years. Second, the many ECEP participants who have generously donated their time and energy to making this project a success. Their contributions are acknowledged with thanks.

Dr. R.J. McLaughlin
Dean, Ontario Agricultural College, University of Guelph, Canada
March 1999

PREFACE

All of the papers presented in this book are products of the Environmental Capacity Enhancement Project. Most of the papers are derived from research reports, others were presented at training sessions and still others reflect the experiences gained by practitioners involved in internship and outreach. This book presents the work of these individuals with the hope that others will benefit from their experience, thereby continuing ECEP's goal of contributing to capacity development in Southern Africa.

There will undoubtedly be debate concerning the selection of papers included in this volume. The diversity of topics is, however, reflective of the diversity of issues associated with land use (for example, agriculture, mining and urban development) and the depth and breadth of issues and approaches associated with planning (for example, public participation, indigenous knowledge and the role of science and technology). There is a central theme, however, of presenting articles that, in their totality, encourage an integrated approach to planning which considers the relationship between people and all aspects of their environment. Beyond this, the book stresses an approach to planning which is practical and fundamentally linked to the needs and abilities of people within their communities, through community involvement and participation. The book has also attempted to present a range of articles that draw from experiences in different countries and different geographic settings (such as rural and urban), in the hope of allowing broad regional application.

This book reflects the efforts of many people who care about issues of land use, the environment and planning. Thanks are extended to the authors who contributed the papers that have made this volume possible. Through their work and willingness to document their experiences, there is an opportunity for many to learn. Stephanie Wells, copy editor, and Irene Staunton, who coordinated the publication of this book in Zimbabwe, are thanked for the expertise they provided. Kathy MacLean, of the ECEP office at the University of Guelph, was helpful in the production of this publication. Finally, a special note of appreciation is reserved for John Wall, whose editing skills helped to make this book a reality.

Wayne Caldwell

CONTRIBUTORS

William Balu-Tabaro
    Engineer
    Department of Geological Survey & Mines
    Entebbe, Uganda

Hillary Bakamwesiga
    Lecturer, Institute of Environment and Natural Resources
    Makerere University
    Kampala, Uganda

Urgessa Biru
    Ph.D. Student (since completed)
    Department of Agricultural Economics and Business, University of Guelph
    Guelph, Canada

Wayne Caldwell
    Associate Professor, School of Rural Planning and Development
    University of Guelph
    Guelph, Canada
  and Senior Planner and Deputy Director
    County of Huron Planning and Development Department
    Goderich, Canada

Albert Chipeleme
    Lecturer, Department of Soil Science
    University of Zambia
    Lusaka, Zambia

Lucy Chipeta
    Lecturer, Department of Geography
    Chancellor College, University of Malawi
    Zomba, Malawi

Andrea Hammel
    B.A. Student (since completed)
    Departments of Sociology and Anthropology, University of Guelph
    Guelph, Canada

Kevin Head
    M. Sc. Student (since completed)
    School of Rural Planning and Development, University of Guelph
    Guelph, Canada
George Kakande
    Senior Environmental Officer
    Kiziranfumbi Youth Environmental Protection Organization
    Kampala, Uganda
Joseph Kakooza
    Geologist
    Tank Hill Quarry Ltd.
    Kampala, Uganda
Wilfred Monte Kaliisa
    Research Associate, Institute of Social Research
    Makerere University
    Kampala, Uganda
Martin Kitilla
    Coordinator for Management of Air Quality and Urban Transportation
    Sustainable Dar es Salaam Project
    Dar es Salaam, Tanzania
Shaibu Mapila
    Deputy Director of Fisheries
    Department of Fisheries
    Lilongwe, Malawi
Isaac Mapaure
    Lecturer, Department of Biological Sciences
    University of Zimbabwe
    Harare, Zimbabwe
Lindah Mhlanga
    Research Fellow, University Lake Kariba Research Station
    University of Zimbabwe
    Kariba, Zimbabwe

Duncan Miller
        Chief Research Officer, Department of Archaeology
        University of Cape Town
        Cape Town, South Africa

Pauline Mitchell
        Research Assistant, Department of Archaeology
        University of Cape Town
        Cape Town, South Africa

Jean Munro
        M. Sc. Student (since completed)
        School of Rural Planning and Development, University of Guelph
        Guelph, Canada

Mutiyenkhu Munyenyembe
        Lecturer, Department of Biology
        Chancellor College, University of Malawi
        Zomba, Malawi

Eugene Muramira
        Environmental Economist
        Environmental Economics Association of Uganda
        Kampala, Uganda

Dezi Ngambeki
        Agricultural Economist
        AIMS Agribusiness Enterprises
        Kampala, Uganda

Susan Pfeiffer
        Associate Professor, Department of Human Biology and Nutritional
        Sciences
        University of Guelph
        Guelph, Canada

Estone Sambo
        Associate Professor, Department of Biology
        Chancellor College, University of Malawi
        Zomba, Malawi

Alex Tindimubona
        Chairman
        African Science and Technology Exchange (ASTEX)
        Kampala, Uganda

Nikolaas J. van der Merwe
        Professor, Department of Archaeology
        University of Cape Town
        Cape Town, South Africa

Peter van Straaten
        Adjunct Professor, Department of Land Resource Science
        University of Guelph
        Guelph, Canada

Christopher White
        B.Sc. Student (since completed)
        Department of Geography, University of Guelph
        Guelph, Canada

Lovemore Zinyama
        Professor, Department of Geography
        University of Zimbabwe
        Harare, Zimbabwe

Chapter 1

ISSUES AND RESPONSE:

LAND USE AND PLANNING IN EASTERN AND SOUTHERN AFRICA

AN INTRODUCTION

by Wayne Caldwell

The future of many countries of Southern and Eastern Africa is inextricably linked to their ability to anticipate, manage and react to change. This change reflects increasingly difficult economic circumstances and ever-threatening environmental constraints. It has implications ranging from national and regional levels to the community and individual family. It includes fundamental change in systems of government and governance. It reflects a reliance on a resource-based economy, with natural resource products accounting for two-thirds of exports and four out of five jobs. Change in these countries is influenced by the combination of high population growth rates and rapid urbanization. Related to these are the issues of water quality and quantity and the inadequate treatment of human waste. These issues, along with many others, transcend both rural and urban boundaries and place great demands on natural resources and their allocation.

The complexity, diversity and magnitude of many of these issues make it difficult for planning and management systems to respond. There is often inadequate coordination of efforts, a relative absence of policy and a shortage of expertise, personnel, and resources. Despite this, however, governments, NGOs and community groups attempt to develop and implement policy, programs and actions that will assist countries, regions and communities in coping with change and preparing for the future. Planning initiatives are particularly relevant in the whole area of land, land use and resource utilization.

Planning practice varies throughout the world. In some contexts, it implies the physical planning of infrastructure, including the efficient and adequate provision of water, sewers and roads. In other contexts, it may involve the

1

protection and enhancement of a sensitive ecosystem or minimizing the occupational and environmental hazards associated with small-scale mining. This book has intentionally adopted a broad definition of planning, under which a variety of tools and approaches are used to understand and influence the processes of change affecting a community. Within this book, these planning tools and approaches are presented in the context of the relationship between people and the land they occupy, the resources they use, and the environment in which they live.

Planning must involve the public and affected communities in decision making. This can help to develop consensus and motivate community action. There is a component of public education involved in helping communities understand and appreciate issues. There is also a component of making those who work with and assist communities aware of the wealth of knowledge and imagination waiting to be tapped within each community. In some instances, the planner's role is not to develop and prescribe solutions, but to help the community understand the changes that are occurring and to help them discover and implement solutions by drawing upon their own indigenous knowledge.

It is essential to understand the basic connection between the people of Eastern and Southern Africa and the land they occupy. The approaches to the management of this relationship are central to this book.

Part I includes three chapters that focus on the issues of land tenure and reform. Zinyama provides an overview of the relationship between land use, land reform and the environment. As Zinyama points out, a change in the distribution of land ownership, or people's rights to use land, frequently results in major changes in patterns of land use, agricultural productivity, and settlement patterns. Chipeta focuses on land management and tenure in Malawi and reviews the various tools of public and private land management. Biru builds upon the issues outlined by Zinyama and Chipeta and reviews the relationship between land tenure and the management of natural resources.

Part II stresses certain components of an appropriate planning approach. The three chapters presented here consider the importance of public participation, biophysical inventories and the local community's role in identifying issues and planning for its own future. Munro stresses the importance of public participation in planning processes. Her focus is on drama as a means to communicate and inform, an approach to planning that is innovative and helps reinforce the need to carefully select an appropriate approach to public participation. Mhlanga and

Mapaure consider the role of vegetation surveys in land use planning. Their detailed methodology and results help to illustrate both the approach to vegetation surveys and their utility for planning. Sambo and Munyenyembe stress the relevance of the local community in contributing to natural resource management. The knowledge which exists within a local community is essential in helping to appraise and identify issues and can be instrumental in the development of appropriate planning responses.

A series of detailed case studies comprise Part III of the book. These are intended to provide an appreciation of different issues, different contexts and different planning methodologies. Kitilla provides a detailed review of strategic development planning for the city of Dar es Salaam. This article reviews some of the failures of traditional urban planning and describes an innovative approach to urban planning, drawing upon the input of the city's residents. Mapila's article stresses the importance of local resident involvement in the context of sustainable development, coastal zone management and fisheries planning. The thrust of Biru's second article is agriculture as a key component of land use and Malawi's economy. An appreciation of the history of agriculture and related land use policy is essential to an understanding of many of the issues that complicate land use and reform in Africa. Chipeleme's article highlights the challenges faced by the residents of Gwembe Valley, whose traditional lands were flooded when a hydro-electric dam was constructed. This chapter examines the people's agricultural adaptations, as well as the ways alternative energy sources could improve their system of ecological agriculture. The next three chapters examine the mining industry. Although a small component of total land use, mining is very important from the perspective of employment and the economy. It does, however, have significant environmental implications. Kaliisa, Kakooza, Kakande, Muramira and Bakamwesiga review a number of issues related to small-scale mining in Uganda. Miller, Hammel, White, Pfeiffer, van der Merwe and Mitchell use several case studies to provide insight into the informal mining sector. Their conclusions include a belief that solutions to the problems associated with artisanal mining will come from a holistic approach that must be built on the cooperation of government, NGOs, international mining companies and the artisanal miners themselves. Van Straaten provides further insight into some of the environmental issues associated with small-scale miners, corresponding risks to their health, and potential measures to reduce human health exposure and environmental contamination. Tindimubona, in his review of the

3

diffusion of science and technology for resource management, provides an interesting focus on opportunities for soil conservation and water management, agroforestry and re-afforestation, sustainable agriculture and animal husbandry. The final chapter also considers the relationship between agriculture and the environment, but in a very different context. Head's approach to planning for drought in Africa is an interesting connection between broad climatic trends at the national or regional level and working with a community to implement an appropriate response to drought.

Chapter 2

LAND REFORM AND LAND USE IN AFRICA

by Lovemore Zinyama

INTRODUCTION

Land reform affects the very core of a people's relationship with the environment. A change in the distribution of land ownership or in people's rights to use land frequently results in major changes in patterns of land use, agricultural productivity, and in settlement patterns.

In most African countries, a large majority of the population depends, either directly or indirectly, on the land for their sustenance. At the same time, the majority of these agriculture-dependent people are living in abject poverty. One of the factors that affects rural living standards is the institutional framework of agricultural production, that is the agrarian structure. A central issue of agrarian structure is land tenure.

Other components of this agrarian structure include the provision of agricultural credit, extension services, transport and marketing facilities. Moreover, in many societies land ownership also defines one's social standing in the community. It carries with it control over rural labour, control over local and sometimes even national political and economic institutions and leadership, access to capital and other scarce resources — resulting in the polarization of wealth and power (West, 1986). It is therefore not surprising that governments in developing countries often give land reform such high priority among measures aimed at promoting economic development and social justice.

This chapter will review the nature of land reform and discuss situations in which it has succeeded and in which it has failed. It will then examine in some detail the cases of land reform in Kenya and Zimbabwe, illustrating the complexities of land tenure in Africa.

DEFINITION AND TYPES OF LAND REFORM

The term land reform remains almost as confusing today as it was some 30-40 years ago during the peak of major government-initiated reform programmes in several countries of the world, most notably in Latin America and Asia. Writing in the early 1970s, both Hirsch (1972) and King (1971) have provided a useful framework for understanding the meaning of land reform and clarified some of the confusion surrounding the concept. King starts by distinguishing between the terms "land reform" and "agrarian reform", as the two are often used interchangeably, but erroneously. According to King, land reform means the redistribution of land for the benefit of the landless, tenant farmers and other small cultivators. He further noted that early experience (e.g. in post-revolution USSR) showed that such land redistribution on its own often leads to drastic falls in agricultural production. There is usually a strong need for complementary services such as the provision of research and extension services, credit facilities and marketing services. The provision of such services goes beyond mere land redistribution. This wider perspective is what King termed agrarian reform.

Agrarian reform may be considered as any reform of the agrarian structure (Warriner, 1957). It may be so broad as to embrace all land tenure reforms together with the institutional framework of agriculture (marketing, extension, credit, settlement and land use changes), or it may be as narrow as just one of these changes. In so far as agrarian reform seeks to raise the living standards of the landless poor and small farmers, it is therefore both an agricultural policy and a social policy (Warriner, 1957). The redistribution of land implies a major social and political change; the complementary measures associated with agrarian reform represent changes in the agricultural policy of the government.

On the other hand, "land reform" means land tenure reform only – that is an improvement in ownership rights and in the way land is held. Land reform involves changing and restructuring the economic, legal and political arrangements governing the ownership and management of agricultural land. In predominantly farming societies, land dominates as the main source of wealth and power, and it reflects the social, economic and political status of those who have rights to land. A restructuring of the land tenure arrangements results in direct changes in the social class and the political and economic power structure of the society (La-Anyane, 1985). A key principle guiding land reform is that the peasants who are the actual cultivators of the land should have greater security of ownership of that land.

Generally, land reform seeks to achieve greater equity and social justice in the ownership of land. It serves both to redistribute land and to achieve increased productivity, the latter being realized through changes in the structure of supporting services (marketing, research and extension, credit, input supply). Land reform or redistribution alone will not bring about lasting benefits and a better quality of life for the people; it must be accompanied by increases in both land and labour productivity. There is now ample evidence that land productivity is much higher on small farms than on large estates (Kinsey and Binswanger, 1993).

From the above, it becomes clear that land tenure reform is of two types:

▶ **land redistribution**, which involves the breaking-up or consolidation of existing holdings (i.e. changes in the scale of ownership); and

▶ **tenancy reform**, which concerns improvement in tenancy contracts (e.g. rent reduction, increasing security of tenure), but without a change in the scale of ownership.

In the case of land redistribution, the unit of production is seen as the problem to be resolved, either through expropriation from those with too much land and its transfer to those with little or no land and therefore likely to involve land settlement as well; or it may be done following the consolidation of fragmented holdings and subsequent re-allocation of the same land to the same owner-occupiers, where land fragmentation is the issue.

Tenancy reform has been most common in Asia – for example, in Burma, Malaysia, and the Philippines – as these countries sought to address tensions between landlords and tenants during the early post-independence years. In much of Africa, it is the first type – land redistribution – which has been the focus of government policies since independence, as the post-colonial regimes sought to redress some of the socio-economic inequities inherited from the colonial period. It is this aspect of land reform – i.e. land redistribution – which the rest of this chapter will focus on.

Land reform that includes redistribution of land ownership usually involves the expropriation of land from large landowners and its redistribution to landless and semi-landless small farmers. After redistribution, new tenure arrangements may take the form of individually held small family farms (as in Kenya), or the land may be held communally or collectively as in the case of Tanzania's *ujamaa* or Algeria's socialist villagization programmes (Coulson, 1978; Hirst, 1978; Sutton, 1984).

In some early land redistribution programmes, especially where this followed a period of political unrest against the propertied class, expropriation of land from

7

the large landowners was total and without compensation, as was the case with some of the revolutionary reform programmes in South America (as in Bolivia and Chile). But more commonly, governments may put a ceiling on the amount of land large landowners can own. The excess above this limit is expropriated, some compensation paid, and the land made available for redistribution to the landless and small farmers. Improvements in land ownership and social equity using these principles are well illustrated in the cases of Japan and Taiwan in the 1950s and 1960s. Whereas before the reforms only 54% of Japan's land was owner-operated, after the reforms the figure had risen to 92%; the respective figures for Taiwan are 60% before, rising to 85% after the reforms (La-Anyane, 1985).

Asia, South America and Africa are full of examples of land reform programmes carried out over the past half century. Few have succeeded and many have failed. One crucial, but often under-emphasized, ingredient for success is the affected parties' acceptance of the need for the land reform and clarification of the modalities for implementation of the reform programme. These different stakeholders include:

- **the government** as the implementer of reform, which should define its targets and allocate resources accordingly;
- **the large landholders**, who stand to lose some or all their lands under the reforms;
- **and the beneficiary small farmers**, who should realize they carry a large responsibility to maintain and improve productivity on their newly acquired land.

MOTIVES AND OBJECTIVES OF LAND REFORM

Most land reform has occurred where there were gross inequalities of wealth and power, especially in the agricultural sector. Often, these inequalities extend into other sectors and the realm of political power. Proposals for land reform are based on the premise that such inequalities are inimical to development. No reform can succeed, however, unless its objectives are clearly spelt out, understood and accepted by both the implementing agency and the people concerned.

Different countries may have different objectives for land reform. While the objectives may be inter-related and complementary, sometimes achieving one objective retards or conflicts with another. The principal conflict usually lies between achieving social equity, while striving for economic and efficient utilization of land and other resources. Frequently, it has proved difficult for governments to marry these two objectives, creating awkward dilemmas for individual households as well as the state. Dividing expropriated large farms into numerous small plots may result in decreased household food production, marketable surpluses and export earnings for the government. On the other hand, if a government does not implement land reform, it may fail to raise the standard of living of many of its people and may, in the long run, create political instability.

The majority of land reform programmes around the world are governed by one or more of three frequently incompatible and contradictory motives: political, social and economic (Hirsch, 1972; King, 1971).

The political motive is usually underplayed in government statements on land reform, but is often a key factor, appealing to the landless peasantry or disempowering landowners perceived as a threat to the ruling class. There are numerous examples of governments using land reform – or the promise or threat of reform – to retain political power.

The social equity motive is often closely linked to the political motive – the government promises to give land to the landless peasants in return for political support.

Even without political motivation, situations of acute landlessness can provide sufficient justification for land reform, arising from inequality, poverty and the resulting social and political tensions. As noted by King with respect to Latin America, poverty is very much a moral and human rights issue. There, the condition of the mass of the peasantry was so miserable that the first objective of any land reform had to be a social one (King, 1971).

The economic motive on its own rests on the premise that land reform will result in greater agricultural production, increased marketable surpluses for domestic consumption and/or export, and higher rural household incomes. The relative weight government gives the socio-political and economic motives can have a large influence on the success or failure of the land reform programme.

LAND REFORM AND LAND USE IN AFRICA

In many countries of Eastern and Southern Africa, traditional or pre-colonial land tenure systems were based on communal claims to land. Title to land was introduced during the colonial period when vast areas were alienated for European settlement – these were usually the ecologically more favourable lands. On the other hand, the indigenous African people were forced to cultivate small plots in regions of marginal agricultural potential. Over time, the so-called native reserves became highly over-populated, resulting in serious problems of environmental degradation, increasing landlessness, and widespread rural poverty (for Zimbabwe, see Whitlow and Zinyama, 1988; Zinyama and Whitlow, 1986).

However, it should be noted that inequitable distribution of land was not confined to former European colonies alone. In Ethiopia, for instance, a feudal landlord-tenant system determined who held land. Before the overthrow of the emperor and the 1975 reforms, some 70% of the arable land in that country was owned by the church, the landed gentry (many of them as absentee landlords), and the central government. An estimated 50% of the farmers were tenants who worked under the most insecure tenurial arrangements which allowed the landlord to claim a large share of whatever they produced.

In an effort to redress these imbalances and the attendant problems of landlessness and overcrowding, the new governments in several African countries embarked on some type of land reform soon after attaining political independence. In some cases, the reforms entailed the abolition of both individual freehold as well as traditional communal title to land, so that henceforth all land was vested in the head of state, with usufruct rights for the cultivators based on long leases (e.g. Ethiopia, Nigeria and Zambia) (Arntzen et al., 1986; Williams, 1992).

The reasons governments gave for the transfer of land rights to the state included an attempt to discourage absentee landlordism, to ensure that all land was efficiently and beneficially occupied and developed, to regulate and improve the process of land use planning, to prevent land speculation and ensure equity in land ownership. However, these motives have been questioned as signifying one element of a broader trend, during the 1970s and 1980s, towards expanding the African state at the expense of other forms of societal authority (e.g. traditional leaders), as part of the struggle for control between the "state" and "civic society" (Williams, 1992).

In other cases, especially where there had been extensive alienation of land for European settlement during the colonial period, the new governments embarked on actual land redistribution. This would involve the acquisition and break-up of former large estates or plantations and their re-allocation for settlement by small farmers (e.g. Kenya, Namibia and Zimbabwe). In Mozambique and Tanzania, the governments also experimented for awhile with socialist ownership and land use.

It is important to note that the beneficiaries of land reform, especially if it involves the break-up of large estates, frequently need to be resettled on or close to their newly acquired lands. Furthermore, the various input supply agencies and service providers may require a nucleated form of settlement close by or within the resettlement land, thereby leading to the development of service centres where none may have existed previously. Thus land redistribution is frequently followed by changes, not only in land ownership and land use, but also in the patterns of settlement.

In the following paragraphs, the varied experiences with land reform in two selected countries from Eastern and Southern Africa are discussed, with particular attention to the impacts of reform on land use, including settlement patterns and the environment. Land reform in Kenya and Zimbabwe differs in several important respects:

▶ the scale of the redistributed land and population resettlement programmes;
▶ the political ideologies that underpinned the programmes;
▶ the strategies adopted by the respective governments to implement the reforms;
▶ the amounts of resources available for the reform programmes;
▶ the resultant changes in patterns of settlement and land use patterns.

Kenya

Land reform in Kenya dates back to the mid-1950s, the time of the Mau Mau uprising. The unrest was most fierce in the Kikuyu reserves, where the people had been resettled after being displaced from their former lands in the Kenya Highlands to make way for European settlement. A major grievance among the Kikuyu was land hunger, especially as the large European-owned farms nearby appeared under-utilized.

The colonial government's response to the state of war was to embark on a major development programme within the Kikuyu reserves, known as the Swynnerton Plan, starting in 1956. The aims of this programme were:

▶ to re-organize Kikuyu agriculture;
▶ to consolidate land holdings that had become too fragmented over time due to over-population;
▶ to redistribute the consolidated land;
▶ to introduce individual ownership of land in place of the traditional communal tenure system.

11

The colonial administration hoped that individual or freehold tenure would bring about greater entrepreneurship among African agriculturalists, increased investment and increased productivity. Increased output would also lead to the creation of more rural on-farm and off-farm employment. Each farmer's smallholding was clearly demarcated and registered, and the land could be used as collateral for agricultural or other loan requirements. The consolidated holdings were planned to take full advantage of the varied agro-ecological conditions in the area, with farms arranged in such a manner that they ran from the interfluves towards the valley floors.

After independence, the colonial programmes of land consolidation and redistribution, survey and registration of individual rights to land were continued and extended to other parts of the country. Most significantly, this included the break-up and redistribution of former European plantations in the Kenya Highlands to smallholder farmers under the Million Acre Settlement Scheme which was started in 1962. The government objectives were clearly mainly socio-political, that is to meet the land needs of the people, thereby contributing to political stability, while at the same time raising rural incomes and creating employment opportunities (Clayton, 1978). By 1969, when the Million Acre Settlement Scheme was completed, some 35,400 smallholder families had been resettled on 492,500 hectares, with average farm sizes ranging between 10 and 15 hectares. (This did not include government-assisted land transfers and private sales of large farms intact from European farmers to African owners).

Once the Million Acre Settlement Scheme was completed, the programme of land consolidation, survey and registration was extended to other regions of the country, in areas previously settled by Europeans and in the traditional African reserves. Later there were some minor variations to suit the social and ecological conditions of the drier northern and eastern provinces of the country, which are dependent on livestock rather than crop production. Okoth-Ogendo (1986) estimated that by the late 1970s, over 70% of all land outside the arid zones had been privatized.

A lot has been written about the Kenyan model of land reform, notably the change from traditional communal holdings to individual tenure and its socio-economic impacts. Most commentators have painted a gloomy picture of its impacts. While acknowledging that food and cash crop production in the smallholder sector has generally improved, they have raised a number of issues which, in one way or another, are attributable to the introduction of private ownership of land and its impact on the long-term distribution of land, employment and rural incomes (Haugerud, 1983; Hazlewood, 1985).

Among these issues are problems of increasing rural indebtedness as farmers failed to pay back loans they had obtained using their privatized farms as collateral, problems caused by speculative trading in land, illegal subdivisions of registered land, and absentee landlordism (Okoth-Ogendo, 1986).

Privatization of land was based on the premise that freehold tenure would encourage sustainable land and water resource utilization, as well as greater output which would create more rural employment, either directly on the farms or indirectly in agro-based downstream processing industries. It has been argued that, instead, agricultural employment has not expanded, as most farmers continue to rely on family labour. Furthermore, growing landlessness and rural unemployment have caused widespread migration to urban areas, especially to Nairobi, compounding the problems facing the Kenyan capital today. Thus, Okoth-Ogendo (1986, p.79) contends that whatever contribution land tenure reform may have made to economic growth in Kenya, the gains have been "completely offset by the emergence of economic disparities, redistribution of political power, and the disequilibration of socio-cultural institutions that have occurred in rural society as a consequence of reform".

However, a recent study by researchers from the Overseas Development Institute, London, and the University of Nairobi provides a more encouraging picture. Among other things, the researchers have argued that privatization of land among smallholders, by changing the farmers' perception of the value of land, had encouraged them to undertake investments in permanent improvements, to adopt and adapt new technologies from multiple sources, and to rehabilitate the environment, provided the government ensured an enabling macro-economic policy framework (Mortimore and Tiffen, 1994; Tiffen et al., 1994). In a study of Machakos district, southeast of Nairobi, they reported that agricultural output per head had risen by more than threefold and output per unit of land about elevenfold over the past half century, and especially since the 1960s. This is in an area where population densities are as high as 650 persons per sq. km.

Zimbabwe

Zimbabwe's land redistribution programme began in 1981, a year after independence. As in Kenya, the origins of the land redistribution programme are rooted in the process of land alienation for European settlement that had taken place from the time of colonization in 1890. Land reform and redistribution is an attempt to redress the inequalities of land ownership under colonial rule. The magnitude of land alienation during the colonial period is illustrated in Table 2.1.

Table 2.1 Division of land by racial group in Zimbabwe, for selected years (% of total land area)

Year	% for Africans	% for Europeans	% Not Assigned	% Forest or National	TOTAL
1894	24.3	15.0	80.7	-	100.0
1911	21.7	19.7	58.6	-	100.0
1931	30.1	50.8	18.5	0.6	100.0
1961	43.5	53.2	-	3.3	100.0
1970	46.6	46.6	-	6.8	100.0
1982	45.6	41.1	-	13.3	100.0

Note: After independence in 1980, the principal divisions became known as large-scale commercial farmland (former European) and communal land (former African).

The European population never constituted more than 5% of the total population of the country even at its peak in the 1960s. Yet they had exclusive right to an increasingly larger proportion of the country, reaching a peak of 53% in the early 1960s. After the unilateral declaration of independence (UDI) in 1965, the European minority government was even talking of parity in land distribution and this idea was embodied in law under the Land Tenure Act of 1969. As a result of land alienation combined with the forced removal of Africans from so-called European areas, especially during the 1950s, the African reserves had become progressively overcrowded and overstocked, resulting in severe environmental degradation (Whitlow and Zinyama, 1988; Zinyama and Whitlow, 1986).

Not only was there an imbalance in the amount of land available to each racial group, but also in the quality of the land for agricultural purposes. Areas allocated for European settlement were located closer to the economic heartland of the country, well served with transport and other infrastructure, close to the main urban markets, thereby enhancing their prospects for development. Even more importantly, European lands were located in the most ecologically favoured parts of the country, especially in terms of soil quality, rainfall amount and reliability. In contrast, the African reserves were located in areas of low and unreliable rainfall, with poor sandy soils of low water retention capacity which required large amounts of fertilizers to make them productive.

Thus, during the war for independence in the 1970s, as in Kenya, land hunger was the biggest grievance of the African population and a rallying point for the liberation movements. Not surprisingly, after independence, the new African majority government was expected – on political, economic and social grounds – to effect some land transfer from the European large landowners. Land redistribution was essential for a number of reasons, notably:

▶ to relieve population pressures in the crowded reserves (which were now known as the communal lands);

▶ to reduce the environmental degradation that was taking place there;

▶ to give the land-hungry African people an opportunity to venture into small-scale commercial agricultural production for the first time.

At the commencement of the land redistribution programme, government had planned to transfer enough land from European farmers to resettle some 162,000 peasant families by the mid-1980s. But this target was not met for a number of reasons. By the end of the 1980s, only some 53,000 families had been resettled on about 3.3 million hectares of land, and by mid-1990s the total number of settler families had risen to about 70,000 on 3.5 million hectares.

However, even though these figures are far below the original targets, they are much better than was the case in Kenya, both in terms of the amount of transferred land and the number of resettled farmers. In Kenya, a total of 61,400 families were resettled on 690,500 hectares between 1962 and 1979. The Zimbabwe government's ultimate objective is to transfer a total of 8.5 million hectares from the large farm sector for redistribution to peasant families, the pace of redistribution and resettlement depending on the availability of resources. Conversely, the large farm sector (now including a small number of African landowners) will be reduced ultimately from 15.5 million hectares at independence in 1980 to only 5 million hectares, mainly for the production of strategic and capital intensive crops such as tobacco, wheat and horticultural products.

The land redistribution programme has had several significant impacts in terms of:

▶ population distribution and settlement patterns,

- ▶ land use patterns, and
- ▶ the environment.

Firstly, the conversion of land to smallholder farming has resulted in changes in the demographic structure of the resettlement areas. Before their transfer, these areas were sparsely populated, with each farm comprising the farm owner's homestead and associated buildings, plus a compound for up to a few hundred labourers and their families. After resettlement, much larger numbers of people have come into these areas, including the settler families, local administrative staff and agricultural extension workers, health and education personnel, as well as small business owners at designated service centres within the resettlement schemes. Thus population densities have increased and the settlements have changed from a dispersed pattern to one comprising nucleated villages and service centres.

Secondly, the reform programme has led to considerable changes in rural land use patterns in the resettlement schemes. Previously sparsely settled and utilized large farms are now criss-crossed by a network of roads and footpaths. Lands which the previous owners had left mainly under bush for commercial livestock grazing have now been converted into large pockets of smallholder cultivation of both subsistence and cash crops.

A third issue concerns the impact of the reform programme on the natural resources within the resettlement areas. Throughout the 1980s, the government was required by certain entrenched constitutional clauses to adhere to the principle of "willing seller-willing buyer" in acquiring land for resettlement. Consequently, a large proportion of the land made available to the government for resettlement was located in areas of low rainfall, rather than in the better ecological regions of the country (Zinyama *et al.*, 1990). This means that land that was inherently not suited for intensive crop cultivation has been opened up for settlement and cultivation by resource-poor farmers who are dependent on subsistence food production. Again, because of the settlers' poverty, many of the resettlement schemes no longer have their previous dense woody vegetation; it has been felled for cultivation, building materials, fuelwood and, in some cases, sold as firewood to merchants from the urban centres.

Unlike in Kenya, where from the outset the government chose individual tenure in both the resettlement schemes as well as in the traditional reserves, in Zimbabwe the issue of tenure remains unresolved in both sub-sectors. Individual rights to land are only recognized in the urban centres and commercial farming areas.

On the resettlement schemes, the settlers reside as tenants of the state and, in theory, can be evicted summarily should the responsible government minister deem it necessary. The settlers' decision-making in the utilization of land and investment are subject to much closer scrutiny and control by government officers, notably the resettlement officers and agricultural extension workers, who normally reside on the schemes. It has been suggested that excessive paternalistic control by government can be detrimental to the long-term prospects of settlement schemes (Kinsey and Binswanger, 1993). Two decades after the land reform programme started, settler farmers in Zimbabwe do not enjoy long-term security of tenure, and especially inter-generational security.

In the communal lands, the farmers have traditional freehold tenure which guarantees them ownership and usufruct rights to arable and residential land for the family, as well as access to communal grazing land, forests, water and other resources. Disputes have increased over the years as agricultural land has become scarce (Republic of Zimbabwe, 1994).

One issue is the fear that the introduction of freehold tenure in the communal lands would result in increased social unrest, especially as many of those made landless through privatization would not be able to find alternative employment in the largely stagnant urban economy. At present, the communal lands effectively serve as a sponge to absorb the large numbers of school-leavers who, after a brief stint searching for a job in town, eventually return to their rural homes to eke out a living from subsistence agriculture.

In 1994, a government-appointed commission of enquiry made several recommendations regarding tenure systems in both the resettlement and communal lands (Republic of Zimbabwe, 1994). Although the government accepted most of the commission's recommendations, to date they still have not been implemented. Among other things, the commission recommended that the communal tenure system be retained and strengthened to improve security of tenure, reduce intra-community disputes over land and enhance local community management of common property resources. The commission was of the view that security of tenure under communal ownership could be improved by strengthening traditional village institutions whose authority had been eroded during the colonial period and in the early post-independence years. For the resettlement areas, the commission recommended that the current tenant system be replaced by the issuance of long-term leases with the option to subsequently purchase one's land.

Thus resettlement land would, with immediate effect, change to leasehold, with a long-term view of progressing to freehold.

CONCLUDING REMARKS

Even today, land reform remains part of the agenda of several African countries, notably Namibia, South Africa and Zimbabwe. It is therefore imperative that it be implemented in a manner which, while striving towards social and economic justice, does not unduly endanger national and household food security. It is only through informed decision-making by policy makers that these countries stand to benefit from their current initiatives to reform the ownership and distribution of land. Countries which have previously attempted land reform provide useful lessons for these countries. Otherwise, land reform can, as has been shown so many times in other countries and on other continents, become an expensive disaster.

The appropriate distribution of land, including the form and type of tenure is a critical issue in Africa's future. Attempted land redistribution and tenure reform provides an opportunity to ensure an equitable distribution of land and, in turn, access to the means of production and improved livelihood. The challenges faced by Kenya and Zimbabwe in attempting to implement land reform programmes provide insight into the complexity of this process.

REFERENCES

Arntzen, J.W., Ngcongco, L.D. and Turner, S.D. (eds.). 1986: *Land Policy and Agriculture in Eastern and Southern Africa.* Tokyo: United Nations University.

Clayton, E.S. 1978: *A Comparative Study of Settlement Schemes in Kenya.* Agrarian Development Studies Unit Occasional Paper No. 3. London: University of London, Wye College.

Coulson, A. 1978: Agricultural policies in mainland Tanzania. *Review of African Political Economy*, No. 10, 74-100.

Haugerud, A. 1983: The consequences of land tenure reform among smallholders in the Kenya Highlands. *Rural Africana*, Nos. 15-16, 65-89.

Hazlewood, A. 1985: Kenyan land-transfer programmes and their relevance for Zimbabwe. *Journal of Modern African Studies*, Vol. 23, No. 3, 445-461.

Hirsch, G.P. 1972: Some fundamentals of land reform. *Oxford Agrarian Studies*, Vol. 1, No. 2, 136-148.

Hirst, M. 1978: Recent villagization in Tanzania. *Geography*, Vol. 63, part 2, 122-125.

King, R. 1971: Land reform: some general and theoretical considerations. *Norsk Geografisk Tidsskrift*, Vol. 25, 85-97.

Kinsey, B.H. and Binswanger, H.P. 1993: Characteristics and performance of resettlement programs: a review. *World Development*, Vol. 21, No. 9, 1477-1494.

La-Anyane, S. 1985: *Economics of Agricultural Development in Tropical Africa*. Chichester: John Wiley & Sons.

Mortimore, M. and Tiffen, M. 1994: Population growth and a sustainable environment: the Machakos story. *Environment*, Vol. 36, No. 8, 10-20 & 28-32.

Okoth-Ogendo, H.W.O. 1986: The perils of land tenure reform: the case of Kenya. In J.W. Arntzen, L.D. Ngcongco and S.D. Turner (eds.), *Land Policy and Agriculture in Eastern and Southern Africa*. Tokyo: United Nations University.

Republic of Zimbabwe. 1994: *Report of the Commission of Inquiry into Appropriate Agricultural Land Tenure Systems*. Harare: Rukuni Commission.

Sutton, K. 1984: Algeria's socialist villages - a reassessment. *Journal of Modern African Studies*, Vol. 22, No. 2, 223-248.

Tiffen, M., Mortimore, M. and Gichuki, F. 1994: *Population Growth and Environmental Recovery: Policy Lessons from Kenya*. Gatekeeper Series No. 45. London: IIED.

Warriner, D. 1957: *Land Reform and Development in the Middle East*. London: Royal Institute of International Affairs.

West, H.W. 1986: Land tenure, policy and management in English-speaking African countries. In J.W. Arntzen, L.D. Ngcongco and S.D. Turner (eds.), *Land Policy and Agriculture in Eastern and Southern Africa*. Tokyo: United Nations University.

Whitlow, R. and Zinyama, L.M. 1988: Up hill and down vale: farming and settlement patterns in Zimunya communal land. *Geographical Journal of Zimbabwe*, No. 19, 29-45.

Williams, D.C. 1992: Measuring the impact of land reform policy in Nigeria. *Journal of Modern African Studies*, Vol. 30, No. 4, 587-608.

Zinyama, L.M., Campbell, D.J. and Matiza, T. 1990: Land policy and access to land in Zimbabwe: the Dewure resettlement scheme. *Geoforum*, Vol. 21, No. 3, 359-370.

Zinyama, L. and Whitlow, R. 1986: Changing patterns of population distribution in Zimbabwe. *GeoJournal*, Vol. 13, No. 4, 365-384.

Chapter 3

LAND MANAGEMENT SYSTEMS IN MALAWI

by Lucy Chipeta

INTRODUCTION

L
and management presumes the existence of a social regime which governs the distribution of beneficial activities on land. The laws of that society may be customary or modern, oral or written, but in any case are determinants of individual perception and evaluation of land. This consciousness of the environment is the basis of land tenure which in turn shapes the economics of how ·land is used and developed (Yahya, 1990).

In Malawi, one of the pressing problems of land administration is the question of land tenure. Several questions arise as to the origin of land tenure and alternatives are being explored to find the most suitable methods of land management for the community as a whole. This, in turn, raises the question of who should own land. This chapter will examine the existing land management systems in Malawi, and how these systems address issues of access to land by low-income households. This will be examined in relation to urban land. Much has been written on rural agricultural land, but not much exists on management and problems associated with urban land. Finally, this chapter provides recommendations on improving the existing land management systems to accommodate the less privileged in the urban fabric.

LEGAL PROVISION

Management and control of land in Malawi is governed by the Land Act, which empowers the state to control all types of land, regardless of tenure. This is enforced through a series of other urban regulations such as the Town Planning Act, Urban Area Act, Malawi Housing Act and building by-laws. Land is clearly a key component in economic development because it constitutes a production tool, a means of exchange, a guarantee for credit and a form of wealth accumulation. Therefore, the state, which has a critical role in the economy of developing countries, seeks mastery over land (Coulbaly, 1990). The Land Act of Malawi designates the state as having uncontested control over land use and distribution. This clearly expressed affirmation of the legislature is nevertheless hampered in actual practice by structural deficiencies.

The Land Act gives the ministers power of control over any type of land, whether customary, public or private. This is expressed in the requirement for permission from the minister by any land owner for all land transactions. In Malawi there are three types of land tenure systems: customary, private and public.

Customary Land is the property of the state and is vested in perpetuity in the president (CAP 57:01 Sec. 25). Section 26 of the same Act empowers the minister to control all customary land and all minerals in, on, or under it for use or common benefit directly or indirectly to the inhabitants of Malawi.

The Land Act also empowers the minister to manage and control the use of any land other than land situated in a municipality or township. Customary land is held and used under customary law applicable in a area. Local chiefs are normally given authority by the minister to authorize its use or allocate it in accordance with the customary law. This land is communal and is accessible to almost everybody in the locality.

However, this type of land tenure does not act as a guarantee for credit. It is regarded as unsafe by financial institutions, yet this type of tenure is common to about 85% of the Malawi population who reside in rural areas. It has been argued that this type of tenure does not guarantee security of tenure, as it carries no legal backing. This view has been refuted by Kishindo (1990). His findings on customary land stated that the customary tenure of land does not act as a barrier to agricultural development because social recognition of the validity of a claim to the land provides the security. The problem of customary land not being viable as a security for development loans is addressed by using other collateral such as cattle. In this case, the barrier to economic development lies in the fact that subdivision and fragmentation of land is not conducive to commercialization. This chapter will not focus on this type of land tenure as it mainly relates to rural areas and agricultural land. However, this tenure exists in disguised form in urban areas where proper compensation has not been provided.

Public Land is a recent phenomenon, along with private/freehold tenure. This type of tenure was adopted under the colonial system. In the case of Malawi, the administration of public and freehold land is based on the English pattern of land administration. All public land is vested in perpetuity in the president. The minister has power to control the use of this land except that which is located within cities, municipalities and Townships. In these areas, land use is controlled by the local authorities, although in practice land management and allocation is still being done by the Minister for Lands through regional offices.

Public land evolved from customary land or private land. This land changes from customary through declaration orders or government acquisition through leases. This includes all land held by the government for the purpose of developing a town, government building or roads and services. Public land may also be obtained through purchase of freehold or from termination of leasehold estates pursuant to breach of contract. This type of land is mostly found in urban areas and is the most mismanaged, because of a lack of clear policies. Mismanagement has led to encroachment upon the land, an issue which will be reviewed later in the chapter.

Private Land refers to all land which is owned, held or occupied under freehold title, leasehold title or a certificate of claim, or which is registered as private land under the Registered Land Act.

This freehold land tenure is a recent phenomenon, introduced in the 19th century. Prior to this, all land in Malawi was held under customary tenure. This concept of land tenure was introduced by the white settlers who purchased land from local chiefs, especially in the Shire Highlands. Freehold tenure was granted on production of proof of purchase. Land claims certificates were issued and these were legally accepted in 1903. It was after this that land became private and subjected to the English law of the time. Private land therefore traces its origin from certificates of claim and indeed today much land tenure can be traced back to such certificates.

Private leasehold tenure is obtained through leasing of public land from the government.

The acquisition of this land follows a cumbersome procedure which is rarely followed by low-income households.

URBAN GROWTH

Land management problems are critical in urban areas, because of the continuous rise in urban population. Few urban issues are not embedded in questions of land ownership and tenure. All societies have rules governing land use, but the treatment of land as a commodity which can be bought or sold for a market price is a relatively new phenomenon in Malawi, as it is in many developing countries. In Malawi, as already stated, land registration and the land market began to emerge a century ago. The land market has emerged in response to the accelerating rise in urban populations, with rural settlements and agricultural land on the urban fringe being absorbed into the urban domain.

Malawi's urban population is growing at an alarming rate of about 6.7%, which means demand for urban land will increase drastically. The population increase has also intensified competition for social, economic and environmental needs in urban areas; increased the potential for title disputes; and aggravated the difficulty of housing the poor. The accelerating rate of urbanization and its ensuing environmental, health and social problems in developing countries has severely strained government budgets. The combined effects of expanding urban boundaries and the growth in wealth of the upper class has lead to competition for land. It is the poor, the least educated, and the least influential who have been the losers.

Table 3.1 Annual mid year projection of population and urban households

Year	Malawi				Urban			
	POP	Annual % Growth	# of Household	Annual % Growth	POP	Annual % Growth	# of Household	Annual % Growth
1989	8,021,700		1,874,559		1,172,700		277,210	
1994	9,461,400	3.6%	2,210,996	3.6%	1,711,200	9.2%	436,345	11.5%
1999	11,227,500	3.7%	2,623,709	3.7%	2,488,300	9.1%	588,199	7.0%
2004	13,270,453	3.6%	3,159,637	4.1%	3,622,401	9.1%	862,476	

Source: National Statistical Office, Malawi Demographic Survey (1997), Analytical Report

This growth in urban population will lead to competition for urban land for various services which will drive up the price of both land and services at an alarming rate. This will fuel land and housing speculation, distorting urban development patterns, frustrating public interest and denying access to secure land tenure and housing for the majority of the urban population who are low-income people.

LAND MANAGEMENT SYSTEMS IN MALAWI

Although the state formally controls all types of land, it cannot do so effectively without land management mechanisms. Several organizations have been mandated to administer land through set mechanisms.

Administration of customary land

Customary land is communal land inherited from ancestors or distributed by the chief. The chiefs, in liaison with the District Commissioner, are the administrators. Customary land is not subject to any utilization controls, unless it contains minerals. Mainly found in rural areas, customary land is generally used for agriculture. This land is now being depleted, due to rising population and the increasing popularity of private estate land. In recent years the administration of this land has been subject to bribery and other corrupt practices which favour high-income estate owners. There is also customary land in Malawi's major urban areas. Although theoretically land within urban areas is declared public, in practice land in the urban fringe is administered as customary land. The Land Act 57:01 Section 28 provides for compensation to individuals for loss or disturbance due to the declaration under Section 27(1) that land required for urban growth should be public. In fact, this has not been done and traditional chiefs in those areas still perform their role of allocating and authorizing the use of land. As will be discussed later, this has been perpetuated due to lack of clear land policy.

Public and private land management

While mandated to strictly control land management, the state is too remote to control local land issues. Other organizations have been established to administer and manage all public land and some have been given land on a freehold basis for the sake of implementing certain government objectives. These organizations are the Ministry of Lands and Valuation, the Malawi Housing Corporation, the Local Authorities such as cities and municipalities, and the Ministry of Survey and Physical Planning. The Local Authorities have been mandated to manage housing estates for low-income groups in Traditional Housing Areas (THAs). Malawi Housing Corporation has been mandated to manage permanent housing estates for both low- and medium-income people. The Ministry of Lands manages public land and oversees private land transactions. The Ministry of Survey and Physical Planning and some Local Authorities are mandated to prepare land use plans as a basis for land allocation and management.

In order to efficiently manage land, several mechanisms have been put in place. These include land registration, land taxation, land use zoning, subdivision control and density control.

Land registration

The Malawi Land Act makes provision for land registration. Ownership of land can only be recognized through title deed, which comes through land registration. Land registration has been put in place to monitor land transactions, to facilitate conveyance, transparency, and keeping records of transactions. Title transparency and evidence of ownership is important for commercial developers who need to use the land as security for borrowing money. Registration for all types of land, freehold or leasehold, is done by the Ministry of Lands and Valuation. Land registration is an important prerequisite for property taxation, as this is the only way one can prove the property exists. Land registration is also done by the Local Authorities and the Malawi Housing Corporation, and these organizations generally provide deeds on a short-term basis. Deeds in Traditional Housing Areas are not recognized as security by lending institutions because of the short-term tenure.

Registration, although an important land management mechanism, benefits the most affluent and wealthy households who are more conversant with the procedure. The procedure for acquiring and registering land is inefficient and bureaucratic, as one must follow several steps in order to finally get a deed. It is time-consuming and very costly, with fees to be paid at various stages (i.e. application, building plans, surveying, acceptance of lease offer). This deters low-income households. The registration procedures through the Malawi Housing Corporation and Local Authorities are simpler but these organizations rarely offer unserviced land, so land is normally not available under their jurisdiction.

Land taxation

Privately owned land is taxed, making it an important revenue resource for the management of sustainable urbanization. Land taxes are normally collected by the Local Authorities, based on the quantity and quality of improvement of land and property. The proceeds are used to service the land. While this provides an efficient land market, it does not guarantee access to land for the poor, who are often priced out of the market and cannot afford to pay the exorbitant land taxes imposed by the Local Authorities. In the past, in most THA projects, low-income householders were exempted from the taxes, a decision which has been reversed because most Local Authorities needed the tax revenue. It is recommended that certain areas reserved for the urban poor should again be exempted from these land taxes or should be subsidized. Most THA projects are heavily subsidized by the government, but these projects have been penetrated by the middle- and high-income households, once again putting the poor at a disadvantage.

Land use zoning

Malawi's Ministry of Surveys and Physical Planning and Local Authorities are responsible for land use zoning, the mechanism which segregates parcels of land or areas of a town and allocates them to activities that may legally be undertaken. Planning for land use has been in the form of rudimentary land use zoning, usually unrelated to any form of land use framework, divorced from infrastructure and engineering considerations, and lacking implementation mechanisms for meeting its goals. Current land use planning is more or less regulatory, as it deals with controls and limitations which are difficult to comprehend. As a result, planning has been dismissed as a futile exercise, irrelevant to the practical needs of settlement management. Zoning has been criticized for being too rigid and denying the urban poor access to land.

Subdivision control

Subdivision control is another land management mechanism which has been applied on private land in urban areas. Any landlord intending to sell or subdivide land requires permission from the Planning Committee, as well as approval from the Minister of Lands. This is to ensure that certain conditions such as provision of access roads, right of way, and stream reserves are in place. In rural areas, this control has been mainly used to control fragmentation of agricultural land.

Density Control

Related to subdivision control, density control is meant to control urban sprawl which may deplete agricultural land and to ensure economic use of land and its distribution. In urban areas, various housing densities have been established to ensure scope for a variety of development. Density control helps safeguard health and privacy by requiring and providing for minimum levels of comfort and environmental protection. It is a mechanism for monitoring overcrowding and under-utilization of available facilities. Existing density standards provide excessive amounts of land for low-density settlement, which is wasteful and depletes urban land, leading to artificial land shortages.

CRITICAL EVALUATION OF LAND MANAGEMENT SYSTEMS

Malawi's land management systems have been criticized for being unsuited to low-income households. It is argued that the systems are inappropriate because their form and content originated in the colonial era and are based on the very different economic and social systems of those times. Land management controls do not facilitate the development of shelter for the poor; they are badly administered and the policies imbedded in them are usually inappropriate. The end result is unaffordable legal housing. The flaws in the sytems usually outweigh the benefits of health, safety, welfare and planning where the poor are concerned (Mattingly, 1990).

The long procedure to obtain formal access to land and development consent makes it very difficult for low-income households to acquire land through formal means. Any commodity market in which the processing of a lawful transaction is burdensome and unduly lengthy creates a supply/demand disequilibrium, with severe consequences for the poor. Furthermore, the scarcity or inaccessibility of land results in most housing markets developing a variety of illogical, illegal, and certainly unfair practices such as under-the-table land deals, collusion among estate agents, excessive transaction fees, price fixing and price jumping, bribery and corruption – all of which affect price and affordability. Because there have been no barriers to participation in housing programmes geared for the poor, these programes have been hijacked by middle- or high-income households. This is a distinct disadvantage for the poor and uneducated who need land and housing, but may not be well informed on the normal procedures to acquire them. As a result, low-income households have found alternative means of land acquisition in squatter settlements where the procedure is simple and straightforward.

The various land agencies in urban areas do not seem to be co-ordinated in any way, making land supply and administration cumbersome and inequitable. The poor have the most to lose as a result of the inefficient management systems. Overall, land development and utilization are very difficult to monitor, given the highly centralized administration of public land.

RECOMMENDATIONS

Decentralization of land administration

Land registration is important. It helps to keep track of land transactions, facilities, conveyance and ensures transparency. The existing registration procedure is too complicated for low-income and uneducated households to comprehend. It is therefore proposed that a simple registration procedure be introduced. The existing administrative procedure is too centralized; registration of all categories of land should be placed in the hands of local authorities, especially in urban areas.

In urban areas, almost all land is public and much of it has been taken over by squatters, a situation which is almost impossible to reverse. A recent Research on Housing Indicators programme revealed that almost 50% of housing is illegal. These structures stand on illegal land, probably public, but there are no concrete records to show who owns what or who allocates the land being used. To regain effective land management, the only solution is to legalise these squatter settlements by following a simple land registration system. This can only be done at the local level, as the central government is too remote to monitor local affairs.

Currently, there is no monitoring or control over public land by the Ministry of Lands in major urban areas. In the case of Zomba, a city northeast of Blantyre in southern Malawi, there is no ministry office or rangers to monitor encroachment on public land. The ministry relies on Town Planning rangers who do have authority over land use, but not over land acquisition. If local authorities take over, there is likely to be greater efficiency and proper monitoring, and the local authorities will probably be able to mobilize revenue from the resources. This will require resources in terms of manpower, as well as proper cadastral maps covering formal and informal land holdings, accurate subdivision maps, up-to-date tenure and property transaction records and electronic recording and retrieval methods. This would lead to more efficient land acquisition procedures and improve the effectiveness of land management.

Relaxed land taxation

While land taxation supports a more efficient land market, it eliminates participation of the low-income population in development. Land becomes too expensive for low-income households and they resort to alternative cheaper land. It is proposed that certain land should be strictly reserved for low-income people, who should be exempted from land taxes and other costs such as survey fees.

Negotiation with government is required to make these exemptions. In the Chinamwali habitat housing project, the government still requires participants to pay survey fees to process their deeds. Chinamwali is project area land which was surveyed by the physical planning department with donor money. The Ministry of Lands should just use the temporary beacons as evidence of landholding and exempt the low-income people from paying fees. This will give low-income urban households access to land.

Relaxed land use zoning controls

Land use planning has concentrated on zoning control, which seems to be too rigid and unrealistic for Malawi's socio-economic structure. It is recommended that flexible plans be adopted to allow a mixture of land uses, especially in areas reserved for low-income housing. Other planning controls in these areas could be relaxed to meet the demands of the inhabitants. This may involve community participation in the preparation of detailed, but simple plans which can be easily interpreted. Land use planning should be more responsive, perhaps being replaced in certain areas by a dialogue based on mutual responsibility for future development. A greater degree of autonomy for the private sector in the development and promotion of individual economic initiatives and residential development can take the form of public-private partnership. Such an approach would be more promotional than restrictive, and will require a considerable change in attitude among planners and implementers.

Promoting access to suitable land

Facilitating access to land and inputs for building settlements is one of the most important prerequisites in developing sustainable human settlement. Although it is difficult to make affordable land available, there are measures which help improve the situation:

Land Sharing: Private land is sometimes appropriated by squatters. In these cases, the government has a double role to play – protecting the squatter as well as the landlord. There is a need to negotiate for compromise in which the landlord can apportion part of the original land to resettle the squatters so that the remainder of the land can be efficiently utilized. This removes the fear of eviction and the squatters can be given small building lots at reasonable prices. This protects the landlord's land from degradation and helps the government supply land to the urban poor. This requires community participation.

Assisted Land Purchase: The government should give the urban poor assistance to purchase land and housing. The urban poor can organize themselves into community groups and be given group loans for housing and land. This requires mechanisms for group land acquisition and development loan facilities. It is recommended that wider applications of democratic community or cooperative land ownership of land be adopted as a decentralized land management strategy. Neighbourhood committees could be formed to handle planning, land allocation, loan acquisition and collection, land registration and enforcement. Such a broad-based and community-focused approach could facilitate transactions for the poor by circumventing the heavy and obstructive bureaucracies common to many developing countries.

CONCLUSION

The procedure for gaining formal access to land and obtaining development consent should be streamlined for more efficient land allocation and delivery. This requires decentralization of land management functions which are vital to ensuring the availability and productive use of land. The state should hand over land control to Local Authorities, which should involve community committees in the allocation and management of land in their neighbourhood.

It is clear that the existing land management systems need to be reviewed. Relaxed management mechanisms should be put in place to facilitate and ensure access to land for low-income urban households.

REFERENCES

Coubaly, B.K. 1990: Land Legislation and Human Settlements Planning in Mali. *Proceedings of the Symposium on Access to Land and Infrastructure for Low-income Shelter in Africa.* Dakar: Shelter Afrique.

Laws of Malawi, Chapters 57:01, 58.

Kishindo, P. 1985: Customary Land and Agricultural Development in Malawi. *Journal of Social Science*, Vol. 38, No. 4, 305-313.

Kishindo, P. 1990: Customary Land Tenure in Malawi: Is it a Constraint on Agriculture in Africa. *African Journal of Social Science*, Vol. 3, May 1990.

Mattingly, M. 1990: Land Use Controls: Catalyst of Retardation. *Proceedings of the Symposium on Access to Land and Infrastructure for Low-income Shelter in Africa.* Dakar: Shelter Afrique.

National Statistical Office. 1987: *Housing and Population Census, Preliminary Report.* Zomba: National Statistical Office.

National Statistical Office. 1997. *Malawi Demographic Survey. 1997 Analytical Report*. Zomba: National Statistical Office.

Office of the President and Cabinet. 1989: *Outline Zoning Scheme*. Zomba: Department of Housing and Physical Planning.

Yahya, S.S. 1990: Selected Issues in Land Management. *Proceedings of the Symposium on Access to Land and Infrastructure for Low-income Shelter in Africa*. Dakar: Shelter Afrique.

Zomba Municipal Council. 1992: *Integrated Development Strategy*. Zomba: Municipal Council.

Chapter 4

LAND TENURE REGIMES IN SUB-SAHARAN AFRICA

by Urgessa Biru

INTRODUCTION

L and tenure influences the management and exploitation of land-based resources. In Sub-Saharan Africa, there are various tenure regimes that have a corresponding influence on resource exploitation. This chapter will review the tenure regimes, their relation to each other, and how they influence the management of natural resources.

MANAGEMENT OF NATURAL RESOURCES

The concept of natural resource management refers to the "obligations" which arise from ownership over one or more parcels of land. It refers to the management aspect of the land tenure concept. In other words, it refers to the behaviour of those who have the rights over use of the land-based natural resources (or person-to-land relations).

In the context of agricultural land, the concept of "management of natural resources" refers to the appropriation of land-based resources such as soils, water and forests by individual households for direct production activities. This includes cultivation or grazing as well as non-agricultural use like homesteads. In economic terms, management of natural resources refers to the use of a "bundle of rights", or the mode of resource exploitation in the production process in order to draw economic benefits from it (Bromley, 1991; Bohannan, 1963; Harris, 1953).

RESOURCE MANAGEMENT REGIMES

This concept of natural resources management refers to the behaviours of property right owners in relation to land. This aspect of land-based management is what Bromley (1991) refers to as "resource management regimes".

Bromley (1991) describes four possible holders of tenure rights (resource management regimes). These are:

- open access or non-property regimes
- common property regimes
- state property regimes
- private property regimes

All these categories reflect the nature of access to, and control over, land resources. In the following section, summaries will be provided of each of these property regimes with a more detailed discussion focused on private property in the context of Sub-Saharan Africa.

Open access is a regime in which there is no property owner. In this case, anyone may have access to property, with no defined, finite group of users (Gordon, 1954; Bromley, 1991).

Common property regimes exist where a group of individuals possess the access and use rights to a parcel of agricultural land. Examples include tribal groups, subgroups, sub-villages, extended families and kin systems. These groupings hold customary ownership of certain natural resources such as farm land, grazing land, and water resources (McCay and Acheson, 1987; McKean, 1986; Bromley, 1991).

A common property regime in this context refers to private property for the group. It refers to the trusteeship between the group of individuals and the social group. Individuals have rights and responsibilities and, as with private property, common properties are characterized by the exclusion of non-owners (Bromley, 1991; Ciriacy-Wantrup and Bishop, 1975).

The property-owning groups in common property regimes may vary in nature, size, and internal structure across a broad spectrum. However, they are social units with definite membership and interaction among members, with some common economic interests and cultural norms. To this end, it is worth noting that the common property regime is fundamentally different from land-based property regimes in collective farms or agricultural cooperatives prevalent in centrally-planned economies (Bromley, 1991). In the latter, land does not belong to the members of the collective as common property but to the state. Contrary to such state-ownership regimes, the customary common property regimes in Africa are characterized by group or "corporate" ownership with management authority vested in the respective group (see also Bromley, 1991; Biru, 1988; Cohen, 1980; Noronha, 1985). Hence, under common property regimes, all four aspects of land ownership: nominal title, control, benefit and management, are shared or are under "corporate" control. Therefore, if tenure institutional change takes place, its effect will be on the group as a whole.

State property regimes are most common in Sub-Saharan Africa, and in this case ownership and control over use of land and land-based resources rests with the state (ibid.).

Private property regimes, as Bromley (1991) described, are those in which ownership and control rest with the owner. However, buried in his description is, on one hand, the Western notion of "private property ownership", and, on the other, the perception that there was no ownership of property under customary land tenure. It is true that the concept of "private property ownership" of land, as defined and understood in the Western legal system, is quite different from the African concept of land ownership.

LAND OWNERSHIP IN TRADITIONAL SUB-SAHARAN AFRICA

The African concept of land ownership was that all belongs to the people and all have the right to use it. To borrow Kettlewell's words, "like air and water, land is not owned by anyone and is held in trust from the dead by the living for the unborn" (Kettlewell, 1965, p. 250). Although the above statement sounds like the concept of "an open-access" regime, the absence of private ownership, as understood in the Western legal system, does not mean there is no ownership of land within customary systems. The key to the concept of "land ownership" in African customary tenure systems is "trusteeship".

Land can be owned, but it is held in trusteeship by either individuals or groups of individuals. Thus, private ownership of land in the African context of customary tenure refers to the trusteeship relations between individuals or groups of individuals and the social entity. In this context, having a share in something which is part of a common patrimony, reinforces feelings of having identifiable social roots and of belonging to a supportive and united human entity.

However, that does not mean individuals do not own land. As Kamchedzera (1992, p. 193) put it, "even under common law, ownership does not only refer to the physical soils, but the control, management, and even benefit of the thing." In this sense, even in customary tenure, private ownership exists if privacy is measured in terms of "access to" (access rights), "control over" (exclusion rights), or the "transfer rights" of farmland, within the socio-political and moral dictates (Machika and Nankumba, 1988; Kamchedzera, 1992).

If privacy of land ownership in customary tenure is measured in terms of *access rights* to agricultural land, each individual is ensured access to agricultural land and the use of it. The general principle underlying the traditional land tenure institution in Sub-Saharan Africa is that each member of the group is entitled to be allocated a sufficient amount of land to support his/her family.

This entitlement is both complicated and made more flexible by the nature of Sub-Saharan African communities. These communities include members who can claim actual or putative descent from other members, and strangers or migrants who have been accepted as members of, and reside with the group (Noronha, 1985). In other words, access to land and other vital resources is not necessarily based on kinship or descent-based ties. It may also be grounded upon loyalty and patronage relations which are often associated with ascriptive forms of status or social identity (Berry, 1984; Meillassoux, 1980).

This means that lineage or social groups with surplus cultivable areas can always accommodate land-hungry outsiders, provided the latter agree to enter into the local network of personal interrelationships and accept the political authority of the local chief. As a matter of fact, the relationship between the stranger and the holder of customary rights of access to land is akin to a contract between a client and his patron: rather than a transaction concerned with land, this is an exchange of persons in the course of which one party makes allegiance to a host group and its leading representative (Gruenais, 1986).

The nature of land allocation decisions varies significantly according to the type of farming system. While shifting cultivation mainly requires that the group leaders decide when the cultivators have to give up their lands to move to new areas, in settled agriculture (dry-land farming, flood-recession agriculture or irrigated farming), their main responsibility lies in guaranteeing the perpetuation of the lineage through the inalienability of its land assets (Minvielle, 1977; Noronha, 1985). However as we have seen earlier, there is no concept of private property rights, as understood in the Western legal practice, in the customary tenure system of rights of access to land (Cohen, 1980; Riddle, 1985; Noronha, 1985).

If privacy of ownership is measured in terms of *exclusion rights*, under customary land tenure, individuals have full control over their farm land. They have a full right to exclude others from the enjoyment of their parcels of farm land within socio-political and moral dictates (Minvielle, 1977; Noronha, 1985;

Machika and Nankumba, 1988; Kamchedzera, 1992).

In terms of **transfer rights** of agricultural land, because land is a "corporate" property, it cannot be freely and definitely transferred by the individual or household which possesses and cultivates the land. He or she is considered a temporary trustee or manager of the "corporate" property of the whole lineage. The allottee is not allowed to dispose of the land freely because it belongs to the higher social entity whose representatives only are empowered to make decisions in land matters.

Nevertheless, land authorities – the village chief or the head of the lineage (when he is not at the same time the village chief) – may allow a reshuffling of land access rights under specific circumstances; for instance, when changes in the size of the household require the land allotments to be adjusted or when some consolidation of holdings can bring benefits to the community or a subsection of it (Noronha, 1985; Gregory, 1982). Furthermore, although land cannot be freely and definitely transferred, as understood in the Western legal system, the customary system has its own mechanism for allowing the transfer of land from one individual to another. A traditional tenure institution allows temporary alienation of land by individuals for determinate or indeterminate periods of time through "lending" and "pledging" (Noronha, 1985; Gregory, 1982).

Lending land may serve the function of adjusting the distribution of land to that of the labour force or to the varying subsistence needs of different households (depending on the family's demographic cycle or exogenous events such as accidents or illnesses, especially in non-stratified societies). Lenders may ask for payment (fixed or variable), expect a gift (predetermined or of the borrower's choosing), or they may consider the loan as part of a reciprocal relationship of economic interdependence (*ibid.*).

Land pledging also comes within the scope of traditional networks of interpersonal, interfamilial, or interlineage relationships. As with land loans, land pledging may correspond to an exchange between persons – to what Gregory (1982) describes as "an exchange of inalienable things between transactors who are in a state of reciprocal dependence". Typically, the operation is then never reversed. As observed by Coquery-Vidrovitch (1982), "the individual who pledges his land is always entitled to recover it, he or his descendants, at least as a matter of principle. He also keeps the initiative of such a move since the beneficiary of the pledge is not allowed to insist on the repayment of the loan taken. As a result, the pledger and the pledgee may remain linked together across several generations" (quoted by Platteau, 1992, p. 94).

In summary, land transfer in the context of traditional Africa serves as part of the social safety net and interdependence. In this regard, the very vocabulary of Western law is inadequate. As Platteau (1992, p. 87) put it, "there is no genuine alienation of the land, land is not definitely parted with, it may change hands for quite a long (and indeterminate) period of time". Land transfer in the context of customary systems in Africa is a gift exchange which establishes a relationship between the subjects, contrary to commodity exchange which establishes a relationship between the objects exchanged (Gregory, 1982; Platteau, 1992).

Therefore, in traditional Africa, land transfer is a mechanism by which communities ensure the distribution of parcels of land to members of the community who need them to support their families. It is a mechanism by which members of the community support each other, and benefit from the informal land transactions by giving temporary use rights to others (through rent, pledges and sales, without fear of losing ultimate ownership of their gardens).

In stratified societies, the practice of land pledging may enable individuals or families who wield control over a sizeable labour force (clients, slaves, servants, etc.) to gain access to large land areas in which this labour force can be made to work (Platteau, 1992). The mobility of land ensured through this mechanism could thus foster "the constitution of a privileged class not, strictly speaking, of big landowners, but of big land managers who succeeded in combining wealth and political power" (Coquery-Vidrovitch, 1982).

CONCLUSION

Under colonial administration, traditional land use and tenure was thought to be based on an open-access regime, which could be sublimated to Western legal principles. This paper argues that in spite of land being held in common, it was held corporately in trust for the benefit and future benefit of the group using and holding the land. This calls into question the propriety of land alienation under the colonial administrations, and subsequent imposition of state-property regimes and private property regimes based on the colonial structure.

REFERENCES

Berry, Sara. 1984. The food crisis and agrarian change in Africa: a review essay. *African Studies Review*, 27 (2), 59-112.

Biru, Urgessa. 1988: *Vulnerability of Agropastoral Households to Environmental Stress in Ethiopia: The Socio-economic Ecological Perspectives with Special Reference to Food Security and the Importance of Livestock*. M.Sc. Thesis submitted to Agricultural University of Norway (NORAGIC), Department of Natural Resource Management.

Bohannan, P. 1963: Land, Land Tenure. In D. Biebuyck (ed.), *African Agrarian Systems*, pp. 101-111. London: Oxford University Press.

Bromley, D.W. 1991: *Environment and Economy. Property Rights and Public Policy*.

Ciriacy-Wantrup and Bishop, R.C. 1975: Common Property as a Concept in Natural Resources Policy. *Natural Resources Journal*, 15, 713-727.

Cohen, J. 1980: Land Tenure and Rural Development in Africa. In R.H. Bates and M.F. Lofchie (eds.), *Agricultural Development in Africa: issues of public policy*, pp. 349-400. New York: Praeger.

Coquery-Vidrovitch, C. 1982: Le regime foncier rural en Afrique noire. In E. Le Roy and F. Leimdorfer (eds.), *Enjeux fonciers en Afrique noire*, pp. 65-84. Paris: ORSTROM and Karthala.

Gordon, H.S. 1954: The Economic Theory of a Common Property Resource: The Fishery. *J.P.E.*, Vol. 62, 124-148.

Gregory, C.A. 1982: *Gifts and Commodities*. London and New York: Academic Press.

Gruenais, M.E. 1986: Territoires autochtones et mise en valeur des terres. In B. Crousse, E. Le Bris and E. LeRoy (eds.), *Espaces disputes en Afrique noire*, pp. 283-298. Paris: Karthala.

Harris, M.D. 1953: *Origin of the Land Tenure System in the United States*.

Kamchedzera, G.S. 1992: Land Tenure Relations, the Law and Development in Malawi. In Guy C.Z. Mhone (ed.), *Malawi at the Crossroads: The Post-colonial Political Economy*. Harare: Sapes Books.

Kettlewell, R.W. 1965: Agricultural Change in Nyasaland 1945-1960. *Food Research Institute Studies*, Volume V, No. 3. California: Stanford University.

Machika, M.R.E. and Nankumba, J.S. 1988: *Dynamics of Land Tenure and Agrarian Reforms in Africa - The Case of Malawi*. Research Report Presented to FAO and

Malawi Government.

McCay, B.J. and Acheson, J.M. (eds.). 1987: *The Question of the Commons: the Culture and Ecology of Communal Resources*. Tucson: University of Arizona Press.

McKean, M.A. 1986: Management of Traditional Common Lands. *Environmental Review*, 6, 63-88.

Meillassoux, C. 1980: *Femmes, grenier et capitaux*. Paris: Maspero. (English translation: 1981: *Maidens, Meal and Money: Capitalism and the Domestic Community*. Cambridge: Cambridge University Press.)

Minvielle, J.P. 1977: *La structure fonciere du waalo Fuutanke*. Paris: ORSTOM (Centre de Dakar).

Noronha, R. 1985: *A review of the literature on land tenure systems in sub-Saharan Africa*. Research Unit of the Agriculture and Rural Development Department. ARU 43. Washington: World Bank.

Platteau, J.P. 1992: *Land Reform and Structural Adjustment in sub-Saharan Africa: Controversies and Guidelines*. Report prepared for the FAO, Economic and Social Policy Department, Policy Analysis Division.

Riddle, J.C. 1985: *Customary Tenure in Malawi*. Mimeo. Madison: University of Wisconsin-Madison, Land Tenure Centre.

Chapter 5

DRAMA AS COMMUNICATION IN PLANNING

by Jean Munro

INTRODUCTION

Communication is key to any planning process, and knowing how to communicate effectively and appropriately is a challenge. Depending on the context, participation may involve detailed communication with a small number of people or broad communication with many people. Planners and others working with the public need to develop culturally creative, appropriate, feasible and effective approaches to communication and public participation.

In the African context, it is particularly important to select the right vehicle for public participation. Issues of literacy, limited resources, and the relative absence of mass media make it important to use methods which lead to direct communication with all members of a community. This chapter reviews the application of drama as a means of communication in the planning process.

Drama is a useful tool that can be used by community leaders, government agents, NGO workers, researchers, and community groups. This chapter describes one project in which drama, combining song, dance and theatre, was used as a technology transfer method. The lessons learned from the evaluation can be transferred to other planning, extension and drama projects.

The case study presented in this chapter is an evaluation of a project entitled "Drama as a Technology Transfer Method" which took place in Uganda. In 1996, the International Center for Tropical Agriculture (CIAT) collaborated with the International Center for Research on Agroforestry (ICRAF) and the Ndere Dance Troupe, a professional drama group based in Kampala, in a technology transfer project. The project had two main objectives:

▶ to gain a better understanding of the role of drama groups in technology transfer;

▶ to increase the adoption of climbing bean production and agroforestry technology by introducing them at the same time.

The director of the Ndere Dance Troupe wrote the script based on a play previously performed by the Abekundire Women's Group. The play was put into written form and the professional drama group provided some acting training for the Abekundire Women's Group. As part of the training, the two drama groups performed together in six different communities to an estimated 13,000 people. A year after the initial performances, the Abekundire Women's Group performed the same play twice on their own. This final evaluation of the drama took place one year, or two harvests, after the first six performances.

THE LOCALE

The Kabale District in southwest Uganda is part of East Africa's highland region. There is concern about the current land management practices of small-scale farmers in the district. In recent years, a fungal disease which causes root rot of the common bush bean has become an increasingly serious problem. This fungus commonly occurs where agricultural land areas have been reduced, leading to intensive cultivation with no fallowing or effective crop rotation. Crop yields in the Kabale District have decreased dramatically and the majority of the rural people are not able to feed themselves adequately. Their protein intake and household incomes are seriously reduced.

Farmers can rectify this problem by planting bean varieties with greater resistance to the disease and by improving the soil fertility. The Uganda National Bean Program (UNBP), with support from CIAT and the Eastern and Central Africa Bean Research Network (ECABREN), have identified suitable varieties and better soil management alternatives to reduce losses to root rot diseases. The bean varieties, originating from the Rwandan National Bean Program, are climbing varieties with high yields and greater pest resistance. This integrated approach to disease management requires not only a shift from traditional bush beans to climbing varieties, but also improved soil fertility and use of stakes. Researchers see agroforestry as a sustainable way to improve farmers' access to the latter two components.

The reduced land base available for small-scale farmers is the result of a population increase related to a number of gender, culture and education issues. Kabale District is one of the fastest growing areas in East Africa. In the past, the people of the district, the Bakiga, were well known for being very hard workers. However, the men are now gaining a reputation for being lazy and drinking heavily (Rwangyezi, 1997). This behavior has a direct impact on overall agriculture production, family well being, and women's workload and responsibilities. As there are direct links between natural resource management and gender roles, it is important to address the issues simultaneously and the linkages clearly illustrated. Dealing with only one component of the issue will not effectively deal with the problem.

The Drama

The play is entitled *Ekikambi*, which literally means a piece of flat tobacco. The title refers to the Bakiga women's habit of chewing tobacco for a few weeks until it has become spent; if a woman does not have another piece of tobacco, she adds rock salt to the old lump of tobacco to revive its sharpness.

Throughout the play, *Ekikambi* is used in reference to the infertile soil of Kabale. As well, the term is used to describe the men of Kabale District, who are portrayed as drunks, and as useless as *Ekikambi*. Solutions to increase soil fertility and change men's lifestyles are equivalent to the rock salt.

The story depicts a hard-working woman named Bakeinyaga who, after being sent away by her drunk husband Rukanyanga, learns from other farmers about how to care for her soil, plant climbing beans and raise a zero-grazing cow. In the end, she improves her life, harvesting huge amounts of beans which enables her to feed her children properly and dress decently. Her husband realizes he is wasting his life while his wife is creating a better life for herself. He asks her to take him back and, after reciting all the "new technology" messages, she agrees.

The main messages are:
▶ improve the soil fertility by planting agroforestry trees and using manure from the zero-grazing cow;
▶ stabilize terraces by planting bunds along the edges;
▶ plant climbing beans which have greater yields and root rot resistance than bush beans;
▶ use the agroforestry trees for staking;
▶ stop or decrease drinking because it ruins families.

Unique Aspects of Project

Some extraordinary aspects of the Drama as Technology Transfer Project make this project unique. It is an unconventional extension method for an International Agricultural Research Center (IARC) to support, and it is not common for two

IARCs to work together to disseminate combined or complementary messages. In addition, the main extension agents are the actors, who are subsistence farmers. Many IARCs focus on research and work with wealthier farmers because they are, in theory, best able to carry out research experiments. In this project, the audience or recipients of the messages are from all wealth categories, while the actors are from the lowest wealth category.

EVALUATION METHODOLOGY

The purpose of the evaluation was to determine the appropriateness and effectiveness of drama as an agricultural extension tool. Appropriateness is measured in terms of how drama fits into the current communication system in rural Kabale communities, how farmers want to be given information, how they learn best and how they view drama in comparison to other extension methods. Effectiveness refers to the conative, cognitive and affective effects that drama has on an agricultural community (Gonzalez, 1991).

The project evaluation was done in eight phases: literature review, reconnaissance visits and rapid rural appraisal (RRA) exercises, Agricultural Knowledge and Information Systems (AKIS) identification and analysis, Communication Survey, Impact of Drama Survey and Extension Services Survey, Data Analysis, Women's Group Self-Evaluation, and Feedback Sessions. The evaluation took place in four communities, three in which the two groups had performed together, and one where the Abekundire Women's Group had performed alone.

A purposive sample of each community was used for the formal surveys. In total, 79 individuals participated: 60 from the communities where the drama was presented in 1997, nine from the Abekundire Women's Group, and ten from communities where the drama was recently performed and where the AKIS was identified. As the study did focus on agriculturists, 80 percent of the respondents were women, the main agriculturists in the area. In addition, the 15 organizations dealing with agricultural issues in Kabale District were interviewed to determine the extension services offered in the district.

RESULTS

Before looking specifically at drama, the farmers' current experience with agricultural extension was explored. In an RRA exercise, women, youth and men saw poverty related to low crop yields as the biggest problem facing communities. However, the communication survey showed that 67 percent of the respondents do nothing about the pests and diseases affecting their crops. Only 19 percent said they had tried a new method of digging, and 46 percent said they had tried, at one time, planting a new seed variety. Most farmers were not aware that certain bean varieties are resistant to root rot and have a greater yield than what is currently grown. As well, the average farmer interviewed did not know that there are agricultural research centers for crops such as beans. Only two percent of the sample had contact with some type of agriculture resource. As well, 43 percent had never had any previous contact with an agricultural extension agent.

Government agricultural extension agents primarily deal with groups of farmers. With restricted budgets and limited staff, this is more efficient than working with individuals. However, concentrating on groups overlooks the high percentage of people who do not belong to groups. In this study, 35 percent of the respondents were not members of formal or informal groups in their community. Those from the poorest and youngest people made up the largest percentage of non-members, while no large differentiation was seen in regards to education level, or gender.

Some women said they did not join groups because they felt they would be judged negatively if they did not have a nice dress, or more than one dress, to wear to meetings. Some said they did not join a craft group because they felt too proud to admit that they did not know how to do that craft.

The farmers, researchers, NGO staff, and Department of Agriculture staff agree that the current extension services are not adequate. There is a need for an extension service which meets the needs of farmers who live far from the town center, those who do not own land and specifically youth and women. However, the service should address the whole community because, although men do little agricultural work, they are part of the agriculture decision making process. In general, respondents felt that one of the best ways to disseminate agricultural information to the whole community was through the local government system.

In an RRA exercise, farmers ranked eight different learning methods according to how they learn best. Overall, drama was not identified by farmers as the best extension method that they learn from or would want to learn from. Drama ranked fourth, coming after learning from extension agents, individual experimenting and learning from other local farmers. Even so, farmers still identified some very positive aspects arising from drama presentations. Some quotes from farmers regarding drama included the following:

- "In the play there is demonstration and if you can learn through demonstration you can make a big change in your home."
- "Drama gets you motivated to work harder or change something."
- "... with drama, you can reflect on what is going on, its being played by the common people and therefore looks very real."
- "A play reinforces what I've already learned in the other extension tools."
- "... they (the actors) have to be demonstrating and you can go and copy what they have been showing you."
- "... because when you see people you can learn and it reinforces ideas that the agriculture officer has already discussed."
- "I can watch a demonstration and then compare what I see in the play to what I see at home."
- "In drama, there are demonstrations which I can carry out on the field."
- "... when acting you follow the play as if it is real. There is more interest in people."

From the comments, demonstrations within drama seem to be a key to both learning and motivation.

Amongst farmers from different categories, there was a strong preference for working with an agricultural extension agent, despite the fact that 43 percent of respondents had never before spoken with an extension agent. Ironically, slightly more people who had never had contact with an agricultural extension agent thought this contact would be the preferred method of learning. Interestingly, the farmers' perception of the "all-knowledgeable" extension worker contradicts many other viewpoints in the agricultural community. A frequently cited problem with extension systems in developing countries is the lack of trained extension agents (Peterson, 1997; McCaslin and Tibezinda, 1997; Halim and Ali, 1997).

In ranking extension preferences, farmers continually included extension methods in the sequence of how they would like to have information delivered, although this was not asked of them. This suggests that in order to achieve optimal understanding, messages need to be presented in numerous ways and through different means. Table 5.1 illustrates some of the findings on specific questions regarding extension preferences.

Table 5.1 Farmers' thoughts on extension

How would you like agricultural information?		What is the best way for government to pass on information to farmers?		Highest ranking choice of agricultural extension method from which you learn best (all respondents)?		Highest ranking choice of agricultural extension method from which you learn best (women)?		Highest ranking choice of agricultural extension method rfom which you learn best (men)?	
28%	Through an extension agent	65%	Through the local government system	45%	Extension agents	41%	Extension agents	50%	Extension agents
14%	Through a family member	15%	Through extension agents	20%	Experimenting	25%	Local farmers	38%	Experimenting
10%	Through local friends	5%	Through the Church	15%	Local farmers	16%	While doing chores	12%	Drama
10%	Through groups			5%	Drama	8%	Experimenting		
Others suggested workshops, government gatherings and experimentation		Others suggested women's groups and the radio		5%	Visiting farmers from outside				

In evaluating appropriateness, some form of agriculture extension is needed and wanted in Kabale District and drama does partially fulfill this need.

EFFECTIVENESS

In the evaluation, three types of effects were researched; cognitive, conative and affective. A cognitive effect pertains to knowledge gain, change in levels of awareness and forms of learning. Conative effect refers to behavior change, while affective effect refers to feelings connected to attitudes, opinions or evaluations. These can be positive, negative, or neutral feelings towards the object (Gonzalez, 1991, p. 45). For the purpose of this evaluation, cognitive effects were focused on, while affective and conative effects were identified but not thoroughly explored.

First of all, the drama's cognitive effects on communities are discussed. Past evaluations of drama projects reveal that drama is an effective method of raising awareness and teaching about issues. However, these evaluations have been primarily of dramas with dominantly social messages (i.e. family planning, AIDS, hygiene, privatization), and not technical messages related to agricultural practice.

The study results demonstrate that drama can be an effective method of both raising awareness and teaching about technical issues. It is estimated that more than 13,000 people saw the six performances, with attendance at each performance ranging from 600 to 4,000 people (Rwangyezi, 1998). Of the survey respondents who saw the drama, 68 percent said they learned something new from the drama, 24 percent said they did not learn anything new, and 8 percent said although they did not learn anything new, the play reminded them of correct practices and motivated them to continue farming.

Although the play was highly entertaining, filled with jokes, songs, dance and acrobatics, the audience still heard all the main messages that they were intended to hear. The first message discussed by those surveyed was to improve the soil, followed by planting climbing beans, planting agroforestry trees and obtaining a zero-grazing cow.

Closer examination found that different people heard and concentrated on distinct messages in the play. Men discussed the entertaining aspects first, followed by planting trees and raising cows; very few mentioned terracing land. In contrast, the women first discussed improving the soil, proceeded by planting climbing beans, planting trees and terracing the land. These findings reflect the traditional roles of women and men in the community. It can be assumed that relevant messages touched home and people connected to what was most prevalent in their minds.

Ten months after the performance, people were still able to describe the whole plot and pick out main messages. There are a number of possible reasons for this high rate of learning and retention. Although Uganda has a tradition of community theater, it is still an exceptional and therefore memorable event to see a Western style performance in the rural areas.

In addition, it seemed that the audience could relate quite closely to the characters. The problems experienced by the main characters were similar to their daily problems, so they were very attentive to the solutions. In one community, people are now using the names of the two main characters (Rukanyanga and

Bakeinyaga) to describe people in their own community. For example, when they see a woman working very hard, they refer to her as Bakeinyaga; when they see a drunkard, they call him Rukanyanga. At a performance in another community, an audience member was crying as the play ended. When asked why, he said he felt the play depicted his own life and it made him very sad.

Some respondents said they listened very hard because they knew the actors had come all the way from Kampala, so they obviously had something important to say. In contrast, others said that because the actors were local farmers like themselves, they knew the solutions must work.

One of the most important aspects was that people were having fun and it was not a serious environment. Although the play dealt with serious community issues, the audience members did not feel that they were being lectured to and were possibly more open to the messages being presented.

When describing the messages in the play, respondents connected the messages. They could picture everything in sequence – getting a cow, using manure to fertilize soil or planting trees to use as green manures, planting high yielding crops such as beans, staking beans using newly planted trees, and, in the end, being able to eat better. This suggests that the drama is truly a systems approach to technology transfer. Through a story, one can see a change in lifestyle and the activities which bring about the changes. Connecting an action like planting climbing beans to an emotion like happiness seemed to be effective.

Agriculture is not purely a technical activity – it has social, economical, political and physical dimensions. Production constraints are not only environmental or determined by land, labour and capital. An agriculturist's social relations affect the opportunities they have within and beyond the household (Cornwall & Scoones in Cornwall et. al., 1993). Therefore, it is important that people see the connections candidly and drama provides a means in which to display the relationships directly.

ADOPTION

The evaluation does show a certain degree of adoption of the new technologies promoted in the drama. Of those who watched the drama, 65 percent of the respondents said they had made a change in their agricultural practice because of the drama. After the drama, 39 percent planted climbing beans, 36 percent did not, and 25 percent were already growing climbing beans. The main reason for not growing climbing beans was a lack of seed (27 percent), no land (13 percent), and only 5 percent stated that staking was the main obstacle. The main reason given for growing the climbing bean was its high yield (46 percent).

After the drama, 48 percent of respondents said they planted trees, 18 percent did not and 34 percent had already planted trees. As for the community's drinking habits, 39 percent felt that there had been a decrease in drinking, 48 percent said there was no change and 14 percent did not know. One young respondent mentioned that after the drama, her father had stopped physically abusing her mother. Some men who were interviewed at the local bar stated that drinking had not necessarily decreased, but they were trying to start drinking later in the day.

To see if the drama sparked initiative to seek out more information about the issues it had raised, participants were asked if they had contacted an organization or government official for more information after watching the drama. The results show that few were motivated to seek more information: 18 percent sought more information, 2 percent were already in contact with an organization or government official, but 80 percent did not seek more information.

To investigate the flow of information, the respondents who attended the drama were asked if they had told others about the presentation and over 75 percent responded that they had. A small percentage (18 percent) of those who did not attend heard all the main messages from someone who had attended, however 47 percent only heard that a theater group had come, and 35 percent did not even know that a group had performed.

It is difficult to measure why there is a behaviour change. Even though the respondents were asked if they changed or started a new practice because of the drama, there are always other factors which influence adoption.

In two of the communities studied, NGOs were working on issues similar to those presented in the play. These communities saw a slightly higher implementation rate than in the communities where there were no NGOs working.

Farmers themselves mentioned lack of seed as the main reason they did not grow climbing beans after the drama. It is difficult to get climbing bean seeds, and project organizers promised to bring seed to the communities a week after the performances. However, the organizers were not prepared to distribute on a mass level and, in the end, only gave seed to a few groups. Ten months later, most villagers were still waiting for seeds to be brought to them.

Other changes in individuals or communities as a result of the drama were also investigated. Interviews with the Abekundire Women's Group revealed unexpected benefits from the drama project. The women had been working with AFRENA-ICRAF since 1990 and were grateful for the work that ICRAF had done with them. They wanted to share the knowledge they had gained from this relationship and the drama allowed them to relate their experience to other farmers. Many of the women gained self-confidence by performing in front of a large audience. The group has become highly respected in the community, even by men. Although these were not the goals of the project, these elements are extremely important in any community development project.

The Abekundire Women's Group inspired other community groups to start their own drama groups. As more local drama groups form, the extension method could become more sustainable.

SUMMARY OF FINDINGS

Table 5.2 highlights the main strengths and weaknesses of the drama project.

Table 5.2 Strengths and weaknesses

STRENGTHS	WEAKNESSES
° partially fulfilled the need for extension	° message design was not participatory resulting
° large amount of beneficiaries	in some inaccurate messages
° does not exclude people	° the project plan was such that there was no
° audience and actors learned about issues that	opportunity to increase communication
are important to them	between researcher and farmer
° high implementation rate	° negative repercussion of broken promise
° most messages that were discussed were	syndrome
very relevant to the audience	° some messages did not address key issues
° actors gained self-confidence and respect	° not a sustainable dissemination method
within community	
° created discussion within community about	
issues that are difficult to discuss	
° encouraged and motivated farmers	
° sparked interest and built awareness of	
possible solutions	

Exploration of strengths

Raising Awareness: In the communication study, it was revealed that the Kabale District extension service and NGOs work with interested groups in the focus area.

The problem with this approach is farmers who are not aware of the technologies will not make the effort to join the group or they will not be invited to join. Therefore, a drama may complement the current extension system by creating awareness of issues and new technologies.

Raising a Sensitive Social Issue: *Ekikambi* focused on excessive drinking, a difficult issue to discuss. Few agricultural extension tools could approach this social issue diplomatically or tie it to the communities' agricultural issues. In some ways, not having direct contact with audience members allowed the audience to listen and not be threatened by the messages. They could assess the issues and process the information as they saw fit. If people were addressed individually or if it were directly stated that the community had a problem, people might feel their lifestyle were being judged. They might take a defensive stance, without reflecting on their habits and the effects of their habits.

Encouraging Community Support: It may be advantageous that the drama is seen by a large group. If an audience member decides to change his or her agricultural practice, the decision would be understood by other community members – at least those who watched the drama. In some communities, it is felt that anyone who makes an improvement in life will be sabotaged. If most of the community is involved in the drama performance, there might be a supportive environment for change. In one community, the men interviewed said they had decided, as a group, to try to start drinking later in the day.

Exploration of weaknesses

Participation: The project was not participatory in many ways. As the implementation and learning rates seem quite high, the participatory factor may not be relevant, but there is reason to believe it is.

Although greater participation may not increase learning or implementation, it could result in a more sustainable methodology, it could evoke more critical thinking, and the messages could be more appropriate.

Firstly, farmers (both actors and audience) were not involved in designing the messages or writing the script. While many of the messages were relevant to the audience, certain points such as the reason for planting agroforestry trees or how to acquire bean seed were not as accurate as the script writer had anticipated.

Secondly, because the Abekundire Women's Group were not included in the logistics of staging a play, they were not prepared to do it on their own means and initiative.

Thirdly, the audience had limited involvement with actors during and after the play. The Abekundire Women's Group is an enormous source of information on agroforestry tree production, soil conservation techniques and climbing bean production, as well as drama. During the performance, the audience was engaged a few times by actors asking questions. Afterwards, however, the opportunity for discussion between actors and audience was not explored. To hold the audience's attention and provoke critical thinking, more interaction is needed. The Abekundire Women's Group has recognized this as a failure and will try to include more audience participation in future performances.

Gap Between Farmer and Researcher: The large communication gap between researcher and farmer is a current issues in extension literature and in the IARCs (FAO, 1995; Cornwall *et al.* 1993). This has prompted the researcher to look at whether drama as a dissemination tool narrows this gap or creates a communication link between researcher and farmer. The way this project was conducted does not address the issue, but adjustments to the project could possibly improve the flow of information, especially from farmer to researcher. This issue is dealt with further in the recommendation section.

Broken Promise Syndrome: During RRA activities, community visits, and while conducting the surveys, farmers asked constantly about the promised bean seed. There cannot be enough said about the effect of broken promises on rural communities. Promising resources to farmers is problematic in many ways, as it creates unnecessary dependency on outside sources. Not following through on promises is even more problematic, as it creates mistrust of organizations. In this case, some farmers consciously decided not to seek out climbing bean seed on their own because they were waiting to be given the seed. Giving information or sources of information and telling people how to secure resources is much more useful and sustainable than handing out or promising resources.

Sustainability: Drama on a large scale is not a sustainable method of information dissemination, as an external body will always have to pay for the performances. One option would be to have the audience pay to see the drama, but this would drastically reduce the number of people receiving the messages, diminishing one of the strengths of this tool. As well, a paying audience may demand to see professionally trained actors, which again diminishes the strength of community drama. Although the Abekundire Women's Group was motivated to perform because they wanted to disseminate information, they do not have the financial resources to continue performing for other communities in the district. They could possibly market themselves as an extension service to NGOs, the Ministry of Agriculture and research centers. Drama may become more sustainable as small, local drama groups are inspired to start their own groups within rural communities.

Risks and Threats: There are a number of risks associated with using drama. First of all, drama can be as powerful, persuasive and coercive a tool as other mass media vehicles. The hazard lies in the messages disseminated. In a project proposal, Rwangyezi refers to the power of drama: "As a result of the attractive, friendly, yet effective methods of communication, learners end up demanding even painful experiences like circumcision and participation in wars" (1995). It is important to recognize that drama is a powerful tool, which can influence people with both positive and negative messages.

Secondly, the image portrayed by actors to their communities can, in some cases, harm the individual. Members of one community commented that a woman seen acting in a play might be shunned because she was not working in her fields. However, some women countered this notion, as they felt that once the community had been exposed to a performance, they would not judge the actors so negatively. Some men said they would not allow their wives to travel in a drama group, because it would appear they did not have control over their wives.

Thirdly, the use of an indigenous tradition by "outsiders", as well as the use of a tradition for unjust intentions, can often devalue the custom. There is the risk of drama becoming a commercial tool in Uganda. Already a theater company in Kampala is hired by companies like Coca-Cola to perform advertisements. In this project, however, the messages disseminated were based on altruistic intentions.

LESSONS LEARNED AND RECOMMENDATIONS

After considering the lessons learned from the project evaluation, the following recommendations are made for planning community based projects using drama:

Messages: As drama can be a powerful, influential tool, it is important that the messages disseminated are correct. A check system should be incorporated in the project plan, with a reliable source verifying all of the technical and social messages before a drama is presented.

In addition, several options for solving problems should be included in the drama. This would reflect the complex decision making process that families normally go through. For example, in the Kabale context, the play could depict women improving their lives in different ways: one woman stopping root rot by improving her soil, another woman planting climbing beans, and one woman rotating crops by growing and selling potatoes and buying beans with her profits.

Some actors and playwrights feel that exaggeration is a key entertaining component in drama. However, when the project's main objective is to inform, there should be a balance between the teaching and entertainment aspects, so that accurate messages are conveyed and the audience remains attentive.

The more people are involved in designing the messages presented, the more appropriate and relevant the messages will be. Deciding how to involve various stakeholders in the process is a difficult issue. Three models are presented in the following section.

Follow-up: In order to ensure that the messages disseminated can be implemented, it is important to plan for all the necessary elements the audience members will need. In this case, climbing bean seed was not available after the performances and one of the main reasons given for not planting climbing beans was the lack of seed.

In addition, the local drama group should keep a record of the community members who were involved in the project for future research on the impact of drama and to monitor the project.

Performance: To make the play more relevant for the audience, local names should be incorporated in the play. There should be much interaction with the audience, in order to hold their attention. For example, they could be asked for advice or asked to help determine the final solution, or there could be a question and answer period at the end of the performance.

The drama should be performed on a day when most people are able to attend, in order to reach the largest possible audience. In Kabale, women can attend performances on market days or Sundays, usually the only days that women do not cultivate.

NGOs working in the community should be invited to the performance so they are aware of the messages and become familiar with the method of dissemination. As previously stated, drama is most effective as a complementary extension tool.

Advertising: The performance should be advertised at least two weeks before

55

the performance. The church and local market are effective venues for advertising in Kabale.

Training: In order for a local drama group to take complete responsibility for the project, there needs to be a training component which covers the logistics of presenting a drama (transport, sound system, advertisement), and how to manage a budget. In some cases, literacy classes may be needed.

Payment: Those participants who are to receive payment should not be paid until there is proof that the service has been rendered. The money for direct costs will need to be paid beforehand, but the service fee should be held back. Prices for drama performances range from 100,000 to 200, 000 Ugandan Shillings (USD $78-$156) depending on the distance the group must travel.

MODELS FOR USING DRAMA FOR COMMUNITY LEARNING

This specific Ugandan project yielded numerous lessons which can be applied to other planning contexts and community projects. Based on the lessons stated above and those from other evaluations of drama extension projects, three models for using drama are presented here. Each involves drama yet uses the mode of communication differently. The three models represent different theories of development, communication and drama. Obviously, many different types of projects can use drama and the three suggested here are not the only available options.

Model 1: Development Worker Driven. This model builds upon the lessons learned in the Drama as a Technology Transfer Project. The objective is to disseminate complementary messages to as many people as possible and to a wide variety of people, as opposed to a certain segment of society. The messages are designed by the research centers or non-governmental organizations, and a local drama group incorporates the messages into a play and performs the drama. The development worker's role is to develop the information package, explain it to the drama group and possibly be available as a resource person. This is the least costly and least time-consuming of the three models, however, in a number of ways, it is the least sustainable.

Model 2: Actor Driven. This is a longer process, in which development workers and a local drama group work together on experiments or demonstration projects. Based on this experience and in consultation with the development workers, the group designs a skit which incorporates the desired messages. After each performance, a question and answer period is held with the audience. The actors' experience in the demonstration will probably have given them the information they need to answer the questions. If they do not have the information, they can direct the person to a source that does. The questions and answers are recorded for the community workers, to keep them informed on current issues. The partnership formed between the actors and community workers is ultimately an equal relationship. Initially, the actors will be gaining confidence in their own knowledge developed through the consultation with the development worker. Gradually, information will flow evenly between the two sources. Over time, this option could become self-sustaining if the drama group were able to establish a business connection based on the messages being disseminated (for example, *Ekikambi* might be supported by a seed distribution center or tree nursery) or market themselves to NGOs as a complementary extension resource.

Model 3: Community Driven. This model uses drama not as a disseminating tool but as a facilitation tool. It is based on the concept of popular theater in which a community uses role play or psychodrama to identify community issues, roots of problems and action plans. Role playing is useful in that there are many things we know, but they cannot be stated. According to Fabian, "... they can be represented – and made present – only through action, enactment and performance." (Fabian in Cornwall *et. al.*, 1993, p. 9). The focus of popular theater is to integrate a community's culture with development needs identified by the community. Seeing how a community handles problems can be a learning process for development workers as well. The flow of information is mainly within the community and from the community to the development worker. This is the most sustainable option as it is community driven. However, it is time-consuming and finding the human resources to facilitate this process may be challenging.

PROJECT EVALUATION CONCLUSION

This evaluation has attempted to illustrate the usefulness of drama as an extension tool in the highlands of Southwest Uganda, as well as its potential as a broader tool for communication and community involvement in planning and development. It suggests that drama is an appropriate and effective method of extension in this district. Drama is able to reach a large number of people in a short time, in a district where there are few extension workers and many farmers who need to address a serious agricultural issue. Although farmers do not perceive drama as the best way to learn, some see it as a motivational and supportive tool and it has the potential to spark community discussion and innovation. The beneficiaries are from all sectors of the community; no one is excluded. The results suggest that drama does have a positive impact on communities, as it informs, involves and motivates people towards positive change.

CONCLUSION

In many cultures, drama is thought of primarily as a form of entertainment. Drama can also raise awareness, provoke thought and discussion, facilitate, inform and motivate. These results are necessary and important in any research and development project or program. Drama is often one of the best communication tools for crossing social barriers of language, ethnicity, class, gender, wealth, politics and religion. These are barriers which often inhibit communications between groups and block a project's success.

In addition, drama is a way to inspire greater community participation in a planning process. The word "participation" is common in current research and development literature. Organizations, development workers, and planners are aware of the importance of involving the main beneficiaries as much as possible in the different stages of projects. It is believed that greater participation will bring about more relevant and sustainable programs that fit the true needs of communities. However, planners struggle with exactly how to effect greater participation. Drama may provide a partial solution.

Drama is an effective way of communicating between groups who have cultural or political difficulty expressing ideas to one another. In places where drama is a traditional way of passing on information or story telling, there is usually respect for actors and the messages expressed. Drama creates an environment in which an audience is able to discreetly filter the information and take in what is relevant and important to them. It provides an opportunity for people to reflect on their own lives, practices and actions. It is effective in raising awareness and encouraging people in their current work. Drama can inform both illiterate and literate people, as well as those schooled and not schooled. It is a useful means to convey messages to large groups and it stimulates action and thought within small groups.

The versatility of drama allows for a variety of applications in the planning process. Organizations or ministries can teach about laws or land regulations using drama. It can be used to put social and moral pressure on people to change habits which affect the entire community. It can teach specific techniques, practices and concepts. As well, drama can encourage people to find their own solutions. It can be used by researchers as a way to facilitate community members determining their own indicators of project or program success. Communities can use drama as a means to facilitate discussion about issues that need to be addressed but are difficult to discuss.

This chapter has focused upon the application of drama in a specific location and context. The findings, however, have a much broader application. The need for public involvement is an important component of virtually all planning and community development contexts. Whether it be the establishment of a health program, the building of a school or disseminating information about soil and water conservation techniques, community involvement is essential in, ideally, all stages of a project. A variety of tools is available to the planner, extension agent or development worker to communicate with and involve a community, and selecting the appropriate tool may very well determine the success of the project.

ACKNOWLEDGEMENTS

This research was financially supported by the Environmental Capacity Enhancement Project (ECEP) based out of the University of Guelph, Canada, and by the African Highlands Initiative (AHI) coordinated by the International Center for Research on Agroforestry (ICRAF). Technical and logistical support was provided primarily by the International Center of Tropical Agriculture (CIAT), with additional support from the Agroforestry Research Network in Africa (AFRENA) of ICRAF in Kabale, AHI and CARE-Uganda in Kabale. Christine Mugisha, as research assistant, and Gladys Tukahirwa, as the chair of the Abekundire Women's Group, provided valuable assistance throughout the process of this study. Dr. Soniia David, Dr. Roger Kirkby and Dr. Charles Wortmann of CIAT are acknowledged for their supportive guidance, insight and expertise throughout this research and in the writing of this report. Finally, those of Kabale District and Kampala who participated in this study are acknowledged as it was their willing participation which ultimately made this research possible.

REFERENCES

Blackburn, D. (ed.). 1994: *Extension Handbook: Processes and Practices*. Toronto: Thompson Educational Publishing Inc.

Cornwall, A., Guijt, I. and Welbourn, A. 1993: *Acknowledging Process: Challenges for Agriculture Research and Extension Methodology*. Brighton: IDS Discussion Paper, No. 333.

FAO. 1995: *Understanding farmers' communication networks; an experience in the Philippines*. Rome: Communication for Development Case Study, No. 14.

Gonzalez, H. 1991: *The Myths of Communication and Development: Why Information Campaigns Fail and How they can Succeed*. New York: IIRR, Communication and Development Research Paper, No. 1.

Halim, A. and Ali, M.M. 1997. Training and Professional Development. In Swanson, Burton *et. al.* (eds.), *Improving Agricultural Extension: A Reference Manual*. FAO.

McCaslin, N. and Tibeinda, J. 1997. Assessing Target Group Needs. In Swanson, Burton *et. al.* (eds.), *Improving Agricultural Extension: A Reference Manual*. FAO.

Peterson, Warren. 1997. The Context of Extension in Agricultural and Rural Development. In Swanson, Burton *et. al.* (eds.), *Improving Agricultural Extension: A Reference Manual*. FAO.

Rwangyezi, S. 1995: Project Proposal titled *Alternative Methods of Technology Transfer – Theater as the Natural Attractive and Friendly Way of Making Long Lasting Impact*. Kampala.

Rwangyezi, S. 1997: Ndere Dance Troupe. (Personal Communication) Kampala.

Rwangyezi, S. 1998: Final Report on Project titled *Alternative Methods of Technology Transfer – Theater as the Natural Attractive and Friendly Way of Making Long Lasting Impact*. Kampala.

Chapter 6

Vegetation Survey and Classification - Their Role in Land Use Planning and Development

by Lindah Mhlanga and Isaac Mapaure

Introduction

This chapter presents case study results of a vegetation survey of selected islands on Lake Kariba, Zimbabwe. The chapter draws mainly from experiences in Zimbabwe, but the concepts discussed may be applicable to other countries in the region and beyond. The researchers contend that vegetation survey and classification should use a unified classification and mapping system for results to be comparable, and vegetation mapping should guide land use planning. It is concluded that data on vegetation structure, composition and condition should be integrated in land use planning.

General background

The objective of vegetation survey and classification should be to accurately describe vegetation in terms of plant associations and identify relationships between the environment and these associations or their constituent species (Muller, 1983). Information on flora of an area should be systematically and objectively collected. Vegetation surveys should describe, delimit and classify existing plant associations on floristic criteria into vegetation types. Such surveys facilitate the assessment of natural resources valuable in land use planning, in determining conservation priorities and in identifying areas suitable for *in situ* conservation of bio-diversity (Rogers, 1994). In countries where pristine/natural vegetation exist, sound and objective classification of vegetation has important practical applications for both management and planning. Such surveys should provide a classification system which is ecologically reliable and readily adaptable to the planning process. This can facilitate efficient and sustainable utilization of natural vegetation, assist in land use planning, and is the only objective way available for selecting nature reserves (Muller, 1981).

Vegetation survey is considered an important activity in physical resources inventory programmes, especially in developing countries (Muller, 1983). Data on vegetation gathered during surveys should be integrated into environmental decision making, together with data on other important relevant resources. Other than being a valuable aid in land use planning, vegetation data form a basis for vegetation resources studies, assist in the proper utilization of vegetation and individual component species, identify conservation areas and areas relatively undisturbed.

FUNCTION OF VEGETATION SURVEYS AND CLASSIFICATION

Role of vegetation in land use planning

Vegetation surveys facilitate the assessment of natural resources valuable in land use planning (Rogers, 1994). The destruction of possible conservation sites due to unplanned development (Muller, 1994) is threatening the environment in most developing countries in Africa. Land use planning and development decisions ought to be cognisant of natural resource inventories, particularly vegetation which is usually overwhelmed by other forms of land use. Vegetation data has to be included in the planning process both from the point of view of its utilization and for the conservation of designated areas.

The function of a vegetation survey depends primarily on the objective of the survey and these can vary from one survey to another. Surveys, however, can be used as basic resource inventories and to determine conservation priorities and target areas for germplasm collection. Vegetation surveys and classification are of paramount importance in objective and comprehensive bio-diversity conservation (Muller, 1994). Muller (1983, 1994) presented a case for vegetation surveys in developing countries and he discusses the main functions of vegetation surveys.

Resource Inventory

Land use in most developing countries is based on the utilization of natural vegetation. In Zimbabwe, two-thirds of the land is non-arable (Muller, 1983) and communities rely on natural vegetation for their livelihood. Rural communities heavily depend on vegetation to graze and browse their domestic livestock, for fruits, fuelwood, construction timber and traditional medicines. Careful planning and rationalized use of vegetation and other resources would ensure sustainability and better livelihoods of most communities. Sound inventories of the vegetation resources providing clear descriptions of the availability of graze, browse, fruit, firewood and pole resources are required for planning purposes. Such information will enable people to determine current use, predict future demand and threats to existing resources, thus enabling planners, decision makers and other stakeholders to institute appropriate management measures. Excessive removal or uncontrolled exploitation of plants would result in loss of vegetal cover leading to environmental degradation and loss of desirable plant species.

Environmental degradation is now a common phenomenon threatening most communal areas in East and Southern Africa. Reliance on vegetation has increased, with growing human populations and localized high densities of livestock putting more pressure on the resource. There is now a gradual realization that vegetation should be considered as a key resource in land use planning in order to avert environmental disasters.

Bio-diversity conservation

Objective and comprehensive bio-diversity conservation requires vegetation surveys and inventories in order to cover all ecological zones and habitats (Muller, 1994). Bio-diversity can be conserved either *in situ* or *ex situ*. Both *in situ* and *ex situ* conservation require ecogeographic data which is primarily collected through field surveys. There is a need to carry out surveys in most developing countries and ensure that such information is made available to planners. The lack of survey-based data is one of the main reasons why *in situ* botanical conservation has not progressed in the Third World (Muller, 1994).

Ecogeographic surveys and ex-situ conservation

Ecogeographic surveys involve ecological, conservation, geographic and taxonomic information gathering and synthesis, the results of which should be predictive and can be used to assist in the formulation of priorities for collection and conservation (Maxted, Van Slageren & Rihan, 1992). This is primarily for plant genetic resources conservation whereby the total genetic diversity of cultivated species and wild relatives has to be collected and preserved. Distribution maps are generated from field data and specific geographical locations and habitat niches favoured by the target taxa identified. This is followed by survey missions, in which localities expected to contain the target taxa are visited by a collector. The area is then divided into grids and surveyed. Specific localities where the target taxa are found are noted in the process. During ecogeographic surveys, the collectors identify areas suitable for *in situ* and on-farm conservation, target areas for germplasm collection, and identify areas of high bio-diversity. Data collected during ecogeographic surveys is used to formulate conservation objectives and strategies. Conservation objectives include an assessment of threats of genetic erosion in the area, availability of resources and political and geographic limitations within the target areas.

Exploration or collection missions rely on data collected during ecogeographic surveys. The information is used as a basis for planning collecting missions in order to maximize the sampling of genetic diversity. The major objective during collecting missions is to maximize the genetic diversity sampled (Maxted *et. al.*, 1992). The collector has to rely on existing information in herbaria to be able to go in the field with clearly defined targets for taxa, areas and habitats.

In situ conservation and nature reserves

In situ conservation in the form of either genetic resources reserves or nature reserves is a form of land use. Ecogeographic data generated during surveys can be used to determine minimum requirements for the conservation of the targeted species. The ecogeographic information should enable the conservationist to determine the number of populations to be conserved, based on the spatial distribution of the species, the size and structure of each population and ecological and environmental conditions that should be covered, and the size of the habitat units. In order to choose sites, extensive inventorying of existing and potential nature reserves is done. Comprehensive and detailed information on botanic taxa growing in the reserve will be generated, as well as general information on existing nature reserves, their location, size and purpose. This information will be overlaid on geological and meteorological data to assess the extent to which existing nature reserves are handling genetic diversity. Information generated during inventories is used as a basis to designate the reserves. The minimum requirements of the target population will determine the physical design of the reserves: shape, size, zoning, boundaries and distances between reserves.

Vegetation surveys can be used to locate, identify and select nature reserves.

In Zimbabwe, most of the effort in conservation has been towards large mammal populations. Less consideration has been given to conservation of plant bio-diversity or areas of botanical interest (Timberlake, Nobanda & Mapaure, 1993). Experiences from Zimbabwe during the vegetation survey of communal areas (Timberlake *et. al.*, 1993) has shown that such areas can be identified and characterized. Four criteria were used to identify small areas with potential for conservation:

▶ **rarity in the country**;
▶ high **plant species diversity** in a comparatively limited area;
▶ **wide variety of habitats** in a comparatively limited area;
▶ **relatively undisturbed condition** or particularly good example of a more widespread vegetation type (Timberlake, Nobanda, Mapaure & Mhlanga, 1991).

Similar criteria can be used elsewhere and surveys can be done to cover the whole country.

After identification and description of flora, it is essential that formal conservation measures are instituted. The major challenge is to bring such information to the attention of appropriate authorities and land use planners so that areas identified are conserved. Botanical conservation should constitute part of land use planning and a clear national policy should be articulated. Land pressures due to increasing population usually threaten high bio-diversity or areas containing rare vegetation types. Local communities can be encouraged to take up the responsibility of managing such sites.

Surveys of national parks and forest lands

Large tracts of protected areas exist in most countries. Most of these parks have not been surveyed and, according to Muller (1994), existing protected areas are due to chance rather than informed planning. Vegetation surveys of protected areas will identify plant species and habitat types that are already adequately protected (Muller, 1981). In Zimbabwe, a survey of the vegetation of national parks is on-going. Hwange National Park (Rogers, 1994), Sengwa Wildlife Research (Craig, 1983), the Chirisa Safari Area (Craig, Martin & Mahlangu, 1984) and Matetsi Safari Area (Worsely, 1988) have been surveyed using aerial photography and Braun-Blanquet approach to vegetation classification (Rogers, 1994). The Forestry Commission of Zimbabwe has also carried out vegetation surveys in some of the

Botanical Reserves and Forest Lands falling under their jurisdiction. Such surveys are useful in providing background information and baseline data for park management and a basis for further vegetation studies (Rogers, 1994).

Vegetation as an indicator

Vegetation is an integration of all environmental factors (Rogers, 1993) and, as such, they can give a good indication of potential for agriculture for an area (Timberlake *et. al.*, 1993). Vegetation surveys can play a significant role in clarifying and mapping agro-ecological zones, giving indications of agricultural potential of an area. Vincent and Thomas (1961) carried out an agro-ecological zonation of Zimbabwe, in which vegetation was used as a guide to general agricultural potential in the five ecological zones of the country. They paid particular reference to soil-vegetation association, such as the Kalahari sands in Zimbabwe, which support Baikiaea plurijuga woodlands.

The close relationship that exists between vegetation and soil was recognized in some pedological work (e.g. Nyamapfene, 1988). The use of vegetation, especially trees, as a guide in soil surveys is advantageous because the patterns which they form are readily identifiable on aerial photographs and trees are recognizable in the field from a distance (Nyamapfene, 1988). Nyamapfeme (1988) gives examples of good soil indicators from Zimbabwe. *Terminalia sericea* is indicative of deep, well-drained sands. *Colophospermum mopane*, a common tree species in Southern Africa, is an indicator of moderately deep soils of good agricultural potential in hot, semi and low rainfall areas in Zimbabwe. *Brachystegia boehmii* and *Uapaca kirkiana*, when co-dominant, indicate the presence of well-drained, shallow, gravelly soils. *Diplorhynchus condylocarpon* occurs on soils that have an inverse calcium to magnesium ratio and toxic levels of heavy metals, notably nickel and chromium. Variations are expected to occur, depending on moisture availability, altitude, rainfall and soil texture. Generalizations across broader spatial scales can not be made. Specific circumstances have to be studied and relationships drawn.

Relationships also exist between vegetation and geology through the influence of geology on the soil. Vegetation can also be used as a guide in locating minerals; geobotany and biogeochemistry (Thomas, Walker & Wild, 1977). Through surveys, plant communities that show associations with rock types can be identified and used as a guide in mineral prospecting projects. More specific examples of vegetation-soil relationships have been documented by Wild (1965, 1968, 1970), with specific reference to vegetation types associated with serpentine, copper and nickel.

Vegetation monitoring

Baseline vegetation data is required for the monitoring of the effects of developments on the vegetation. Environmental degradation, particularly destruction of woodlands and forests is a common phenomenon in developing countries. There is, however, no baseline vegetation data against which degradation can be measured (Timberlake *et. al.*, 1993). Vegetation data from observable points enables future monitoring of ecological changes.

Methods and approaches used in vegetation surveying and inventory

Vegetation classification systems are of two main types: physiognomic and floristic or phytosociological (Mueller-Dombois & Ellenberg, 1974). Physiognomic classification describes the growth form and structural appearance of the vegetation. Forms denoted by woodland, shrubland or grassland are physiognomic or structural types. Such classification can be useful in country-wide mapping and in approximate habitat descriptions (Muller, 1983) which require more information on the floristic composition.

The National Herbarium of Zimbabwe has developed and adopted a standardized phytosociological classification system that can be used in research, land management and land use planning. The classification system was used during the communal lands vegetation survey (Timberlake *et. al.*, 1993). The method relies on extensive collection of species cover data. The underlying factors were (a) the vegetation classification obtained must be based on floristic criteria; and each of the categories or types produced must correspond, where possible, to one particular type of each environment (b) the need for a common approach to vegetation classification by all concerned with the management of natural vegetation and (c) the methods used to sample and classify have to be objective so that results obtained by different people in different places are comparable (Muller, 1983). The classification includes each type of vegetation found in the country. It can be used on small areas and, as long as a similar approach is used, a country map can be produced. A detailed description of the methods is in Muller (1983), Craig (1983) and Timberlake *et. al.* (1993). The method is largely an improvement, modification and hybridization of some of the earlier systems used by various researchers. The method is based principally on floristic composition of the woody species rather than vegetation structure alone.

The inventory approach from which the classification was adopted involves interpretation of panchromatic aerial photographs in order to stratify the vegetation into reasonably homogenous units, which are used as a framework for sampling. This is followed by plotless field sampling covering all the stratified types in areas of reasonably representative vegetation. A random starting point is selected at each site and a circular area covered from the central point. All woody and grass species occurring in the areas are recorded and the area is expanded until no new species are encountered. Care has to be taken not to transgress any obvious environmental boundaries.

Woody species are assessed for cover-abundance using a modified Braun-Blanquet Scale (Table 6.1) (Mueller-Dombois & Ellenberg, 1974).

Table 6.1 The modified Braun-Blanquet Scale

Species frequency and estimate aerial cover	Braun-Blanquet symbol
Few with small cover	+
Numerous but less than 5% cover or scattered with up to 5% cover	1
Any number with 5-25% cover	2
Any number with 25-50% cover	3
Any number with 50-75%	4
Any number with more than 75% cover	5

The Braun-Blanquet approach is based on three assumptions:
- classification and interpretation of communities can be based on floristic composition;
- some species in a community give a more sensitive expression of relationships than others;
- these indicator species will be used to organize communities into a hierarchical classification (Whittaker, 1975).

Cover abundance for grasses is determined using 1 x 1 m quadrants placed at each sampling site. Environmental data such as landscape type, soil type, grazing intensity and burning are also recorded. Soil samples can also be collected and analyzed for physical and chemical properties.

Data collected is analyzed for classification using various methods. Two Way Indicator Species Analysis (TWINSPAN; Hill, 1979a), a computer programme developed specifically for vegetation classification, can be used. It is a divisive hierarchical vegetation classification technique and a dichotomized ordination analysis (Hill, 1979b). TWINSPAN compares the species composition of each sample with every other sample and places similar samples together in a sample by species matrix (phytosociological table) (Rogers, 1993). Species-cover data can also be analyzed by DECORANA (Hill, 1979). Detrended Correspondence Analysis (DCA; Gauch, 1982), a direct gradient analysis technique, determines similarity relationships among vegetation and among samples and calculates axes score for each sample (or species). Ordination diagrams are produced. Hierarchical Cluster Analysis can also be used to produce classification of vegetation, using species presence-absence data. Hierarchical Cluster Analysis divides the samples into a hierarchy of dissimilar entities and the results can be presented as a dendrogram. Relationships between vegetation and environmental variables can be analyzed by Canonical Correspondence Analysis (Ter Braak, 1991). This method is an egenvector technique for relating community composition to known variations in the environment.

Description of vegetation types is based on interpretation of the results from either of these methods as well as field observations. The vegetation are described, according to Pratt, Greenway & Gwynee (1966), in terms of the typical vegetation structure. This physiognomic classification can be adapted to suit varying situations. For the vegetation types in Zimbabwe, thirteen physiognomic types were distinguished by Timberlake et. al. (1993). These include moist forest, dry forest, bushland/woodland thicket, closed woodland, woodland, bushland, wooded grassland, bushed grassland, moorland, grasslands, permanent swamp, barren land and cleared land. Details on the description of each physiognomic type are in Timberlake et. al. (1993). Types can be described in terms of their typical vegetation structure, determining and characteristic species, important associated species (including grasses), distribution in the country, variation, differences from similar vegetation types, topographic features, underlying geology, soil type, past and present land use, general ecology and possible determining factors (Timberlake et. al., 1993). Vegetation maps of the surveyed area can be produced. Data on aerial photographs is transferred to base maps and vegetation maps produced.

Case Study: A Floristic Classification of Selected Islands on Lake Kariba, Zimbabwe

Creation of Lake Kariba

The formation of Lake Kariba, a vast artificial body of water, resulted in the inundation of 5,180 km^2 in the Zambezi River valley (Lake Kariba Coordinating Committee, 1960). The flooding of the valley floor left the crests of ridges and hills now exposed as islands in the lake. There are 190 islands on the Zimbabwean side and 103 on the Zambian side. Most of the islands in Lake Kariba originated from geological faulting and therefore occur in chains especially southwest of the Chete gorge and in the Sibilobilo area. Their total surface area is 147 km^2 and their shoreline totals 604 km. Most of the islands have steep shores and are covered with sandstone boulders and solid outcrops of sandstone, while some are sandy plateaux. They vary considerably in size with the smallest, Pimple, being 2 ha and the largest, Chete Island, which is 2,637 ha in extent. Sizes of the islands vary annually and smaller ones appear and disappear with fluctuations in the lake level. When the lake level falls drastically, islands near the mainland are reconnected.

The islands are not evenly distributed in the lake. Seven major groups can be distinguished (Lake Kariba Coordinating Committee, 1960). A group of 52 islands occur along the northern shore between Lufua and Kariba, 25 are found along the Sanyati gulf and 43 extend from Sibilobilo fishing camp up to Kotakota narrows. The lower end of the lake has groupings of 22, 44, 34, and 20 islands in the Bumi River estuary, Sengwa River estuary, Binga east-Sinazongwe west Chete gorge area and Sebungwe River estuary, respectively.

Previous vegetation studies

The vegetation type of the Zambezi valley, in which the islands fall, is predominantly savanna woodland dominated by *Colophospermum mopane* interspersed with thicket vegetation (Wild & Barbosa, 1967; Child, 1968; Balon & Coche, 1974). The terrestrial vegetation of the flooded valley was principally deciduous except for a narrow fringe of evergreen trees on fertile alluvium along rivers (Balon & Coche, 1974). Most of the vegetation surveys on the islands have been confined to either one or a few islands. Schramm (1978) found the predominant vegetation type on Dinosaur Island was *Colophospermum mopane* woodland, but he distinguished ten micro-community types according to species

70

dominance. Dyer (1985), in his study of Dinosaur Island in the Sibilobilo area, also found that *Colophospermum mopane* was not the dominant species in the ecological units he defined. Instead, the vegetation is described as savanna woodland with several communities determined by underlying geology. Attwell & Bhika (1985) classified the vegetation on Starvation Island into two major vegetation types. The main vegetation type covering most of the island was dominated by *Karomia tettensis, Combretum elaeagnoides, Combretum apiculatum* and *Diospyros quiloensis* and was heavily damaged by elephants. Frost (1987) described the vegetation on Zebra and Antelope Islands as being dominated by *Colophopermum mopane* with smaller numbers of *Kirkia acuminata, Adansonia digitata, Diospyros queloensis* and *Combretum species*.

The recent communal land vegetation survey by Timberlake *et. al.* (1993), which emphasized a vegetation type/habitat basis to determine soil-plant relations found that *Colophospermum mopane* woodland in Kariba District was mostly confined to the heavier soils. *Conibretum* shrubland was found to be common on the basalt soils in Omay. In view of the above, we therefore hypothesized that the vegetation types on these islands are complex, their structure and composition being determined by a wide range of factors, including underlying geology, type and depth of soil, distance from the nearest land mass, size of the island and the impact of large herbivores.

This study's main objectives were to describe and classify the vegetation of selected islands on Lake Kariba, using classification techniques to determine possible factors that influence species composition and richness and to draw possible conservation and management issues from the findings.

Study area

The study was carried out on Lake Kariba, situated on the border between Zambia and Zimbabwe, in Southern Africa. Lake Kariba stretches for 276 km in an east-west direction. A total of 47 islands were studied in Basins 1 to 5.

The geology of the Zambezi valley and the islands are described in detail by the study carried out by Lake Kariba Coordinating Committee in 1960. The lake lies mostly over sandstone and shales of the upper Karoo System. The major portion of the lake lies in the great trough of the Zambezi formed by the rifting movements and is composed almost entirely of sedimentary rocks of the Karoo System, although some volcanics are found in the Sibilobilo area. The great

71

majority of the islands consist of sandstone boulders and solid outcrops of sandstone. Sandy soils predominate with some Kalahari sands in the upper reaches and clay soils derived from shales on the southern side near Kariba (Lake Kariba Coordinating Committee, 1960).

Kariba's climate can be divided into four seasons based on temperature and rainfall; the cold dry season (June to August), hot dry season (September to November), hot wet season (November to March), cool dry season (March to May) (Bowmaker, 1973). The mean temperature during the hot wet season is 28°C and during the cool dry season is 17°C. Annual precipitation over the lake is between 250-1,000 mm and falls generally between November and April. The mean annual potential evaporation from the lake is 2,500-3,600 mm (Balon & Coche, 1974).

METHODS AND MATERIALS

Data collection

Preliminary stereo-photo interpretation of black and white aerial photographs (1:80 000, 1989; 1990) of larger islands was done in order to stratify the vegetation into reasonably homogenous units, which act as a framework for sampling. This was followed by field sampling which covered all the stratified types in areas of reasonably representative vegetation. Sampling was plotless. A starting point was selected at each site and the investigators moved from that point, covering an approximately circular area from the central point. All woody and grass species occurring in the area were recorded and the area was expanded until no new species were encountered. Care was taken not to transgress any obvious environmental boundaries. All woody species were assessed for cover-abundance using a modified Braun-Blanquet Scale (Mueller-Dombois & Ellenberg, 1974). Cover abundance for grasses was determined using 1 x 1 m quadrants randomly placed in the same area. Environmental data such as landscape type, soil type, grazing intensity and burning were also recorded. Soil samples were collected and analyzed for exchangeable bases (potassium, magnesium, and calcium), free iron, cation exchange capacity, organic carbon and physical characteristics.

Data analysis

Hierarchical Cluster Analysis was used to produce a classification of the vegetation after application of the method on species presence-absence data. Hierarchical

Cluster Analysis divides the samples into a hierarchy of dissimilar entities and the results can be presented as a dendrogram.

RESULTS

Vegetation classification

A Hierarchical Cluster Analysis performed on 87 representative sites from the surveyed islands resulted in several clusters of vegetation plots. Interpretation of the resultant clusters coupled by observations in the field yielded 18 vegetation types, one of which has two sub-types and two of which comprise one plot each. The grassland types were clearly separated out whilst the shrubland and woodland types sometimes had their plots mixed up. The vegetation types are described in detail in Mhlanga and Mapaure (1998).

Vegetation types on Lake Kariba Islands

Eighteen major vegetation types were identified on the islands surveyed. This represents only those types occurring on 47 islands surveyed in Basins 1 to 5. Vegetation was classified according to species composition and physiognomy. A catenary sequence was noticed on all islands surveyed. The grassland communities are confined to the bottom slopes between the water edge and woodland types, where the soil is moist. This is followed by woodland types on the mid-slopes and tops of islands.

This section will briefly review the categories and types of vegetation classified in the study area. For a full explication of the findings of the study, the reader is referred to Mhlanga and Mapaure (1998).

Type	Dominant/Co-dominant species	Subdominant Species	Other Information/ Characteristics
Type 1 - Mixed Woodlands	*Colophospermum mopane*	*Combretum elaeagnoides* (in shrub layer). Well developed herbaceous layer *(Hibiscus micranthus, Desmodium sprostreblum, Indigofera trita var. sibula* and *Sida cordifolia).*	Found on coarse loamy sands and on medium to coarse sandy loams.
Type 2 - Woodlands	*Colophospermum mopane -Combretum apiculatum*	Can be divided into sub-types, based on presence of *Aristida adscensionis* or *Andropogon sp.* (in grass layer).	May shift from co-dominance of major species to single dominance of either. Most extensive vegetation on islands in the Sibilobilo area and Sanyati basin.
Type 3 - Mixed Woodland	*Colophospermum mopane-* (sometimes) *Afzelia quanzensis*	Tree species: *Combretum elaeagnoides, Combretum apiculatum, Commiphora mossambicensis.* Shrub Species: *Karomia tettensis, Markhamia zanzibarica, Erythroxylum zambesiacum, Diaspyros quiloensis* and *Dalbergia martinii.* Herbaceous layer: *Tephrosia purpurea, Sida alba, Commellina benghalensis, Justicia kirkiana.* Grass cover: *Panicum maximum, Heteropogon contortus, Melinis repens.*	May include occasional shift of dominance between *Colophospermum mopane* and *Afzelia quanzensis.* Found on med-slope to top of island on Chasayi and Mambaleza Islands.
Type 4 - Mixed Woodland	*Combretum apiculatum*	*Combretum apiculatum, Colophospermum mopane, Diospyros quiloensis, Pteliopsis myrtifolia, Afzelia quanzensis* and *Albizia harveyi.* Middle layer: *Karomia tettensis, Carphalea pubescens, Grewia monticola* and *Erythroxylum zambesiacum.* Herbaceous layer: *Blepharis maderaspatensis, Spermacoce chaetocephala, Justicia kirkiana* and *Jacquemontia tamnifolia.* High density of lianes. Grass layer dominated by *Panicum sp.*	Occurs on medium sandy soils on 40 Mile Island and deep, fine sandy soils on Long and Sampakaruma Islands.
Type 5 - Mixed Woodland	*Combretum zeyheri, Combretum elaeagnoides* and *Combretum apiculatum*	Herbaceous layer: *Chamaecrista mimosoides, Striga gesnerioides* and *Calostephane divaricata.* Grass layer: *Heteropogon contortus* and *Loudetia simplex.*	May occur as either a shrubland or a woodland. Occurs on sandy loams and on medium to coarse loamy sands.
Type 6 - Mixed Woodland	*Combretum elaeagnoides*	Tree species: *Commiphora africana, Afzelia quanzensis* and *Triplochiton zambesiacus.* Herbaceous layer: *Tephrosia purpurea, Tephrosia euprepes, Justicia kirkiana.* Grass layer: *Setaria pumila, Alloteropsis cimicina, Panicum heterostachyum* and *Aristida adscenscionis.*	Grasses are very tall, up to 2 m high. This type occurs on Kampaka, Samunomba, Masuko and Diamond Islands. It occurs on sandy loams and on medium to coarse loamy sands.
Type 7 - Woodland	*Acacia nilotica,* sometimes co-dominant with *Dichrostachys cinerea*	Shrubs: *Grewia monticola* and *Colophospermum mopane.* Species rich herbaceous layer with *Indigofera tinctoria cominant.* Grass layer: *Melinis repens, Panicum maximum* and *Eragrostis vicosa.*	Occurs on medium sandy loams on Samunomba, Tsetse and Mubende Islands. This type was a previous grass community, invaded and colonized by *Acacia nilotica,* perhaps as a result of previous cultivation.
Type 8 - Mixed Woodland	*Acacia nigrescens-Afzelia quanzensis*	*Combretum mossambicense, Terminalia sericea* and *Markhamia zanzibarica.* Shrub layer: *Grewia flavescens, Turraea nilotica, Catunaregum spinosa* and *Commiphora glandulosa.* Grass layer: *Panicum maximum,* with *Panicum repens* and *Phragmites mauritianum* in areas near water.	Well-defined on Snake Island. This vegetation type is relatively pristine and is found on coarse to medium sandy loams.

Type 9 -
Thicket	*Karomia tettensis.* May co-dominate with *Combretum elaeagnoides* and *Combretum apiculatum.*	Herbaceous layer: *Cardiospermum halicacabum* var. *microcarpum, Tarrena luteola, Hibiscus rhabdotospermus, and Crotalaria reptans.* Grass layer: *Panicum maximum, Panicum heterostachym* and *Setaria pumila.*	Results from degradation of *Colophospermum mopane* woodlands by large herbivores, esp. elephants. Found on coarse loamy sands and coarse to medium sandy loams on the mid-slopes to top of islands. It is common on Nandavwi, Masuko, Mbeta, Petrol, Mamembere, Patridge and Elephant Islands.
Type 10 -
Thicket	*Dospyros quiloensis*	Shrub layer: *Sida cordifolia,* and multi-stemmed *Diospyros quiloensis* shrubs; may include *Colophospermum mopane, Karomia tettensis, Combretum apiculatum.* Grass layer: *Eragrostis viscosa* and *Perotis patens.*	Results from heavy utilization by large herbivores. Found on Starvation Island.
Type 11 -
Woodland Thicket	*Combretum celastroides.* Sometimes *Karomia tettensis* becomes co-dominant, forming impenetrable thickets in the shrub layer.	Few emergent *Colophospermum mopane, Adansonia digitata, Pteliopsis myrtifolia* and *Sclerocarya birrea* trees indicate original vegetation type. Shrub layer: *Lonchocarpus eriocalyx* subsp. *Wankieensis, Markhamia zanzibarica, Erythroxylum zambesiacum* and *Terminalia prunioides* are maintained at <3m by constant browsing by elephants. Grass layer: well developed, with *Setaria sphacelata, Panicum maximum* and *Urochloa trichopus* dominant.	Occurs on all islands in the Sinamwenda area; Christmas, Elephant and Zinyama Islands in Binga. It occurs on a wide range of sandy soils with variable textures; coarse sands, coarse and medium loamy sands and coarse to medium sandy loams. The structure of this type has been influenced by elephant browsing.
Type 12 -
Woodland Thicket	*Guibourtia conjugata.* Sometimes *Combretum elaeagnoides* becomes co-dominant.	Shrub layer: *Meiostemon tetrandrus, Combretum celastroides* and *Karomia tettensis.* Herbaceous layer includes *Amorphophallus abyssinicus, Indigofera setiflora* and *Jacquemontia tamnifolia.* Grass layer: well developed, with *Setaria pumila,* tufts of *Loudetia simplex, Panicum heterostachyum, Brachiaria deflexa* and *Panicum maximum* dominant.	Found on mid-slopes to the tops of Nandavwi and Mambaleza Islands.
Type 13 -
Shrubland	*Pteliopsis myrtifolia.* Sometimes *Meiostemon tetrandrus* and *Karomia tettensis* becomes dominant.	Species rich vegetation type, with up to 61 species recorded at one site. Few emergent trees: *Colophospermum mopane, Adansonia digitata* and *Kirkia acuminata.* Shrub layer: *Carphalea pubescens, Commiphora glandulosa, Lonchocarpus eriocalyx* subsp. *Wankieensis* and *Pterocarpus antunesii.* Herbaceous layer: *Hibiscus rhabdotospermum* and *Hibiscus micranthus.* Grass layer generally well developed with less dense patches: *Panicum maximum, Dactyloctenium aegyptium, Setaria pumila* and *Brachiaria deflexa* dominant; in less dense patches *Eragrostis viscosa* is dominant.	Found on Kudu, Elephant, Marker, Masuko, Kangamani, Mubenda and Masuntu Islands. It occurs on coarse sands and coarse loamy sands from the mid-slope to the top of the island.
Type 14 -
Shrubland	*Indigofera tinctoria.*	Grass layer: *Melinis repens, Urochloa trichopus* and *Panicum repens* co-dominate. Occasional shrubs of *Colophospermum mopane, Kirkia acuminata* and *Lonchocarpus eriocalyx* occur. Herbaceous layer dominated by legumes, including *Tephrosia purpurea, Tephrosia euprepes, Indigofera colutea, Indigofera mummulariifolia* and *Indigofera strobilifera* subsp. *strobilifera*	A secondary vegetation type resulting from *Indigofera tinctoria* invading grasslands. Occurs on the bottom slopes of islands featuring the grass layer described. Found on Mambaleza, Mbeta, Diamond, Kangamani, Christmas, Termite, Garden, Elephant, Tower and Marker Islands. Occurs on a

			wide range of soil types: coarse sandy soils, coarse loamy sands and medium to coarse sandy loams.
Type 15 - Wooded Grassland	*Melinis repens*	Associated grass species: *Eragrostis viscosa, Panicum repens* and *Panicum maximum.* Herbaceous species include *Rhynchosia minima* var. *minima, Tephrosia purpurea, Indigofera tinctoria* and *Indigofera setiflora.*	Found on coarse sands and coarse to medium sandy clay loams on the bottom slopes of Rhino, Kangamani, Nandavwi, Sampakaruma, Mubende, Samunomba and Masuko Islands. Soils where this type is found are generally shallow, and in some places covered by rocks and boulders.
Type 16 - Grassland	*Panicum repens*	Other grasses include *Andropogon eucomus, Eragrostis viscosa, Melinis repens, Pogonarthria squarrosa* and sedges *Cyperus articulatus* and *Bulbostylis* sp. Small shrubs of *Mundulea sericea, Colophospermum mopane, Ziziphus mucronata* and *Mimosa pigra* are occasionally found. Herbaceous layer: well developed, including *Indigofera astragalina, Indigofera gairdneri, Indigofera tinctoria* and *Rynchosia minima.*	Resulted from the formation of Lake Kariba and is confined to the bottom slopes of most of the islands, near water. Buffaloes spend much of their time grazing in this vegetation type. It is found on coarse sandy soils and sometimes grows from crevices when the surface is covered by rock. On Christmas, Marker, Long, Nandavwi and Snake Islands, it is found on fine sandy soils.
Type 17 - Grassland	*Aristida adscenscionis. Panicum repens* sometimes co-dominates in areas close to shore.	Associated grasses include *Heteropogon contortus, Aristida congesta* and *Melinis repens.* Herbaceous layer comprises a few individuals of *Indigofera schimperi* and *Tephrosia purpurea.* Sometimes shrubs of *Mundulea sericea, Colophospermum mopane* and *Flueggia virosa* are found.	Most extensive grassland type on islands within the Sibilobilo area: Namagwaba, Namembere, Lubangwa, 40 Mile, Weather and Patridge Islands. It occurs on clay soils, fine to medium sand clay loams, medium sands and on fine loamy sands. Soils where this type occurs are generally shallow with boulders, stones and pebbles on the surface.
Type 18 - Wooded Grassland	*Urochloa trichopus*	Extensively and heavily invaded by *Indigofera tinctoria.* Other grasses include *Echinochloa colona, Sporobolus pyramidalis* and *Panicum maximum.* Diverse and species rich herbaceous layer with up to 22 species recorded. Common species include *Tephrosia euprepes, Tephrosia purpurea, Indigofera colutea* and *Walteria indica.* Shrubs of <2m sometimes occur: *Terminalia prumioides, Mundulea sericea, Acacia tortilis* and *Erythroxylum zambesiacum.*	Found on the bottom slopes of Christmas and Termite Islands in Sinamwenda area, on medium sandy loams to medium loamy sands.

DISCUSSION

Vegetation classification

To a large extent, the grassland plots were clearly separated out by the clustering technique, while woodland and shrubland types sometimes had their plots mixed up. This is due to the occurrence of some important indicator species in the vegetation types, whose dominant species were different. These observations are expected, as the technique is based on species presence/absence data, rather than physiognomy. This implies that, for instance, a woodland plot dominated by *Colophospermum mopane* would be grouped with a shrubland plot dominated by the same species, with many other species common to both. This was a common observation particularly with transitional vegetation types discussed below.

Vegetation types

In general, the predominant vegetation type on the islands consists of *Colophospermum mopane* woodland (Type 1) or *Colophospermum mopane - Combretum apiculatum* woodland (Type 2). This varies from open *Colophospermum mopane* woodland to scrub *Colophospermum mopane* in rugged higher areas. *Colophospermum mopane* and *Combretum* species tend to integrate with each other forming *Colophospermum mopane-Combretum apiculatum* woodland (Type 2). Various *Combretum* species, especially *Combretum apiculatum, Combretum elaeagnoides*, and *Combretum celastroides* mix with each other forming *Combretum apiculatum* mixed woodland (Type 4), Mixed *Combretum* spp. woodland (Type 5) and *Combretum elaeagnoides* woodland (Type 6). Woodland types are either disturbed or undisturbed. When undisturbed, well developed *Colophospermum mopane* woodland, *Colophospermum mopane-Combretum apiculatum* woodland, *Acacia nigrescens-Afzelia quanzensis* mixed woodland or *Combretum apiculatum* mixed woodland are found. Disturbed types consist of shrublands, thickets and woodland thickets.

Species dominance and richness seem to be influenced by soil characteristics, mainly soil type and depth. This implies that the soil and the parent rock from which it is formed have a strong influence on the species composition and structure of vegetation (Schmidt, 1992). On basaltic soils in Basins 4 and 5, the predominant vegetation type on the islands is dominated by either *Colophospermum Colophospermum mopane* and/or *Combretum apiculatum*. On these islands, *Colophospermum mopane* is the dominant tree species and the woodlands are characterized by low species richness, with a range of 3-10 species per plot, most of them shrubs. According to Timberlake *et. al.* (1993), this can be ascribed to the aggressive rooting habit of *Colophospermum mopane*, with its well developed lateral root system which outcompetes most other species. These islands are generally rocky with large solid outcrops on high ground, which also probably makes it difficult to support other species of deeper rooting systems.

Most of the islands surveyed from Sinamwenda to Binga have sandy Karoo soils derived from the underlying sandstone. The soils are of variable texture and seem to influence the vegetation. *Combretum celastroides* woodland thicket and *Pleliopsis myrtifolia* shrubland occur on these soils. When undisturbed, they are usually dry layered forests ("Jesse bush") and are scattered across the Zambezi valley, generally on Karoo sediments at altitudes of 900 m or less (Timberlake *et. al.*, 1993). On the islands, elephants have caused major damage to this vegetation type, resulting in a change in vegetation structure, from an original dry layered thicket to dense woodland thickets with a few emergents. Well developed Jesse bushes are found on deeper sands. None of the islands surveyed supported an undisturbed Jesse bush. A similar type is found in the north and northwest of the Dande Communal Land and to the north of the Dande Safari Area, where they occur as well developed dry layered forests (Timberlake & Mapaure, 1992). In an undisturbed state, emergent trees of *Pteliopsis myrtifolia, Pterocarpus lucens* and *Entandrophragma caudatum* reach up to 18 m but most of these large trees on the islands were damaged by elephants. It appears that this type is prone to elephant damage resulting in its conversion to woodland thickets. Surveys elsewhere such as East Gokwe (Timberlake *et. al.*, 1993), Busi Sengwa (Muller & Timberlake, 1992) and in Mana Pools National Park (Muller & Pope, 1982) have indicated the same phenomenon.

The structure and species composition of Jesse bush is determined by the poor moisture retention in the sandy soils and the acidic subsoils, which results in shallow rooting system of the majority of species in Jesse bush (Timberlake *et. al.*, 1993). Timberlake *et. al.* (1993) suggest that when the shallow-rooted shrub layer becomes dominant, as on the islands, it prevents enough moisture infiltration through the surface layers. This results in deeper-rooted species being competitively disadvantaged, and such areas will remain as thickets unless they are subjected to a very destructive fire which opens up and destroys the shrub layer.

Guibourtia conjugata woodland thicket on Nandavwi and Mambaleza Islands is similar to Timberlake *et. al.*'s (1993) Type C4 (*Guibourtia conjugata* woodland thicket). They represent the driest forest. This type was found on deeper coarse sand soils and also on coarse loamy sand to coarse clay loams. Timberlake *et. al.* (1993) recorded a similar type in North Binga, which is the mainland area adjacent to Nandavwi and Mambaleza Islands. In Binga, *Guibourtia conjugata* thickets occupy slightly elevated areas on unconsolidated slightly coarse sand which probably originated from Karoo sandstone strata. It appears to be a relatively common vegetation type along the shoreline on the mainland adjacent to Nandawvi and Mambaleza Islands (Mhlanga & Mapaure, 1998). An intensive survey of the area will be required to determine extent of cover as well as the status of the woodlands.

Terrain seems to influence the vegetation types on some of the islands. Snake Island in Sibilobilo area supports an *Acacia nigrescens-Afzelia quanzensis* mixed woodland (Type 10) which is different from the rest of the vegetation types in the area. The island is conical, steep and is covered by boulders. There is poor substrate for plants to grow. The moisture retention capacity of the soil is low. The type therefore supports a mixture of trees with different ecological affinities ranging from those favoring mesic conditions to those that can tolerate low moisture levels. This type is undisturbed since the island is relatively inaccessible to large herbivores.

Four types of grasslands are described and these can be categorized into two main groups. Group 1 consists of near natural or grasslands that have not been invaded by leguminous plants (Types 16 and 17). The dominant grass species in this group are *Panicum repens* (Type 16) and *Aristida adscensionis* (Type 17). The difference in species dominance appears to be determined by soil type. *Aristida adscensionis* occurs mainly on clay soils, sandy clay loams, loamy sands and sometimes on medium sand. *Aristida adscensionis* dominates on fine to coarse sand, favours wetter soils and is confined near water. It thrives on moist sandy soils (Surrell, 1987) and can withstand prolonged periods under water (McLachlan & McLachlan, 1971). It is restricted more or less to the inundation zone where it is constantly subjected to drought and inundation when the lake level rises and falls (Surrell, 1987). The second group (Types 15 & 18) consists of wooded grasslands that have been invaded by leguminous species due to overgrazing and degradation. Persistent overgrazing leads to encroachment of *Acacia nilotica, Indigofera tinctoria* and *Dichrostachys cinerea*.

Conservation and management considerations

Detailed identification, classification and mapping of the vegetation of an area is required in order to assess the conservation status of the vegetation in particular and optimal resource utilization in general (Fuls, Bredenkamp and Van Rooyen,

1992). Vegetation data on Lake Kariba islands on species composition and vegetation structure from locatable points was previously not available. Monitoring of future ecological processes on the islands will require baseline data for comparison. Information and data gathered in this study act as a basis for monitoring vegetation change in future on the islands.

The biggest threat to the islands' vegetation is elephants. Large numbers of elephants are capable of inflicting widespread damage on vegetation (Mapaure & Mhlanga, in press). Dry forests thicken up and become more of a thicket, while *Colophospermum mopane* woodlands are converted to shrublands. Mapaure and Mhlanga (in prep.) found that 50% of the *Colophospermum mopane* examined on selected islands were damaged, and constant browsing and breaking of plants by elephants is trapping *Colophospermum mopane* trees in smaller height and girth classes. This is more apparent in islands within the Sibilobilo area: Namembere, Namagwaba and Patridge. The impact of overutilization by animals is clearly illustrated on Starvation Island, where both woodland structure and species composition has been modified. *Diospyros quiloensis* has assumed single dominance. Bhika (1983) noted that Starvation Island was supporting seven elephants *(Loxodonta africana)*, nine hippopotamus *(Hippopotamus amphibius)*, 35 kudu *(Tragelaphus strepsiceros)* and about 375 impala *(Aepyceros melampus)*. It is clear that the animal population has increased to a level that is altering vegetation patterns, and decisions need to made on the management of this situation.

Isolation from the mainland has not influenced species richness (Mhlanga & Mapaure, in press). In botanical terms, the islands on Lake Kariba are still too young to show differences in species composition due to isolation. An understanding of processes operating on the islands can be useful in ecology on a longer term, as islands are less complex than mainland situations. This study therefore provides a basis on which to build, develop and investigate other scientific concepts.

ACKNOWLEDGEMENTS

The editor would like to acknowledge the assistance of Lisa McLaughlin in editing this chapter.

REFERENCES

Attwell, C.A.M. and Bhika, M. 1985: Feeding Ecology of Impala on Starvation

Island, Lake Kariba. *South African Journal of Wildlife Research*, 15 (2), 41-48.

Balon, E.K. and Coche, A.G. (eds.). 1974: *Lake Kariba: A Man-made Tropical Ecosystem in Tropical Africa*. The Hague: Junk Publishers.

Bhika, M. 1983: *Diet, condition and foraging behaviour of impala (Aepyceros melampus) on Starvation Island, Lake Kariba*. M.Sc. Thesis. Harare: University of Zimbabwe.

Bowmaker, A.P. 1973: *An hydrobiological study of Mwenda River and its mouth, Lake Kariba*. Ph.D. Thesis. Johannesburg: University of Witwatersrand.

Child, G. 1968: *Behaviour of large mammals during the formation of Lake Kariba*. Salisbury: Trustees of the National Museums of Rhodesia.

Craig, G.C. 1983: Vegetation survey of Sengwa. *Bothalia*, 14, 579-763.

Craig, G.C., Martin, C.M.L. and Mahlangu, Z. 1984: *A vegetation map of Chirisa Safari Area*. Unpublished report. Harare: Department of National Parks and Wildlife Management.

Dyer, C. 1985: *A preliminary survey of vegetation and soils of the Dinosaur Island, Lake Kariba*. B.Sc. Dissertation. Johannesburg: University of Witwatersrand, Faculty of Science, Department of Botany.

Frost, P.G.H. (compiler) 1987: *Damage to Colophospermum mopane in relation to elephant density at Kariba*. A Report of Working Group B (Animal Ecology), BZ2 Field Trip to Kariba, May 1987. Harare: University of Zimbabwe, Department of Biological Sciences.

Fuls, E.R., Bredenkamp, G.J. and Van Rooyen, N. 1992: The plant communities of the undulating grassland of the Vredefort-Kroonstand-Linley-Heilbron area, Northen Orange Free State. *South African Journal of Botany*, 58, 224-230.

Gauch, H.G. Jr. 1982: *Multivariate Analysis in Community Ecology*. Cambridge: Cambridge Press.

Hill, M.O. 1979a: *TWINSPAN - a FORTRAN program for arranging multivariate data in an ordered two-way table by classification of the individuals and attributes*. Ecology and Systematics. Ithaca: Cornell University.

Hill, M.O. 1979b: *DECORANA - a FORTRAN program for detrended correspondence analysis and reciprocal averaging*. Ecology and Systematics. Ithaca: Cornell University.

Lake Kariba Co-ordinating Committee. 1960: *Kariba Islands Survey*. Salisbury: Roberts, Mullins and Bannett Consulting Engineers.

Mapaure, I. and Mhlanga, L. (in press). Elephants and Woodlands. The impact of elephant to *Colophospermum mopane* on Namembere Island, Lake Kariba, Zimbabwe. *Zimbabwe Science News*.

Mapaure, I. and Mhlanga, L. (in prep). *Patterns of elephant damage to Colophospermum mopane on selected islands in Lake Kariba, Zimbabwe and its management implications*.

Maxted, N., Van Slageren, M.W. & Rihan, J.R. 1992: The use of ecogeographic techniques in efficient plant conservation. IPBGR/FAO/IUCN Collection manual.

McLachlan, A.J. and McLachlan, S.M. 1971: Benthic fauna and sediments in the newly created Lake Kariba (Central Africa). *Ecology*, 52, 800-809.

Mhlanga, L. and Mapaure, I. 1998 (in press): Vegetation studies of selected islands and adjacent mainland on Lake Kariba, Zimbabwe. *Working Paper Series*. Harare: University of Zimbabwe, Institute of Environmental Studies.

Mueller-Dombois, D. and Ellenberg, H. 1974: *Aims and Methods of Vegetation Ecology.* New York: John Wiley & Sons.

Muller, T. 1981: A case for a vegetation survey in Zimbabwe. *Zimbabwe Science News*, 15, (10), 271-274.

Muller, T. 1994: The role a botanical institute can play in the conservation of the terrestrial biodiversity in a developing country. *Biodiversity and Conservation*, 3, 116-125.

Muller, T. and Pope, G. 1982: Vegetation report for the impact assessment of the proposed Mupata Gorge and Batoka dams on the Zambezi river. In R.F. du Toit, (ed.), *A preliminary assessment of the environmental implications of the proposed Mupata and Batoka hydro-electric scheme (Zambezi River, Zimbabwe)*, pp.53-67. Harare: Natural Resources Board.

Muller, T. 1983: A case for a vegetation survey in a developing country based on Zimbabwe. *Bothalia*, 14, 721-723.

Muller, T. and Timberlake, J. 1992: Areas for plant conservation in Zimbabwe. *Zimbabwe Science News*, 26 (10/12), 88-95.

Nyamapfeme, K.W. 1988: A note on some Zimbabwean soil-vegetation relationships of important indicator value in soil survey. *Kirkia*, 13 (1).

Pratt, D.J., Greenway, P.J. & Gwynee, M.D. 1966: A classification of East African rangeland, with an appendix on terminology. *Journal of Applied Ecology*, 3, 369-382.

Rogers, C.M.L. 1993. *A woody vegetation survey of Hwange National Park*. Harare: Department of National Parks and Wildlife Management.

Rogers, C.M.L. 1994: The woody vegetation of Hwange National Park. *Transactions of the Zimbabwe Scientific Association*, 68, 15-24.

Schmidt, A.G. 1992: *Guidelines for the management of some game ranches in the mixed bushveld communities of the north-western Transvaal, with special reference to Rhino Ranch*. M.Sc. Thesis (Wildlife Management). Pretoria: University of Pretoria.

Schramm, E. 1978: *A preliminary survey of the vegetation and distribution of the Loranthaceae of Dinosaur Island (Island 126/127) Lake Kariba, Rhodesia*. B.Sc. Dissertation. Johannesburg: University of the Witwatersrand, Faculty of Science, Department of Botany.

Surrell, K. 1987: *The shore types of Lake Kariba, Zimbabwe: A case study using Landsat MSS*. Report from a minor field study. Working paper 47. Upsala: Swedish University of Agriculture.

Ter Braak, C.J.F. 1991: *CANOCO - a FORTRAN programme for canocical community ordination by partial detrended canonical correspondence analysis, principal component analysis and redundancy analysis*. The Netherlands: Agricultural Group.

Thomas, P.I., Walker, B.H. & Wild, H. 1977: Relationships between vegetation and environment on an amphibolite outcrop near Nkai, Rhodesia. *Kirkia*, 10, (2), 503-541.

Timberlake, J.R., Nobanda, N. & Mapaure, I. 1993: Vegetation survey of the communal lands-north and west Zimbabwe. *Kirkia*, 14 (2), 171-270.

Timberlake, J. & Mapaure, I. 1992: Vegetation and its conservation in the Eastern Mid-Zambezi Valley, Zimbabwe. *Transactions of the Zimbabwe Scientific Association*, 66, 1-14.

Timberlake, J.R., Nobanda, N., Mapaure, I. & Mhlanga, L. 1991: *Sites of interest for conservation in various communal lands of north and west Zimbabwe*. Communal Lands Vegetation Survey. Report 1. Harare: National Herbarium and Botanic Gardens.

Vincent, V. & Thomas, R.G. 1961: *An Agricultural Survey of Southern Rhodesia: Part 1. Agro-ecological Survey*. Salisbury: Government Printer.

Whittaker, R.H. 1975: *Communities and Ecosystems*. New York: Macmillan.

Wild, H. 1965: The flora of the Great Dyke of Southern Rhodesia with special reference to the serpentine soils. *Kirkia*, 5, 49-86.

Wild, H. 1968: Geobotanical anomalies of copper bearing soils. *Kirkia*, 7, 1-71.

Wild, H. 1970: Geobotanical anomalies in Rhodesia 3-the vegetation of nickel bearing soils. *Kirkia*, 7, 1-62.

Wild, H. & Barbosa, L.A.G. 1967: *Vegetation Map of the Flora Zambesiaca Area*. Supplement to Flora Zambesiaca. Harare: M.O. Collins.

Worsely, S. 1988. *Vegetation Survey of the Matetsi Complex.* Unpublished report. Harare: Department of National Parks and Wildlife Management.

Chapter 7

Indigenous Knowledge Systems in the Natural Resources Management Plan for the Lake Chilwa Basin, Southern Malawi

by Estone Sambo and Mutiyenkhu Munyenyembe

Introduction

Knowledge is key to any planning process. The ability to accurately identify issues, consider options and make decisions is critical. In some instances, the development of information and planning strategies has been left to "experts" who have, at times, undertaken this important work in isolation of the needs, aspirations, and knowledge of the local community. Increasingly, however, there is a realization that there are important advantages in consulting with the community to develop information and identify actions. This chapter provides a focus on integrating indigenous knowledge systems into the development and presentation of information that is essential for natural resource management. Although technical, this chapter provides a detailed appreciation of the sophistication of local knowledge systems.

In the Lake Chilwa basin in southern Malawi, field research on Indigenous Knowledge Systems was carried out through interviews with farmers, as well as through field observations. A total of 117 farmers were interviewed, using a questionnaire containing both open- and closed-ended questions. The data collected included, among other things: farmer characteristics, landholding sizes, food and cash crops grown, trees planted or cared for by the farmer, cultural practices concerning natural resource utilization along the rivers, plant and animal resources utilization and conservation, habitat conservation and land management practices.

Physiography and ecology of the Lake Chilwa basin

Lake Chilwa is a shallow (4 to 5 m depth), endorheic and saline body of water located in southeastern Malawi. It is an important ecosystem supporting part of the country's valuable bio-diversity, including plants, invertebrates, fish and waterfowl. Kalk, MacLachlan & Howard-Williams (1979) listed 29 species of fish grouped into 10 families, and 232 species of invertebrates from 6 phyla. They also listed 266 species of plants in 179 genera and 55 families while the lake's floodplain grassland, marsh, swamp and open water support 156 species of birds, of which 111 species are waterfowl and 39 species are Palaearctic migrants. Recent field studies of Lake Chilwa regarding the vegetation, ecology, birds, fish, vertebrates, invertebrates, and land-use changes (Van Zegeren & Munyenyembe, 1998) have added new information and obviated the importance of monitoring the environment as a tool in the management of this wetland.

Lake Chilwa is of great importance to the Malawi fisheries, contributing between 20 and 33% of Malawi's total fish production although its approximate area of 2,250 km^2 makes up only 10% of the total wetlands area. The lake's high productive capacity is attributed to a rich nutrient content within its shallow waters. More than 6,000 people fish there. In recent years, at a time when population pressure has been increasing rapidly, the fisheries have unfortunately been declining.

The drainage of the Lake Chilwa basin system (Figure 7.1) has a catchment area of around 8,349 km^2. The lake receives water inflow from the Zomba plateau and Mulanje massif, along major rivers like the Sombani, Phalombe, Namadzi, Thondwe, Likangala and Domasi on the Malawi side, and the Mnembo on the Mozambique side. The lake is characterized by periodic drying, which has disrupted human activities, and it completely dried out in 1967 and 1995.

The basin system has lost both habitat and bio-diversity because of extensive deforestation for firewood as well as agricultural expansion. These activities have increased in the face of the high rate of population growth (national average of 3.2% per annum). It is clearly evident that soil erosion has intensified in recent years and compounded the unexplained periodic drying of the lake. White (1971) pointed out that, in general, "there is no sufficient understanding of basic relationships among precipitation, evapotranspiration, water movement in the soil, and water movement in the stream to permit clear-cut generalizations about the effect of land use of vegetation".

One clear effect in the Lake Chilwa basin, however, is that changes in land use and vegetation loss are causing streams to carry large deposits of silt into the lake and the plains around it, so that floods are becoming common and it is feared that sediments may be filling the lake at unprecedented rates. According to 1992 World Bank estimates, Malawi is losing soil from cultivated land at a rate of 20 t/ha/yr (Watts, 1996).

Figure 7.1 Lake Chilwa Drainage Basin

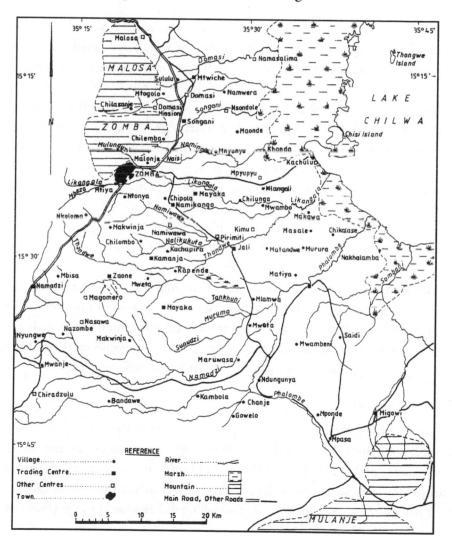

Need for development of a management plan

These scenarios demand a comprehensive management plan for the basin. A draft Management Plan for the Lake Chilwa basin was the subject of a workshop (Njaya, Chiotha & Kabwazi, 1996), which was followed by a study to collect baseline data for the lake for accession to the RAMSAR convention (Van Zegeren & Munyenyembe, 1998). Lake Chilwa became a RAMSAR site in 1997. A component of the Management Plan that should be urgently addressed is soil erosion reduction, which can be achieved by proper agricultural practices, afforestation and reforestation programmes.

Community-based solutions are more likely to succeed than those imposed from outside as, historically, rural communities have acquired detailed knowledge, skills, practices and strategies based on their interaction with the local environment over long periods of time. "Indigenous Knowledge Systems" (IKS) is a term used to describe such accumulated collective knowledge (Matowanyika, Garibaldi & Musimwa, 1995; Matowanyika, Sibanda & Garibaldi, 1995). In the past decade, many organizations, such as the World Bank and IUCN (International Union for the Conservation of Nature and Natural Resources), have begun to address environmental issues by promoting environmental sustainability in development efforts and emphasizing country ownership (Asibey, 1995). IUCN views indigenous knowledge as valuable for new biological and ecological insights, natural resource management, conservation education, protected areas, and environmental assessment (IUCN, 1996).

Because little attention has been paid to the role of IKS, the way communities have sustainably managed their natural resources is poorly understood. It is important to balance the interests of all the stakeholders, understand their future development plans as well as what they perceive to be constraints on their activities. A participatory approach is the best way to rehabilitate affected areas.

The research problem

The aim of this research was to survey people in parts of the Lake Chilwa basin to identify their indigenous ecological knowledge and understanding of their environment, particularly in relation to traditional methods of natural resource management. The study shows that, in the context of what people already know about natural resource management, controlling soil erosion through afforestation can be effectively intensified, using mechanisms that overcome resistance to foreign interventions.

The Lake Chilwa basin is dissected by major rivers which drain into the lake. The last 30 years have seen major changes in land use patterns in the basin, including new tobacco estates, gardens and farms, as well as government rice irrigation schemes on the plains around the lake. Pressure on the environment has resulted in riverbank deforestation and general depletion of indigenous forests on customary land. It can be safely concluded that before these dramatic changes, communities were utilizing natural resources much more efficiently and sustainably.

Development of the basin region can be said to have broken down IKS controls and caused environmental degradation which has affected the ecosystem. The lake and basin system are threatened by soil erosion which depletes land fertility and silts the lake. Other threats include agricultural chemicals, poisonous contaminants from roads and effluent from urban areas running off into the rivers and streams which feed the the lake. The ecosystem is particularly vulnerable because the lake has no outlet.

The problem is complex. This research focused on the local communities' natural resources management, particularly reducing soil erosion by planting trees to rehabilitate the river banks. The research identified local people and practices (both traditional and modern) which have played an important role in maintaining vegetation cover along major rivers, the reasons behind these practices, as well as attitudes towards introducing interventions. It was important to understand what the people in the area perceive as valuable in natural resources management.

Objectives

The research was designed to reach a number of objectives:

1. To survey land holdings on which there has been active practice or promotion of vegetation conservation along banks of major rivers.
2. To make botanical identifications of the species of trees and shrubs that have been preserved along the river banks.
3. To identify the reasons why those trees and shrubs have been retained or planted along the river banks, especially in the context of indigenous knowledge systems.
4. To establish why resources have been overexploited.

5. To explore farmers' traditional knowledge of the tree and shrub species they regard as important and why, and determine how the farmers rank the importance of those species.
6. To identify obstacles to river bank rehabilitation.

MATERIALS AND METHODS

Study sites

The objectives were achieved through field surveys and assessments. The research covered the major river systems west of Lake Chilwa and their tributaries, originating from the Zomba Plateau and the surrounding hills. These are the Domasi, Mulunguzi, Likangala, Mbedza and Thondwe. The Namadzi and Mulanje Massif river systems were not covered, due to time or budgetary constraints.

Indigenous Knowledge Systems

For both the wooded and cultivated areas along the river banks, farmers were interviewed, using a questionnaire designed to determine land-use practices and farmers' perceptions of conservation issues and afforestation. A sample of up to 35 farmers was randomly selected from the upper, middle, and lower sections of each river, making a total of 117 farmers interviewed. Some of the older farmers were of particular interest.

The farmers were prompted to provide information on traditional knowledge, both which is used or is no longer used, regarding sustainable use of woodland resources. This knowledge includes ecological information, hunting practices, fruit collection, harvesting of wood and non-wood products, etc. The questionnaire had six sections:
1. Particulars of the farmers;
2. Cultural values concerning the river systems;
3. Plant resources utilization and conservation;
4. Animal resources utilization and conservation;
5. Ecosystems/habitat conservation;
6. Land management practices.

As vegetation is the basis for environmental stability, more detailed information was obtained by conducting botanical field surveys to support information coming out of the questionnaire.

Plant resource utilization and conservation

Two approaches were employed in studying the utilization and conservation of plant resources along the rivers under consideration:

1.   Botanical surveys were conducted along the rivers and on farms, using standard field equipment to establish the status of the vegetation and floristic composition. Identification of species was done in the field and confirmed at the National Herbarium and Botanic Gardens of Malawi (NHBG). Intact wooded areas along the river banks were identified. Checklists were compiled of tree and shrub species within a belt of 100 metres along both banks of the rivers, and the agricultural practices (crops grown, etc.) were recorded.

2.   Farmers were interviewed, using a questionnaire comprised of both open-ended and closed-ended questions. The data collected included:

     ▶ names of indigenous and exotic trees species found on the farm or in the landscape and their uses;

     ▶ who planted the trees;

     ▶ whether some trees were prohibited by cultural beliefs (taboos) or were known to be poisonous;

     ▶ which plant species were conserved and why;

     ▶ tree management methods;

     ▶ whether some trees were rare or had disappeared and causes of disappearance;

     ▶ preferences for trees species.

QUESTIONNAIRE FINDINGS

Demographic structure

The 117 farmers interviewed came from along the five river systems in the following proportions: Thondwe (32.5%), Domasi (29.9%), Likangala (26.5%, Mbedza (7.7%), and Mulunguzi (3.4%). The Mulunguzi and Mbedza are both tributaries of the Likangala and so are much shorter, but they are important. For example, Mulunguzi passes through and supplies water to the major town of Zomba (projected 1998 population 75,000).

Tables 7.1 and 7.2 show characteristics of the smallholder farmers cultivating land near the banks of these rivers. The survey covered more female (58%) than male (41%) farmers. They were all above 20 years of age, and half of them above

40 years. Most of them (72%) were married. Small-scale farming was the main source of income for a considerable proportion of the farmers (72%), but more females than males engaged in small-scale business to supplement their farm income. On the other hand, a lower proportion of the females (32%) than the males (47%) achieved annual incomes of more than MK2,000 (US$130). In general, the farming community had a low level of education. While 61% of the farmers had basic literacy education, 33% had no formal education at all, and only 5% had post-primary education. The small proportion of people with post-primary education reflects the fact that people with secondary or higher education migrate to towns in search of employment. Within the 33% sample showing no formal education at all, the greater majority (76%) were female. These figures show a clear gender bias favouring male access to education and resources.

Farming systems

Landholding sizes in the area are generally small. Many farmers (86%) had about 0.4 to 2 hectares, and only 3% had over 4 hectares. Maize, or maize and beans, took up 0.4 to 1 hectare in 88% of the cases. About 55% of the farmers had no other crops, while 35% did. Fallowing was not practiced by 76% of the farmers, while 24% allotted at most one hectare. Use of land for woodlots was limited, with 60% of the farmers indicating that they had none, 35% saying they had less than half a hectare and 5% having more. Most farmers (91%) did not set aside land for grazing purposes, but the majority of them (98%) had allocated some farmland to the home compound, although in all cases this was less than half a hectare. In addition, a considerable proportion of the farmers (67%) had access to the river valleys where they cultivated their river valley *(dimba)* gardens although most of these farmers (56%) had *dimba* holdings of less than half a hectare.

Intercropping of beans and maize or maize and pumpkins was common. Also common was the use of follow-up crops such as the legumes pigeon pea *(Cajanus cajan)* and lablab bean *(Lablab purpureus)*, which are not only an important protein source, but also help to maintain soil fertility by fixing nitrogen.

Table 7.1 Smallholder farmer characteristics

Characteristics		Frequency (%)
Sex	Male	41.4
	Female	58.6
	Total	100.0
Age (years)	< 20	2.6
	21-40	50.4
	> 40	47.0
	Total	100.0
Education	None	33.3
	Primary (Std 1-8)	61.5
	Secondary (Form 1-4)	4.3
	College	9.0
	Total	100.0
Marital status	Never married	7.8
	Married	71.6
	Divorced	9.5
	Widowed	9.5
	Separated	1.7
	Total	100.0

Table 7.2 Distribution by gender

Characteristic	Male (%)	Female (%)	Total (%)
Annual Income (MK)			
0-500	8.5	6.2	7.1
500-1000	14.9	32.3	25.0
1000-2000	29.8	29.2	29.5
>2000	46.8	32.3	38.4
Total	100.0	100.0	100.0
Main source of income			
Small scale farming	85.4	63.2	72.4
Small scale business	2.1	19.1	12.1
Temporary employment	10.4	13.2	12.1
Other	2.1	4.4	3.4
Total	100.0	100.0	100.0
Education			
None	18.8	42.6	32.8
Primary (Std 1-8)	77.1	51.5	62.1
Secondary (Form 1-4)	4.2	4.4	4.3
College	0	1.5	0.9
Total	100.0	100.0	100.0

Crop yields

Crop yields were low, with most (58%) having only up to 1 metric tonne of maize. Rice growing is confined to areas near Lake Chilwa, which explains why 85% of the farmers said they harvested no rice. However, of the remaining farmers who did grow rice, only 5% harvested more than 500 kg. Although tobacco is one of the few important cash crops in Malawi, only 20% of the farmers surveyed grew the crop.

Livestock production

Goats, cattle, sheep, and pigs were owned in small numbers (up to ten animals) by 39%, 13%, 6% and 3% of the farmers, respectively. The small number of pigs raised is perhaps due to the widespread Islamic faith, which considers pork unclean. Although chickens are traditionally raised, 33% of the farmers had none, 36% had up to ten and 31% had more than ten. Of special interest was the practice of apiculture by two farmers (2%), who had up to five beehives. Some of the constraints to livestock production could be the prohibitively high prices of domestic animals, insufficient grazing land, and cultural and religious taboos.

CULTURAL VALUES REGARDING THE RIVER SYSTEMS

It has been shown that belief systems have an effect on resource use (Gadgil, 1991; Gadgil, Berkes, & Folke, 1993; Alcorn, 1993; UNEP, 1995). There were a number of cultural beliefs pertaining to the rivers in the basin. Farmers indicated they believed the rivers came into existence as a result of creation (62%), flash floods *(napolo)* or land slide (23%), fountains or springs (6%), *dambo* (4%), pools or rain water (3%), or were dug (1%). While the majority (90%) indicated that the rivers were created by God or spirits, a few indicated that other forces were involved, such as heavy rains or floods. Reasons for creation of the rivers ranged from being a source of water (93%), God's will (3%), source of fishing (2%), and traditional rites of passage or initiation ceremonies (3%). These beliefs may also be the results of external influences such as major religions.

Benefits derived from rivers

Domestic use of the rivers as a derived benefit was cited by 30% of the respondents, while others cited *dimba* gardens (6%), fishing (3%), and irrigation (2%). Many farmers listed multiple benefits. About 44% of the farmers indicated that the benefits were increasing, 28% said they were decreasing and 27% said they were static. Reasons given for diminishing benefits were that the farmers found "easy acquisition of resources no longer possible", "perennial rivers or sufficient water had deteriorated", "drying up of water occurred so not enough of it was available", "more people were using water", and "crops were being washed away by flooding".

Cultural activities at the rivers

Approximately 89% of respondents affirmed, while 11% denied, that cultural activities such as *chinamwali* (traditional rites of passage for women and men) took place at the rivers. Participants in these cultural activities were given as: villagers around the river; members of the Yao tribe from the neighbourhood; all people undergoing initiation; elders; and chiefs. Regarding traditional religious practices carried out at the rivers, 65% of the respondents said there were none, while 24% said baptisms were done and 13% said offerings for calamities were carried out there.

Role of spirits in the rivers

While 35% of the farmers believed there was no role of spirits in the rivers, 20% said spirits were present in the past but do not exist today, whereas 45% believed that spirits were present even today. There were significant differences between tribes regarding the role of spirits in the rivers, but gender, age and religion did not make significant differences in these beliefs.

It was found that the majority (81%) personally feared the spirits, while the rest did not. Gender differences were significant: of those who did not fear spirits, 14% were male and 86% were female; of those who did personally fear spirits, 48% were male and 52% were female. Those who indicated that they feared the spirits had significantly different reasons for their fear, with 96% saying they had been told of the dangers. Of the people who harboured no fear, 60% gave their reason as "not believing in spirits".

Sacred fears or stories associated with the rivers

Respondents gave a number of fears or stories associated with the rivers but some (31%) said there were none. Others (29%) cited mythical and mysterious events, presence in the rivers of mysterious snakes and crocodiles that will bite to death

(12%), floods (24%) and people encountering beings that beat them up (4%). Although gender, age, religion and tribe did not influence the outcome, there were significant differences between rivers regarding fears or stories held.

Activities traditionally prohibited at the rivers

While 26% of the respondents said no activities were prohibited at the rivers, the majority (51%) cited bathing and washing as prohibited, 17% said use of chemicals or damming was prohibited, and 5% said farming along rivers was prohibited.

PLANT RESOURCES UTILIZATION AND CONSERVATION

Field botanical surveys

The rivers studied differed, not only in their topography and land use (e.g. there is no estate agriculture on the Domasi River, whereas there are some large estates along the Likangala and Thondwe Rivers), but also in their vegetation cover. While the lower parts of the Domasi River have been stripped of most woody vegetation, the Likangala River has some patches of forest left along its entire course. The only patches of woody vegetation along Thondwe River are found on estate land. In places where patches of forest remained, vervet monkeys could often be seen. The composition of indigenous tree and shrub species along the rivers differed only slightly, with most species occurring in all the river systems in varying abundance.

Tree and shrub species common to all the river systems included *Erythrophleum suaveolens (mwabvi)*, *Breonadia microcephala (chonya)*, *Nuxia oppositifolia (chipoloka)*, *Syzygium species. (nyowe, mafua, katope)*, *Ficus species. (mkuyu, kachere, tsambe)*, *Chrysophyllum (mbimbinyolo)*, *Newtonia buchananii (mkweranyani)* and *Albizia versicolor (mtangatanga)*. All these are riverine species. Other species common to the river systems are: *Kigelia africana (mvunguti)*, *Trichilia emetica (msikidzi)*, *Khaya anthotheca (mbawa)*, *Bridelia micrantha (msopa)*, *Diospyros kirkii (msakalawe)*, *Pteleopsis myrtifolia (mcheleule, nakamoto)*, *Sclerocarya birrea (mfula, mtondowoko)* and many others.

Some very rare tree species were found in only one of the rivers. *Sterculia quinqueloba (msetanyani)* and *Croton macrostachys (mbwani)* were found only in the Domasi River in very localized areas. *Anthocleista grandiflora (nkungubwi)* and *Swartzia madagascariensis* (snake bean, *dzungu*) were found only in the Likangala River and its tributaries. The latter was particularly rare, with only one specimen found.

Large estates had large tracts of undisturbed riverine forest, while on customary land the river banks showed endless landscape stripped of trees. The estates also had woodlots of exotic species such as eucalyptus, *Cassia* species, etc., from which they harvested wood for their needs. From the remnants of arborescent vegetation, it was evident that the banks of all five rivers were at one time covered with dense forests composed of some of the species mentioned above. A checklist of tree species found along the river systems of Domasi, Likangala, Mulunguzi, Mbedza, and Thondwe contained 116 species, including 12 exotic species.

Indigenous and exotic trees on farms and in the landscape

The questionnaire established that local people had a fair knowledge of both indigenous and exotic trees in their areas. For example, local farmers along all the five rivers studied named a total of 104 tree species, of which 80 species were indigenous and 24 exotic. Farmers were able to name an average of 4 indigenous tree species. The maximum number of trees a farmer could name was 15. The majority of farmers could name between 2 and 6 indigenous tree species.

Almost the same exotic trees were found in all the five river areas. On average, 3 exotic trees were named by a farmer; most farmers would name between 1 and 5 exotic tree species.

Farmers' knowledge of trees differed significantly between the river systems. Farmers along Domasi and Likangala Rivers were particularly knowledgeable about plant names. The other three rivers are in the vicinity of Zomba town and the farmers there may have settled in the area recently. Ethnic composition near Zomba town seems to confirm this. Elderly people who had lived in the villages almost all their lives knew more tree species than younger people. There were no significant gender differences as to who could name the indigenous tree species. There were, however, some gender differences in the ability to name exotic tree species, with women respondents mentioning more trees.

Location of trees

When asked whether trees were located in the homestead, *dimba*, cropland, woodland or in a number of these, farmers indicated that most trees were found in the homestead, followed by cropland. A number of tree species were found in various locations, for example in the homestead, cropland and woodland. The number of tree species in the homestead ranged from 1 to 14, with an average 5 per homestead. A number of tree species found in the homestead were also found in the woodland, especially *Ficus natalensis (kachere)* and *Annona senegalensis (mpoza)*. Exotic and fruit trees such as eucalyptus, *Cassia* species, toon, guava, pawpaw and orange trees, were found in multiple locations: in the homestead, in cropland and in *dimba*.

Some populations of indigenous tree species such as *Bauhinia thoningii (chitimbe)* and *Pterocarpus angolensis (mlombwa)* (mostly saplings) were located in the homestead, cropland and woodland.

Plant utilization

It was found that the demand for timber, firewood and building poles was the reason for much of the riverbank deforestation. Some tree species were preferred more than others, leading to their depletion in study area. For example, big *chonya* trees (used for timber) were extremely rare along all five rivers. Other overexploited species included *mbawa* and *mkweranyani*. Parts of river beds were dotted with numerous huge rotting tree stumps, evidence of once well wooded riverbanks that had been invaded by sawyers.

Field studies and interviews established that many farmers had deliberately left some trees on their farms for various purposes. Trees that were most commonly found on farms included indigenous species like *Kigelia africana (mvunguti)*, whose copious foliage provides shade; *Combretum molle (chisimbiti); Terminalia sericea (naphini); Ficus natalensis (kachere); Adansonia digitata (mlambe); Sclerocarya birrea (mtondowoko); Faidherbia albida (msangu); Trema orientalis (mpefu)*. Common exotic tree species included fruit trees such as *Persea americana* (avocado), *Citrus* species (oranges, lemons, grapefruit, lime), *Mangifera indica* (mango), *Psidium guajava* (guava), *Prunus persica* (peach) and *Casimiroa edulis* (Mexican apple). Other exotic tree species commonly found planted on farms or around homesteads included *Eucalyptus, Toona ciliata* (toon), *Melia azedirach* (indya), *Senna siamea* and *Ceiba pentandra*.

Local farmers mentioned several main uses of plants: for soil fertility (e.g. *Faidherbia albida, Cajanus cajan, Lablab purpureus* and *Mucuna pruriens* subspecies *utilis*), fodder, human nutrition, medicine, fuelwood, building, timber and other uses. The use of trees for food was mentioned by 80 to 100% of the respondents, for fodder by 2-3%, medicine by 4-6%, fuelwood by 2-36%, building by 3-18%, and timber by 1-44%. Many trees were mentioned that had 2-3 uses. Some of these were *masuku (Uapaca kirkiana)*, avocado *(Persea americana)*, *mpoza (Annona senegalensis)*, *mlambe (Adansonia digitata)*, *msetanyani (Sterculia sp.)*, indya *(Melia azedirach)*, toon *(Toona ciliata)*, *njenjete (Albizia harveyi)*, peach *(Prunus persica)*, *ngwalangwa (Borassus aethiopum)*, *naphini (Terminalia sericea)*, and *nkolong'onjo (Combretum imberbe)*. The last two tree species had the most reported uses for fuelwood, building and timber. In terms of the respondents' gender or location, no significant differences were found.

Most farmers reported that the use of indigenous and exotic fruits had decreased in their lifetime, because of seed scarcity or people were unwilling to plant them.

Trees prohibited by cultural beliefs or poisonous fruits

Approximately 28% of farmers knew of at least one tree species prohibited because of its poisonous fruit. *Gmelina arborea* and *Solanum* species were mentioned by some farmers as having poisonous fruits. Most trees with poisonous fruits were reported from Domasi and Thondwe Rivers. *Nkhadze (Euphorbia tirucalli)* was cited by 21% of the farmers as having poisonous latex. A few trees were cited as prohibited by cultural beliefs, among them *mpoza (Annona senegalensis)* and avocado *(Persea americana)*. Female farmers provided most of the names of poisonous and culturally prohibited trees. This can be explained by the fact that the women look after children and spend more time with them than the men do, and impart knowledge about poisonous plants to the children.

During the study, the value of certain traditional beliefs in bio-diversity conservation was appreciated. For instance, along the Domasi and Likangala Rivers, there are many cemeteries which are green areas surrounded by bare land. In these cemeteries, the representatives of the area's original vegetation have been preserved because it is a taboo to cut down trees in graveyards, which are sacred sites.

Tree management for sprouting potentiality

Four tree management methods were presented to the farmers: pollarding, pruning, lopping and coppicing. Farmers were asked which of the methods, or combinations of methods, they used. 91% used coppicing, 46% lopping, 32% pollarding and 10% pruning. Where tree management required a combination of these methods, coppicing and lopping were used most frequently (mentioned by

19% of the farmers).

Tree management methods

Some village nurseries were raising seedlings of both indigenous and exotic tree species. The common indigenous species in these nurseries were *Khaya anthotheca (mbawa)*, *Faidherbia albida (msangu)*, *Pterocarpus angolensis (mlombwa)* and *Afzelia quanzenzis (mngongomwa)*. Exotic tree species commonly raised in nurseries included *Cassia* species and *Eucalyptus* species.

Farmers were asked about six management methods they used for young and mature planted trees, namely manuring, fertilizing, mulching, watering, spraying and protection from animals. Many farmers were aware of the importance of the use of manure on young trees, as well as watering and protecting them from animals (Table 7.3).

Tree species preferred for conservation

Farmers indicated that they would prefer to conserve 46 tree species which are currently not being conserved. Among these, *Khaya anthotheca (mbawa)* topped the list with 23% of the farmers mentioning it. This valuable timber tree is supposed to be protected by law in Malawi, but the protection is not effective. Other species preferred for conservation were *Terminalia sericea (naphini)*, *Pterocarpus angolensis (mlombwa)*, *Faidherbia albida (msangu)* and *Afzelia quanzensis (mngongomwa)*.

Table 7.3 Tree management methods used by farmers

	Tree stage		
	No. of Respondents (%)		
Method	Young	Mature	Both
Manuring	61	7	4
Watering	58	1	1
Mulching	28	0	1
Fertilizing	10	2	0
Spraying	7	0	1
Protection from animals	48	1	0

Most of the reasons given for being unable to conserve the species had to do with domestication. It was said that seeds were scarce (mentioned by 53% of the farmers), germination was problematic, trees were destroyed by animals or other factors of the physical environment, the trees needed special management techniques, or land was scarce.

In terms of gender, age and location, there were no significant differences in the reasons for not being able to conserve the species. Most farmers who were unable to conserve the preferred tree species did not have woodlots on their farms. Some species were rare along particular rivers. For example, *Faidherbia albida* and *Terminalia sericea* were quite rare along the Domasi River.

Trees used as termiticide and trees detrimental to crops

Some tree species were reported as having termiticidal properties, for example mango, orange, *Trichilia emetica (msikidzi)* and *Tabernaemontana elegans (mkwale)*.

Ninety-six percent of farmers indicated that some trees were detrimental to crops, including: *Gmelina arborea* (mentioned by 81% of the farmers), *Eucalyptus* (cited by 80%), mango, toon, *Cassia* spp. and *Ficus natalensis (kachere)*. According to the farmers, the most common detrimental factor was shading and they said *Gmelina*, bamboos and *Jacaranda* deprived crops of direct sunlight. These trees also competed with plants for moisture. *Gmelina* was also said to cause loss of soil fertility. Toon was said to produce chemicals harmful to crops. Most of the trees identified as detrimental were found in homesteads and croplands along Domasi, Likangala and Thondwe Rivers. It is interesting to note that, apart from *Ficus natalensis*, most trees identified as detrimental to crops were exotic.

Scarce trees

Several trees were identified as being scarce or as having disappeared. Some of these were *Uapaca kirkiana (masuku), Lonchocarpus capassa (mpakasa), Breonadia microcephala (chonya), Khaya anthotheca (mbawa), Terminalia sericea (naphini), Diplorynchus condylocarpon (thombozi), Pterocarpus angolensis (mlombwa)* and *Julbernardia globiflora (mchenga)*. The scarcity or disappearance of the trees was blamed on over-exploitation for various purposes and wanton tree cutting, but no one gender or age group was considered responsible.

Farmers' attitudes towards growing trees

The majority of farmers (92%) were in favour of growing trees if given the opportunity. They were asked to name the five trees they would plant, if they could, and the group named a total of 58 trees. The most popular were *Ecalyptus*, pawpaw, orange, mandarin, mango, *Cassia*, avocado, *Gmelina, Annona senegalensis (mpoza)*, *Faidherbia albida (msangu)*, *Leucaena* sp., *Khaya anthotheca (mbawa)*, *Terminalia sericea (naphini)* and *Pterocarpus angolensis (mlombwa)*. The reasons most of the farmers gave for ranking these species were domestic use and income generation, as well as medicines and termiticides. Farmers from Domasi and Thondwe Rivers mentioned the largest number of indigenous trees.

ANIMAL RESOURCE UTILIZATION AND CONSERVATION

A total of 33 animal species were found along the five river systems. The ten most known (by percentage farmers reporting them) were *Papio cynocephalus* (*Nyani*/Baboon), *Cricetomys gambianus* (*Bwampini, Ngwime*/Giant Rat), *Hystrix africae-australis* (*Nungu*/Porcupine), *Potamochoerus porcus* (*Nguluwe*/Wild Pig), *Sylvicapra grimmia* (Common Duiker), *Lutra maculicollis* (Spotted-necked Otter), *Lepus whytei* (*Kalulu*/Hare), *Thryonomys swinderianus* (*Ntchenzi*/Cane-rat), and *Felis lybica* (*Likongwe, Bvumbwe*/Wild Cat). The most reported use of these animals was for food (reported by 80% of the farmers). The mean number of animals indicated for use as food was two per farmer, with a maximum of six. The habitats reported for the animals were forests, trees, shrubs, grasses (mentioned by 87% of the farmers), water (15%), and caves, tunnels (6%). This emphasized vegetation as an important habitat.

Methods of hunting animals

Methods used by farmers to hunt or collect animals included fish line and hook (mentioned by 1%), traps/net/basket/digging pit (mentioned by 6%), gun/spear/stone (2%) and using dogs (16%). None of the farmers indicated use of bait as a method of hunting. More farmers (19%) mentioned setting of traps in forests/water/trees/compared with farmers who said caves/tunnels (4%), or farmers who said water (1%).

Birds in the Lake Chilwa basin

Some 50 bird types were mentioned by the farmers. The 14 most common types were *Cisticola* sp. *(Katiti)*, *Numida meleagris* (Nkhanga), *Dendrocygna bicolor* *(Chipiyo*/Fulvus Duck), *Cisticola* sp. *(Timba)*, *Egretta* sp. *(Kakowa)*, *Pycnonotus barbatus* *(Pumbwa*/Black-eyed Bulbul), *Streptopelia* sp. *(Njiwa*/Dove), *Francolinus afer* *(Nkhwali)*, *Scopus umbretta (Katawa, Nantchengwa*/Hammerkop), *Phalacrocorax africanus* (Mphipi), *Plectropterus gambensis* (Tsekwe), *Euplectus* sp. (Mpheta), *Corvus albus* (Khwangwala/Pied Crow), and *Sarothrura* sp. (Mapingo). Most respondents (94%) said these birds were used for food, while about 4% mentioned other uses such as preying on aquatic biota. Up to a maximum of 8 birds were mentioned by a single farmer. Habitats for birds listed by 98% of the farmers included trees/grasses/forest; water (mentioned by 25%); and rice paddy/sugarcane field (mentioned by 1%).

Methods of hunting birds

The proportion of farmers identifying methods for hunting or catching birds were 20% for use of trap/net/*ulimbo* (birdlime); 2% for catapult/stone/gun; 2% for dogs; and 1% for dogs and catapult/stone/gun. *Ulimbo* is a processed latex that turns extremely sticky to catch the bird when it lands on it because the bird is unable to leave. A small trap *lungwe* is a U-shaped piece of twig firmly driven into the ground. A noose is suspended vertically and disguised with grass so that an unsuspecting bird walks through the noose in which it gets caught. Baits used to catch birds were given by a small proportion (up to 2% of the farmers) and included small fish, earthworm and pawpaw. The only locations for bird hunting were given as forest/trees/grasses.

Fishes in the Lake Chilwa basin

Farmers mentioned 18 fish types. Of these, the six most common types were *Oreochromis shiranus chilwae* (Chambo), *Synodontis nyassae* (Nkholokolo), *Gnathonemus catostoma* (Mphuta), *Clarias gariepinus* (Mlamba), *Labeo cylindricus* (Chonjo), and *Barbus paludinosus* (Matemba). Fishes in the basin were reported to be used for food only. Up to a maximum of 8 fishes were mentioned by a single farmer.

Methods of catching fish

The following proportions of farmers indicated use of various methods to catch the fish: damming water (18%); trap/net/basket and others (16%); fish line and hook (2%); and a wide-mouthed but tapering long basket (*mkungwi*) (2%). They also indicated use of bait as follows: maize bran/maize meal cake (*nsima*) (10%); earthworm (8%); and larvae (*minyontha*) found in trees in encased structures (3%). The preferred locations for catching fish were water (33%) while mud (2%) and caves/tunnels (1%) were also mentioned.

Depletion of animals

A high percentage of respondents (67%) indicated that the animals in and around the rivers will not be depleted to the point where none are left, but 33% said depletion would occur. The reasons the farmers gave as to why the animals would not be depleted were that breeding would continue, some animals escape (stated by 64%), animals were confined to the forest (stated by 12%), and most people were not engaged in hunting (stated by 3%). Those farmers who said depletion will occur felt that animal depletion was already well underway (10%), there is too much prevailing destruction of animal life (4%), more are killed than are born (6%) and persistent drought might wipe out the animals (4%).

Depletion of birds

Over half the farmers (57%) stated that bird life would not be depleted because there is continued breeding. Other reasons given were that birds migrate to other areas, so only a few of them will be hunted. Those who said that bird life will be depleted attributed this loss to migration, hunting, killing more than are born, and habitat destruction.

Depletion of fishes

Most of the farmers (56%) felt that fish life depletion will not occur for the main reason that spawning is frequent and vigorous. Other reasons stated were that fishing is regulated, and fish will appear when there is plenty of water. Those who said depletion will occur based their reasons on the fact that the water level is too low for many fish, fish are to a great extent already depleted, all fish of the same size are being netted, and chemical use is killing fish.

Methods to avoid killing animals destructively

The great majority of farmers (99%) felt the need to kill only some animals, but not all of them. Methods were given by the farmers to achieve this for domestic animals, wild animals, birds and fish.

a)   **Domestic animals**. The two methods given were to kill quickly (mentioned by 50% of the farmers) and to kill few animals and leave many behind (stated by 35% of the farmers). The remaining 15% did not know any method which could be used.

b)   **Wild animals**. Five methods were mentioned, the most frequently cited being the need to stop hunting (mentioned by 66% of the farmers), followed by killing a few to leave behind more of the young (14%), allowing enough time to pass between killings (9%), avoiding the use of nets in favour of using simple traps to catch one at a time (4%), and protection by law (2%).

c) **Birds**. The methods given were the wise killing of birds to leave some (mentioned by 75% of the farmers) and avoiding destruction of nests and eggs (7%).

d) **Fish**. About half the farmers (51%) did not suggest any method to avoid destructive killing of the fish. However, 32% indicated that fish should be caught and killed quickly using the right methods, while 13% said that use of fish poison and small-meshed nets should be avoided.

Threat to animal resources

Farmers reported 27 animal species which were considered scarce or completely gone. Of these species, ten were mentioned by at least ten farmers as scarce or not available at all (Table 7.4). Similarly, there were 13 fish species identified as scarce and five of these were mentioned by at least six farmers (Table 7.4). Again, 23 bird species mentioned were said to be scarce, of which five were mentioned by at least three individuals (Table 7.4). Almost all respondents (94%) attributed the scarcity or lack of animal resources in the basin to the disturbance of river systems, forests and other habitats; the animal population moved away or was depleted because conditions were unfavourable.

Solutions to animal resource conservation

Farmers cited five sources of information on animal resource utilization and conservation: own initiative (mentioned by 51%) was the most common response, followed by parents/chief/village headmen/others (36%), radio (12%), school (1%), and literature (1%). They also stated what they saw as major problems of animal resource conservation in and around the river systems. These were: non-appreciation of the significance of resource conservation; not giving enough room for reproduction; availability of minimal proper veterinary/general care; people failing to conserve and preserve the natural and favourable environmental conditions; and scarcity of fish for rearing.

In providing solutions to the problem of conservation of animal resources, farmers (40%) cited avoidance of wanton killing; refraining from destruction of habitats by fire and from farming along river banks etc (15%); allowing for reproduction and proper care (11%); civic education for the masses (6%); prescribing laws/punishment to regulate the use of resources (6%); empowerment of the people to control habitats (5%); and establishment of legally protected areas for reproduction (3%).

Although the farmers' methods of using animal resources are basically sustainable, population growth may eventually lead to wildlife depletion by direct hunting, habitat destruction or both.

Table 7.4 List of animals, fish and birds mentioned by farmers as being scarce during the survey

Scientific Name	Local/Common Name	Frequency (%)
Mammals		
Panthera leo	Mkango/Lion	35
Hystrix africae-australis	Nungu/Porcupine	25
Panthera pardus	Kambuku/Leopard	20
Sylvicapra grimmia	Common Duiker	16
Tragelaphus scriptus	Mbawala/Bush Buck	16
Loxodonta africana	Njobvu/Elephant	13
Tragelaphus strepsiceros	Ngoma/Kudu	13
Crocuta crocuta	Fisi/Spotted Hyena	12
Syncerus caffer	Njati/Buffalo	10
Papio cynocephalus	Nyani/Yellow Baboon	10
Fish		
Oreochromis shiranus chilwae	Chambo	23
Clarius gariepinus	Mlamba	16
Barbus paludinosus	Matemba	13
Gnathonemus catostoma	Mphuta	6
Labeo cylindricus	Chonjo	6
Birds		
Egretta sp.	Kakowa	5
Francolinus afer	Nkhwali	4
Dendrocygna bicolor	Chipiyo/Fulvous Duck	3
Scopus umbretta	Katawa(Nantchengwa) / Hammerkop	3
Plectropterus gambensis	Masekwe/Spurwinged Goose	3

ECOSYSTEMS/HABITAT/CONSERVATION

Respondents identified the following habitat types in and around the rivers: forest, trees, grasses, *dambo*, mud, sand, water pool, caves, tunnels, rocks. The habitats which they did not think were overexploited included wooded areas of farms, estates and graveyards (mentioned by 27% of the farmers); water (11%); and, to a lesser extent, along river banks (mentioned by 6%). However, a considerable proportion of the farmers (55%) did not seem to know the conservation status of the habitats. Similarly, 46% did not know if any habitats had completely disappeared, while the *dambo/dimbaland*, forest, water and dam, mentioned by 26%, 20%, 6% and 2%, respectively, were said to have largely disappeared.

The reasons given for habitat loss included: careless cutting of trees; soil erosion; ignorance of the importance of habitats/ecosystem structure; decline in river water levels; use of poisons for killing fish and other aquatic life; and the search for land for settlement, agriculture etc.

Responsibility for habitat care

The perception of many farmers (34%) was that caring for the habitats was previously the responsibility of the government, but some farmers (20%) felt that this was under the chiefs, while others (3%) suggested that it was the white people and estate owners. Many farmers (37%) did not know whose responsibility this had been in the past, but all the farmers had opinions as to who is responsible for habitats now. They stated that it was the village headman (42% of respondents), villagers themselves (15%), the government's Forestry Department (8%), village headman with Forestry Department (6%), village headman with villagers and with Forestry Department (4%), villagers with Forestry Department (3%), village headman with others (3%), or others (18%).

The majority of respondents (63%) also stated that the authorities have been effective in looking after the habitats, but the rest (37%) said they have not. Where the authorities were said to have been effective, farmers mentioned three reasons: habitats have been legally preserved up to now (stated by 45% of respondents); those who contravene are punished (7%); and people have been given mandate over the habitats (3%). Those who felt that authorities have not been effective (44% of respondents), said that people do not abide by the law so that over-exploitation is still high.

If the farmers were given a chance to choose who should be given the responsibility to take charge of conservation of the habitats, prioritization was as follows: the villagers themselves (advocated by 28% of respondents); village headman (21%); villagers with the Forestry Department (10%); the Forestry Department (4%); village headman and Forestry Department (3%); village headman and villagers (3%); village headman with villagers and with Forestry Department (2%); village headman and others (2%); or others (27%).

In their own efforts to date to conserve habitats, the majority of the farmers (40%) indicated that they did so in their farmland and gardens, while others said they conserved woodland (26%), homestead (5%), around the river (2%), and grazing land (1%). A considerable proportion (27%) said they did not conserve. For those who stated that they did use conservation measures, the reasons were for: subsistence agriculture (37% of respondents); timber, building material and fuelwood from the woodland (28%); living place (3%); heritage of offspring (3%); aquaculture (2%); and grazing land (1%).

The methods farmers used to conserve habitats included: following good and modern methods of land practice and crop husbandry (mentioned by 40% of respondents); prohibition of unlawful cutting down of trees (29%); and afforestation (4%). The proportion of those who did not indicate any measures comprised 27% of respondents.

LAND MANAGEMENT PRACTICES

Land ownership and control

The majority (60%) of the interviewed farmers indicated that the land they were on was owned by the village, while 24% said that it was their own, 2% said it belonged to the government, and 14% said that ownership was other than the above (for example, it belonged to landlords). Land was acquired through inheritance from parents and next of kin (indicated by 68% of respondents), through the village headman (22%), through the District Commissioner (5%) and by purchase (5%).

As for who decides how the land is used, the majority (76%) of the respondents said this was done by the owner holding title to the land, while others said it was the village headman (13%), family members (10%), or both village headman and owner (2%). Farmers also stated that those providing labour on the farm were the owners themselves (mentioned by 55% of respondents), family members (41%), or other persons (4%).

Traditional land husbandry/management practices

Farmers listed land husbandry practices which they considered traditional, the most common being: construction of ridges, storm drains, weeding, banding etc; burying of plant remains; and fallowing, including avoidance of debris burning. Other practices mentioned were: planting ground cover (e.g. bananas); storage of seed for planting next season; defoliating physically mature maize plants in the field. Traditional land husbandry practices which farmers said they actually employed included crop rotation, intercropping, fallowing, construction of ridges, box ridges, storm drains, banding etc.

Land husbandry practices which farmers mentioned were no longer practiced in their locality included burning land to open up a new piece of field and burning plant residues, showing a high degree of awareness that the practice is undesirable. Growing crops without fertilizer and without making ridges was also said to have been abandoned. Farmers stated several reasons why they thought traditional practices had been abandoned, among which were: decline in soil fertility, necessitating dependence on fertilizer and manure; adoption of modern methods which are better; scarcity of land, disregard for tradition.

When asked to state what farmers considered to be modern (as opposed to traditional) practices, the use of pesticides during crop storage (such as actellic on maize) was the most obvious.

Soil erosion and soil fertility

Most of the farmers showed awareness of the causes of soil erosion in and around their village and near the river. They cited four ways: not following modern farming methods (mentioned by 46% of respondents); too much river flooding carries soil away (22%); too much destruction of ground cover such as trees (19%); and steep or slopey land (13%). Measures reported to be used to control soil erosion were: adoption of good crop husbandry practices, such as planting on ridges across slopes (mentioned by 53% of the farmers); afforestation (6%); and a combination of both (32%). Some farmers (10%) did not know what measures needed to be taken.

Farmers also seemed to know clearly the causes of loss of soil fertility and stated the following: rainfall impact; gathering, heaping and burning of crop residues; lack of crop rotation and fallowing; general poor land husbandry; fertility drained by vegetation; leaching of minerals. Measures the majority (64%) of the farmers came up with in attempting to maintain soil fertility reflected known crop husbandry messages through extension, such as those discussed in the last section. Afforestation (mentioned by 21% of the respondents) was known as one such measure. There was an apparent contradiction regarding use of fertilizer on farms, some advocating its use and some discouraging it. Some farmers, though probably a minority, strongly believe that use of inorganic salts has damaged their soils and should be re-examined.

Information and communication on reducing soil erosion

Farmers stated several sources of information on methods to reduce soil erosion and loss of soil fertility. These included: being innovative; through peers; through parents; from radio broadcasts; and through agricultural extension.

CONCLUSIONS AND RECOMMENDATIONS

Need for a management plan for the Lake Chilwa basin

A pre-appraisal of the Lake Chilwa Wetland and Catchment Management Project funded by DANIDA (1997) focuses on natural resources management, environmental conservation, institutional strengthening, decentralization to the lowest appropriate levels, poverty and gender. It identifies the strong institution of traditional authority, a common social structure in rural southern Africa, as a forum for decision-making on natural resource use. The present study is a contribution that provides information for development of the plan.

Resource management should be planned on the basis of accurate inventory. Protective measures are needed in order to ensure that resources are continually renewed and do not become exhausted. As policy, all conservation areas in Malawi should have a well researched and prepared master plan. Even in Malawi's protected areas, such as forest reserves, very few have written management plans. It appears that only Dzalanyama Forest Reserve has one. Thorough work is needed in both reserves and proposed conservation areas to determine the richness of flora and fauna.

Developing the capacity of village-level institutions, such as the Village Natural Resource Management Committees (VNRMCs), in which the prime incentive should be equitable benefit sharing, is key to the sustainability of future natural resource management. The new Forestry Policy (1996) and new Forestry Act (1997) make important provisions in light of the modern thinking of co-management and ownership of trees that should make the VNRMCs viable. However, the high rate of illiteracy among smallholder farmers in Lake Chilwa basin implies that any strategy addressing sustainable utilization of natural resources should be accompanied by comprehensive civic education.

Issues concerning land husbandry are central to the Lake Chilwa Management Plan, in particular identification of the rate, extent and source points of siltation. Obviously, these are linked to the loss of tree cover in the catchment. The river systems studied in the present research revealed very few forested areas and extensive cultivation on river banks. Only large estates had managed to preserve indigenous forests. Afforestation by estates and smallholder farmers was found in some cases to have used inappropriate species, such as eucalypts, along river banks and around certain river sources.

Research results

This study has shown the following:

1. Local farmers in the five river systems studied have a wealth of knowledge about plant and animal resources in their areas, and women appear to be more knowledgeable in some specialist areas regarding vegetation.
2. There is a sense of awareness that some plant and animal resources are being depleted, and local communities have clearly shown that they know the causes.
3. There is willingness on the part of farmers to conserve many plant and animal species.
4. From the tree preferences, which are heavily in favour of exotic species, it is evident that some knowledge about indigenous plant species, especially fruit trees, is being lost.
5. Certain agricultural practices, such as the preservation of some tree species on farms, assist in conservation of biological diversity.
6. From results of crop yields, livestock production, and income distribution, it is clear that the majority of smallholders were resource-poor farmers. There is a lack of off-farm activity to generate income, such as the already existing small-scale business enterprises, rearing of commercially viable livestock, etc.

7. Many farmers still show respect for cultural beliefs and traditional values related to natural resource utilization (such as initiation rites, herbal medicines, etc), providing a basis for building conservation solutions. Respect for cemeteries as sacred sites is very important for future bio-diversity conservation efforts, such as the utilization of the rich genetic resources from these areas for reafforestation programmes.

Recommendations

1. Reafforestation of the riverbanks should be initiated through promotion of regeneration by fallowing and reintroduction of indigenous species from village tree nurseries and cemeteries, backed by an extensive civic education campaign.

2. Further work should be done to develop and include more species, especially indigenous, in the village tree nurseries than are being raised at present, e.g. *Trichilia emetica (msikidzi), Newtonia buchananii (mkweranyani), Albizia versicolor (mtangatanga), Erythrophleum suaveolens (mwabvi), Breonadia microcephala (chonya), Bridelia micrantha (msopa),* and fruit trees such as *Uapaca kirkiana (masuku), Annona senegalensis (mpoza), Syzigium cordatum (katope, nyowe, nchisu), Parinari curatellifolia (muula), Parkia filicoidea (mkundi),* etc. Some of these are typical riverine species that existed before degradation occurred.

3. Further socio-cultural research should be carried out with special attention to more intensively exploring gender differences in natural resource utilization and mechanisms that can be put in place as incentives to reafforestation, such as pricing and marketing of wood and non-wood products in the Lake Chilwa basin.

4. Other river systems in the Lake Chilwa basin should be covered. Research into characterizing more fully elements of environmental degradation in all the major river systems, e.g. major sources of siltation, should be carried out.

5. Promotion of off-farm income generation is needed to address the fundamental cause of environmental degradation, i.e. poverty.

CONCLUSION

This chapter has shown that it is possible to collect detailed biophysical information from local community members. This information can be critical in helping to understand an area's ecology, appreciate natural systems, identify issues and in turn develop appropriate natural resource management strategies.

ACKNOWLEDGEMENTS

This report covers research carried out with financial support from the Canadian International Development Agency, through a research grant made available as part of a regional programme for Southern Africa under the Environmental Capacity Enhancement Project executed by the University of Guelph with the University of Cape Town. We are grateful for the funds which enabled us to accomplish our tasks.

We wish to acknowledge the efforts of our Research Assistants, Miss Brenda Mapemba and Mr. C. Chiwanda who acted as enumerators, the drivers, and the many guides who assisted us to find our way from village to village. We thank Mr. D.R. Kafumbata for the many hours he spent going through the questionnaires, coding and entering data into the computer for SPSS analysis. The data analysis done by the statistician Mr. P. Kazembe is greatly appreciated as well as his supervision of questionnaire analysis. We all made a good team.

REFERENCES

Alcorn, J.B. 1993: Indigenous peoples and conservation. *Conservation Biology*, 7, 424-26.

Asibey, E.O.A. 1995: Indigenous knowledge systems and prudent natural resource management. In J.Z.Z. Matowanyika, V. Garibaldi and E. Musimwa (eds.), *Indigenous Knowledge Systems and Natural Resource Management in Southern Africa.* Report of the Southern African Regional Workshop, Harare, Zimbabwe, 20-22 April 1994. IUCN-ROSA, Indigenous Knowledge Systems Series No. 1.

DANIDA. 1997: *Lake Chilwa Wetland and Catchment Management Project: Phase I, Malawi. Draft Pre-Appraisal Report*. Internal unpublished report.

Gadgil, M. 1991: Traditional Resource Management Systems. *Resource Management and Optimization*, 18, 127-41.

Gadgil, M., Berkes, F. and Folke, C. 1993: Indigenous knowledge for biodiversity conservation. *Ambio*, 22, 151-56.

IUCN. 1996: Integrating indigenous knowledge systems into land management. Resource paper for the Workshop on *Integrating Indigenous Knowledge Systems into Land Management in the SADC Region, held at Maseru, Lesotho, 4-9 March 1996, IUCN-ROSA.*

Kalk, M., MacLachlan, A.J. and Howard-Williams, C. (eds.). 1979: *Lake Chilwa: Studies of change in a tropical ecosystem. Monographiae Bibliogicae Volume 35*. The Hague: Dr. W. Junk bv Publishers.

Matowanyika, J.Z.Z., Garibaldi, V. and Musimwa, E. (eds.). 1995: *Indigenous Knowledge Systems and Natural Resource Management in Southern Africa.* Report of the Southern African Regional Workshop, Harare, Zimbabwe, 20-22 April 1994. IUCN-ROSA, Indigenous Knowledge Systems Series No. 1.

Matowanyika, J.Z.Z., Sibanda, H. and Garibaldi, V. (eds.). 1995: *The Missing Link: Reviving Indigenous Knowledge Systems in Promoting Sustainable Natural Resource Management in Southern Africa*. Proceedings of a Regional Workshop, held in Midmar, Kwazulu-Natal Province, South Africa, 23-28 April, 1995. IUCN-ROSA, Indigenous Knowledge Systems Series No. 2.

Minae, S., Sambo, E.Y., Munthali, S.S. and Ng'ong'ola, D.H. 1995: Selecting priority fruit-tree species for Central Malawi using farmers' evaluation criteria. In J.A. Maghembe, Y. Ntupanyama and P.W. Chirwa (eds.), *Improvement of indigenous fruit trees of the miombo woodlands of southern Africa. Proceedings of a conference held on 23-27 January 1994 at Club Makokola, Mangochi, Malawi, pp. 84-99.*

Munyenyembe, M.P. and Sambo, E.Y. 1998: The Vegetation of Lake Chilwa. In K. Van Zegeren and M.P. Munyenyember (eds.), *The Lake Chilwa Environement, a Report of the 1996 RAMSAR Site Study*, p. 39-71. Zomba: University of Malawi, Chancellor College.

Mwakalagho, R.J.M, Saka, A.R. and Sambo, E.Y. 1996: Indigenous knowledge systems in land management initiatives in Malawi. Paper presented at a workshop on *Integrating Indigenous Knowledge Systems into Land Management in the SADC Region, held at Maseru, Lesotho, 4-9 March 1996, IUCN-ROSA.*

Njaya, F.J., Chiotha S.S. and Kabwazi H. 1996: Management Plan for Lake Chilwa and its Catchment. *Proceedings of a workshop jointly organised by the Department of Fisheries and University of Malawi, held at Chancellor College, 11-12 January 1996.*

Sambo, E.Y. 1991: *Indigenous fruit trees for smallholder farmers in Malawi: their utilisation, propagation and some aspects of their growth*. SADC/ICRAF Agroforestry Project. Final Report. Nairobi: ICRAF.

Sambo, E.Y., Khaila, S. and Chiotha, S.S. 1996: Applications of indigenous knowledge systems. Paper presented at the *5th Annual Conference of the University of Malawi Research and Publications Committee, held at Mangochi, 2-5 September 1996.*

UNEP. 1995: *Global Biodiversity Assessment*. Cambridge University Press.

Van Zegeren, K. and Munyenyembe, M.P. (eds.). 1998: *The Lake Chilwa Environment, a Report of the 1996 RAMSAR Site Study. Zomba*: University of Malawi, Chancellor College.

Watts, R. 1996: Drainage factors and erosion in Malawi. Paper presented at the 5*th Annual Conference of the University of Malawi Research and Publications Committee, held at Mangochi, 2-5 September 1996.*

White, G.F. 1971: *Strategies of American Water Management.* Ann Arbor Paperbacks, The University of Michigan Press.

Chapter 8

STRATEGIC URBAN DEVELOPMENT PLAN FOR DAR ES SALAAM

by Martin Kitilla

INTRODUCTION

Dar es Salaam is the premier city and potentially the main engine of socio-economic growth in Tanzania. With a population of about 3 million growing at a rate of 8% per annum and a physical expansion rate of about 7.2% per year, it is one of the fastest growing cities in Sub-Saharan Africa.

Under the Country and Town Planning Ordinance, the city's future growth and development should be guided by a Master Plan. Dar es Salaam's current Master Plan was prepared in 1979 by the Canadian consulting firm Marshal Macklin Monagan. The plan is a good guide to where and when certain areas should be developed as the population grows, but this has not generally been implemented. When one compares the 1979 Master Plan with the city of today, they are completely different.

As a planning tool, the Master Plan failed to deliver the anticipated results. Discussed here are only a few areas where the Master Plan could not guide the city's development:

Solid Waste Management: The Master Plan had identified several adequate dump sites to receive the city's wastes and these were to be managed as sanitary landfills. None have been developed as planned; large amounts of garbage were dumped in open public spaces and on street corners. The garbage blocked drains, which caused flooding and ground water pollution. Where industrialists and residents burned their wastes, incomplete incineration polluted the air with toxic gases, dioxins and acrid smoke. Moreover, because the Master Plan lacked an implementation mechanism, only 3% of the 2,000 - 2,500 tonnes of solid waste generated daily in the city were being collected and crudely dumped. These poorly managed council dumps were a health hazard and the disposal sites were closed by court order.

Management of Liquid Wastes: With less than 5% of the city's population served by 130 km of sewers, about 1.8 million people relied upon pit latrines and septic tanks (which were rarely serviced due to the council's inadequate suction tanker fleet). Approximately 300,000 people lacked even elementary sanitary facilities. Most of the city's residential areas are located high on the ground water table, aggravating the sanitation problem as foul water is forced to flow out along the streets and gullies, especially during the rainy season. The surface waters flowing through the city became increasingly polluted with domestic and industrial wastes, either from direct discharges or contaminated ground water. Fears were growing as to the impact this pollution had on the city food chain, as it contaminated urban agriculture and offshore fisheries. There were also fears that the marine ecosystem was being degraded by the increasing pollution and coastal erosion.

Unplanned Settlements: When the Master Plan was being prepared in 1979, unplanned settlements in the city occupied only 40% of the city's built up area. The plan anticipated that by the year 2000, those settlements would have been reduced to about 20%. But by 1992, the unplanned settlements had grown to more than 60% of the city's area, accommodating about 80% of the city's population. The pressure of rapid urbanization has resulted in denser (and more unhealthy) unplanned settlements, and the settlements had spread into hazardous lands such as river floodplain and hillsides. Worse still, 80% of the planned areas are unserviced. Residents in these areas have no formal service provision and must rely on individual connections at an unnecessarily high personal cost.

Transportation: While traffic congestion is prevalent on arterial roads, most housing in unplanned high-density areas is not accessible by motorized transport. With less than 25% of the city's roads paved, the dust generated by a rapid rise in vehicle ownership (due to trade liberalization and removal of vehicle import restrictions) further aggravated respiratory health problems. Heavy traffic congestion resulted in reduced vehicle speeds and increased air pollution. The Master Plan anticipated that the parastatal organization providing public transport would be strengthened to adequately serve the majority of the city's commuter population. Unfortunately, by 1992 this organization had almost collapsed and most commuter service (90%) was offered by the private sector.

Hazard Lands: In the Master Plan, certain parts of the city were designated as "hazard lands" – flood and erosion zones and unstable hills. Unfortunately, the

Master Plan did not give development options in these areas, and they were invaded and developed as unplanned settlements.

Shopping Areas: The Master Plan called for shopping centres and markets based on neighbourhood corner shops and community centres. However, with rapid urbanization and trade liberalization, those shops and centres could not meet increased service demands. These demands, coupled with lax development control and regulation enforcement, led to a mushrooming of shopping centres, small-scale industries, garages, etc. in areas which were not designated for such land use — leading one to wonder if Dar es Salaam had a Master Plan at all!

Petty Trading and the Informal Sector: Due to "urban pull and rural push", large numbers of youths have flocked into the city looking for employment. The city's industries did not have the capacity to absorb them and the central government was undergoing a retrenchment exercise. The incoming youths and the retrenchees employed themselves in activities such as street vending. As the Master Plan did not foresee such activities, it did not provide any sites for them. The mushrooming of informal sector activities caused severe congestion on roads and pedestrian pathways.

REASONS FOR THE FAILURE OF THE MASTER PLAN

The Master Plan failed as a planning tool for guiding growth and development in Dar es Salaam city because it was:

- **too comprehensive.** It failed to prioritize the key development areas, and had no detailed action plans to help implement the proposals.

- **too focused on land use.** It failed to involve other institutions, agencies and people in its implementation. It had no institutional mechanisms to coordinate the various public, private and popular sector parties involved in urban development. There was no participatory mechanism for preparing plans, so as to give all parties a sense of ownership and commitment to its implementation. While the National Urban Water Authority (NUWA) was providing water in one zone, the Ministry of Work was constructing roads in another zone, while the city council was busy sub-dividing plots in yet another. At the same time, the National Housing Corporation (NHC) or private investors might be constructing high-rise buildings in the city without considering the implications of the generated traffic (congestion, parking needs, etc.), sewerage, water supply, power supply, etc. Development was sector-oriented and not integrated.

- **too ambitious**. It was based on a "best possible city" scenario, which tried to lower population densities, introduce cluster housing, design neighbourhood centres, etc., without recognizing existing resource and management constraints. Perhaps the most important reason the Master Plan failed is that planners did not realize they cannot create a "perfect world". Many forces determine the speed and directions of urban development: private investors know exactly where and when they want to invest; residents looking for shelter prefer certain areas to others; community groups are perfectly able to manage their own environment; and utility agencies and parastatals mainly follow market demands when providing their services. Planners should realize that all they can do is facilitate and coordinate what is going to happen in a more environmentally sustainable manner. Facilitation and coordination are needed to avoid duplication and conflicts and to create an environment in which all participants in urban development can play their roles.

- **too control oriented**. The plan set rigid building standards which deterred development and, in the end, could not be enforced. There was an overdependence on rigid enforcement strategies, without clear policy guidelines. Rules and regulations do not work if there is no clear way to enforce them.

- **lacking consideration of the environment:** Master planning has always excluded environmental considerations. Development has always focused on infrastructure changes and provision, with little consideration of the environment. To support this, Grigg (1988) says:

    In all human societies the quality of life depends first on the physical infrastructure that provides basic necessities such as water, shelter, waste disposal and transportation.... When infrastructure is not present or does not work properly, it is impossible to provide basic services such as food distribution, shelter, medical care and safe drinking water....

These failures, combined with an almost total lack of investment in the city's infrastructure over the last 10-15 years and a concurrent collapse of city planning and management, resulted in deteriorated environmental conditions which adversely affected the health and welfare of the city's residents.

New Planning Approaches:

The Sustainable Dar es Salaam Project and Environmental Planning and Management

The city of Dar es Salaam needed a different planning process with a more coordinated approach to its future management, involving all parties who are investing in its future. The process had to be more flexible, responsive and pragmatic, with the full spectrum of people, agencies, institutions and government actively involved in guiding growth and development in an environmentally sustainable way.

The Sustainable Dar es Salaam Project (SDP) was launched in 1992 and introduced the Environmental Planning and Management (EPM) Process, with the ultimate objective of preparing a Strategic Urban Development Plan for the city. The overall goal of the SDP was to strengthen the city council's capacity to plan and manage growth and development — in partnership with other public sector parties and the private and popular sectors.

While cities all over the world have very different environmental settings, development pressures and administrative capabilities, they all face enormous environmental problems and have a growing commitment to resolve them. There is also a growing understanding that effective and sustainable solutions must be found locally, based on and expanding upon local technical capacities and financial resources.

The EPM process is rooted in these principles. The process is implemented by working groups which prioritize environmental issues, generate pragmatic interventions, prepare action plan proposals, agree on implementation mechanisms and resolve conflicts between stakeholders. Each group is made up of individuals and representatives from institutions, communities, and organizations which are affected by problems, contribute to the problems and have the institutional responsibilities, tools and resources to manage the problems.

The EPM process achieves results because it:

▶ is a capacity-building process driven by local needs and opportunities;
▶ supports learning to advance collective know-how among participating cities;
▶ strengthens local governance through stakeholder involvement in participatory environmental planning and management of cities;

▶   is a practical response in the universal search for cities' sustainable development.

Project aims and objectives

The long-term objectives of the project focused on enhancing the availability and promoting the sustainable use of natural resources and reducing exposure to environmental hazards in and around Dar es Salaam. It would also strengthen local abilities to plan, coordinate and manage urban development.

In the shorter term, the project would define the most pressing environmental issues affecting (and affected by) the city's growth and development. It would establish environmental planning and management capacity with the city council, based upon improved multi-institutional coordination between local and central government in partnership with the private sector and non governmental and community based organizations (NGOs and CBOs).

The stakeholders would prepare detailed physical, financial and institutional action plans to address the priority environmental issues identified, and aggregate those plans into a dynamic Strategic Development Plan for the city. They would work to assist responsible institutions to implement the action plans, and through them implement, monitor and adjust the city's Strategic Development Plan. Finally, the environmental planning and management process would be extended to other municipalities.

Project principles

Improving Coordination: Recognizing that the previous sectoral/regulatory top-down approaches to urban management have not worked, new broad-based bottom-up participatory approaches need to be tried, especially if inter-agency coordination is to be improved. By establishing environmental issue working groups, the project brings together participants from all institutions at both levels of government, as well as the private and popular sectors which must be involved. This approach will consolidate scattered information, focus a variety of ideas, harness scarce skills in different institutions, mobilize a variety of resources for plan preparations and implementation, and emphasize true transparency for everyone involved.

Capacity Building: A long-term perspective is required, incrementally supporting human resource development and the establishment of appropriate urban management frameworks. Within these frameworks, a variety of participants formulate and implement their own ideas and action plan proposals, so as to create a basis for institutional sustainability.

Action Oriented: As resources are very limited, there is a need to prioritize issues early (and continuously), as well as to ensure that proposals can be implemented within present and anticipated resources, by preparing detailed physical, financial and institutional action plans. The project supports those environmental issues that have high-level local/central government support, indicated through active resource mobilization. A number of demonstration projects will be developed to test out new ideas and their application within the city itself, to ensure that the overall Strategic Development Plan is based on proven urban management techniques.

Project operation

A National Project Coordinator (NPC) now heads the SDP (formerly headed by a Chief Technical Advisor). Environmental issue coordinators assist the NPC by guiding a number of working groups dealing with specific environmental issues. To consolidate the process within the city council, the City Director is the Project Director.

The working groups draw their members from those affected by the problems, those who create the problems, and those who have institutional responsibilities in managing the problems. In addition, the working groups include relevant professionals from various institutions, NGO/CBO representatives, councillors and interested groups and individuals.

In other words, these groups represent all the stakeholders whose cooperation is required in order to:

▶ clarify various environmental issues;
▶ agree on joint strategies and coordinate action plans;
▶ implement technical support and capital investment programmes; and
▶ institutionalize a continuing environmental planning and management routine.

Project approach

To achieve these objectives, the SDP adopted a four-stage approach.

First, the city's most pressing environmental issues were prioritized by public, private and popular sector representatives during the August 1992 City Consultation. A declaration on priority intervention agreed on the following:

- Improving Solid Waste Management
- Upgrading Unserviced Settlements
- Serving City Expansion
- Managing Surface Waters and Liquid Waste
- Air Quality Management and Urban Transportation
- Managing Open Spaces, Recreational Areas, Hazard Lands and Urban Agriculture
- Managing the City Economy and Integrating Petty Trading
- Coordinating City Centre Renewal
- Managing Coastal Resources

Second, a series of mini-consultations were held on each of the above issues to bring together and involve key stakeholders representing the public, private and popular sectors in order to:

- prioritize the most pressing problems;
- agree on environmental strategies of intervention;
- agree on immediate and medium term of actions by the representative institutions for each component of the strategy;
- formulate, mobilize and launch cross-sectoral and multi-institutional working groups to prepare detailed spatial, financial and institutional action plans for each strategy component.

Third, in partnership with other public, private and popular sector institutions, the working groups' action plans were (and continue to be) implemented as demonstration or pilot projects in selected areas of the city, in order to strengthen city management functions. These projects have two strategic purposes: they are instrumental in demonstrating new approaches and solutions to a problem in a specific geographic area, with the potential for application in other parts of the city; and they are able to respond to issues in specific areas, building credibility and support to the process.

Fourth, a Strategic Urban Development Plan was to be prepared for the City of Dar es Salaam, which integrates the agreed intervention strategies and provides the coordinating mechanism to replicate successful demonstration projects city-wide.

Strategic Urban Development Plan (SUDP)

Dar es Salaam is the first city in the world attempting to prepare what is called a Strategic Urban Development Plan (SUDP) by applying the new EPM approach to urban planning. To date, there is no formal definition for the SUDP but, simply put, it is a management tool which is flexible, manageable, easily updated and responsive to different spatial priority areas according to various environmental issues.

To prepare the SUDP, the Sustainable Dar es Salaam Project (SDP) had to adapt and replicate the working group demonstration projects citywide in a coordinated manner. This required bringing all stakeholders together to discuss the implications of this replication and prepare the SUDP in partnership. Throughout the preparation of the SUDP, the city council has continued to play the leading role, supported by the Prime Minister's Office and other relevant ministries, with technical assistance and logistical support from UNCHS (Habitat)/UNDP through SDP.

It is vital to forge strong partnerships with all key stakeholders at the beginning and throughout the consultative process, to ensure a truly consensual plan, with commitment to subsequent implementation and review.

Umbrella organizations of the public, private and popular sector agencies are called in periodically to discuss their current and future plans, investment opportunities they envisage, their land and services needs, and the problems they have faced with the city council in the past.

There are six different stakeholder groups who play an important role in Dar es Salaam's urban development. As they were all to be actively involved in preparing the SUDP, it was important to first strengthen partnership to secure their commitment to the process. This was achieved through a series of working sessions in which they presented their views on city development and management, as a basis for participation in subsequent consultations on conflicting environmental strategies. The groups include:

City Councillors and Staff: As the leading stakeholders in the urban development process, the councillors were briefed by the city department heads in a seminar. They discussed the application of the EPM process and the status of the SDP and introduced the present methodology for preparing the SUDP, with more detailed follow-up briefing for key respective Council Standing Committees.

The Utility Agencies: The utility agencies included the National Urban Water Authority (NUWA), Tanzania Electric Supply Company (TANESCO), Tanzania Harbours Authority (THA), Tanzania Railways Corporation (TRC), Tanzania Telecommunication Company Limited (TTCL), Tanzania Posts Company (TPC) and the National Housing Corporation (NHC). Also included were the Tanzania Chamber of Commerce Industries and Agriculture (TCCIA); Directorate of Roads of the Ministry of Works; the Ministry of Water's Departments of Sewerage, Sanitation and Drainage; the Dar es Salaam City Council and the Urban Planning Division of the Ministry of Lands, Housing and Urban Development.

The utility agencies came up with a common problem – thay had never been involved in the planning process for managing the city's growth and development. As a result, each utility agency had usually embarked on its own plans, isolated from other agencies. This led to uncoordinated provision of services.

When called to form their own working group, they agreed to use that forum to reconcile their plans and work out common strategies towards investment priority areas, within the context of the Strategic Urban Development Plan. This promoted a crucial spirit of institutional collaboration and coordination of all the agencies' present and future projects.

Each agency presented its present and future programmes and projects and how they related to the 1979 Master Plan, which was also presented to assess its implementation. The working group mapped out areas of agreements and areas of conflicts, which were then deliberated with a view of striking consensus. The results were later related with other sectors' priorities as an input to the SUDP.

Private Sector: As the private commercial sector is a driving force in city development and expansion, it was important to recognize its role, identify its demands and determine what public sector support is necessary to maximize investment returns.

Initially the private sector institutions were sceptical and concerned about the sudden shift in the preparatory process of urban development plans. Once they understood that the new planning approach was being introduced to counter the failure of the Master Plan, they accepted the process. The private sector community began to see the city council as a partner they could rely on, because it was examining issues from a projected perspective, incorporating planning and environmental functions. Private sector participation in city management was to be ensured by having them work with the city council in the planning and implementation stages of programmes and projects agreed upon through the EPM process.

When the private sector understood the intention of the SUDP, their association – the Tanzania Chamber of Commerce, Industries and Agriculture – agreed to present their plans to the city council. These were to be discussed in various working groups for integration with the plans of other sector agencies.

In its endeavour to promote private sector participation in planning, coordination and implementation of varied citywide functions, the city council agreed to second members from key private institutions to its standing committees to offer policy inputs.

The Popular Sector: During the briefing session, it was found that the non governmental and community based organizations (NGOs and CBOs) were comfortable with their role of reconciling conflicting interests between community needs and government policies, and acting as a cushioning agent, translating government policies so that they are readily understood by the public and, in turn, translating the needs of the people to relate to government policies.

Over the past five years, the number of NGOs and CBOs has grown rapidly. Because they work closely with grassroots communities, partnerships between these groups and the public sector can reduce construction costs, increase cost recovery, promote sustainability and respond better to the need of the users.

Government: The government (central as well as local) will always be the major stakeholder in urban development. Although many government officials had already been involved in the SDP, it was still very useful to brief them on the latest developments and introduce the principles of the SUDP. The SUDP needs full endorsement of all the relevant government officials to be an effective tool to manage urban growth and development.

Donors: Although operation and maintenance costs of both the project support and investment proposals are being integrated into the council's annual budget cycles for financial sustainability, donor countries have played (and continue to play) an important role in assisting the city council. Therefore the donor community should also be involved in the preparation of the SUDP.

Preparing the Strategic Urban Development Plan

To launch the preparation of the SUDP, a three-day city consultation on "Coordinating City Development and Management" was held in October 1996.

This major consultation agreed on the partnership approach, institutional framework and methodology for all stakeholders to participate in preparing SUDP. The consultation reviewed the successes of the Environmental Planning and Management (EPM) process, as well as the constraints which needed resolution to ensure the participation of all stakeholders. The consultation produced

▶ a mandate for all participants to continue preparing the SUDP;

▶ commitment of all participants to participate in preparing the SUDP; and

▶ a clear overview of each group's roles and responsibilities.

In addition, the various stakeholders prepared proposition papers in which they presented their views of their roles and responsibilities in city development and management, key environmental conflict areas, institutional problems which needed to be addressed and strategies to be included in the SUDP.

The launching of the SUDP was followed by a series of mini-consultations on prioritized areas of conflict:

▶ While **urban agricultural activities** make important macro and micro contributions to the city's socio-economic development by supplying increased and cheaper food, improving nutrition and creating employment, they need extensive areas of quality land. Can reserving such areas for agriculture be justified in the face of the need for serviced land as city population grows? If so, what management strategy is necessary, what institutions need to be involved in the city development process – and are those institutions committed to implement such a strategy?

▶ Similarly, city growth and development require a wide range of **building materials** (sand, clay, limestone, aggregates, etc.). Current extraction practices, however, have a detrimental effect on surface drainage systems and beach management and, ultimately, on urban growth development. Negotiated agreements are necessary to reserve extraction sites and establish a suitable management strategy.

▶ **Hazard land encroachment**, especially in flood-prone areas, is accelerating as city expansion remains uncoordinated. The city needs a negotiated balance between engineered protection, alternative resource utilization of the river valleys (for urban agriculture/recreation) and household relocation – and an agreed implementation strategy.

▶ **Agreed directions for city expansion,** supported by committed investment and land management strategies, are required to mitigate the current problems of unplanned and unserviced settlements. Past city expansion has followed the arterial roads, with no regard for the environmental costs of developing hillsides or the opportunity costs of depleting natural resources.

▶ Meanwhile, **population density in all parts of the city continues to increase**, with little consideration of the resulting demands on city services. Private and public sector investments are made without adequate services (water, access, power) and no waste disposal mechanisms (solid, liquid, storm water). Again, specific redevelopment areas need to be identified so they may be developed in partnership between the land "owners", investors and the servicing institutions, in order to maximize more equitable returns from such investments.

The SUDP Procedure

All the inputs from the relevant groups of stakeholders, land use priorities from the mini-consultations, and the sector agencies' present and future programmes were considered in the preparation of the SUDP. These were combined with the action plans and strategies developed by the SDP working groups on various environmental issues. All of these inputs were mapped, and the maps were systematically overlaid to determine the potential of different areas in the city.

Different areas within the city have differing characteristics for development potential. To determine the suitability of city land for future development, the following factors were considered:

▶ Degree of competition, hazards and conflicts between various existing land uses and activities, such as urban agriculture, building materials extraction, and residential, industrial and institutional uses;

▶ Availability of utility services, such as water, electricity, accessibility and sanitation;

▶ Levels of hazard, such as steep slopes, flooding and high ground water;

▶ Available natural resources, such as forests, rivers, coastline, etc.

To determine the suitability of land for city expansion, maps were made of the areas of urban agriculture, hazard lands, building materials, sanitation and transportation. These were systematically overlaid to determine the levels of conflict or competition. The overlapping land uses were ranked according to the degree of competition or conflict. The areas with least degree of competing or conflicting uses were identified as potential or available areas for city expansion.

Based on the levels of competition, conflict, hazard, and service (considering accessibility, availability of water and power supplies), all the land in the city was categorized into seven zones as follows:

- ▶ **ZONE A** has the least land use competition and conflict and is highly available for city expansion;
- ▶ **ZONE B** has already been developed, but not intensively, and is moderately available for city expansion;
- ▶ **ZONE C** has a high degree of natural constraints, such as flooding, erosion and serious land use conflicts, so it is the least suitable for city expansion;
- ▶ **ZONE D** is comprised of land currently committed to building materials extraction and is very difficult to acquire for city expansion;
- ▶ **ZONE E** is comprised of land under river valleys;
- ▶ **ZONE F** is forest reserve land;
- ▶ **ZONE G** is an intensively built-up area characterized by primarily old planned residential areas and is only suitable for densification and/or redevelopment.

In each zone, environmental analysis was carried out which considered in detail the following issues:

- ▶ Existing and competing land uses;
- ▶ Potential in terms of building minerals, urban agriculture and urban development;
- ▶ Levels of hazards, such as floods or erosion, which would constrain development;
- ▶ Levels of available services, such as accessibility, water supply, power supply and sanitation.

On the basis of this analysis, the zones were sub-divided into sub-zones indicating their physical areas and sizes. Eventually, each sub-zone was designated its prioritized land use and activities, with corresponding requirements and conditions for its development. This resulted in the Strategic Urban Development Planning Framework which provides the information needed for detailed planning in the various parts of the city.

A map was prepared showing all first-priority land uses for future development in each sub-zone. When this was overlaid with maps showing the existing and proposed services, prioritized city expansion areas were determined. Careful consideration based on the data obtained enabled the identification of land use zones such as industrial and greenbelts. This then gave the strategic development plan for the city of Dar es Salaam.

CONSTRAINTS

As Dar es Salaam was the first city to adapt the EPM process, it lacked the opportunity to learn from others and was bound to make some mistakes and encounter constraints/problems as discussed below.

Institutional Problems: Despite being physically housed in the Dar es Salaam City Council (DCC) premises, the SDP was perceived as an "external project" and was not fully integrated into the council. The majority of the project staff who were supposed to be seconded by the DCC were only released a long time after the project was initiated. The DCC's initial lack of awareness, which would have supported ownership and commitment, brought operational difficulties to SDP and hampered the project's objective of full integration into DCC's day-to-day operations.

Another problem was related to the selection of representatives from the stakeholder institutions and agencies which made up the various working groups. In some cases, the institutions nominated junior members who could not make decisions on behalf of their institutions. This led to hurdles and delays, especially when working group action plans were to be implemented.

Technical Problems: When SDP was established, the DCC had a shortage of qualified personnel and could not provide the project with the required technical staff. The DCC had to look for outside staff, which took almost a year and significantly delayed the start of the project.

Financial Problems: The prepared demonstration projects were supposed to be implemented to determine whether or not the proposed interventions were feasible. Most of them could not be implemented because the DCC did not have the funds. This greatly frustrated the working groups, who wanted to see their action plans translated into reality on the ground.

Political Problems: Many of the government power centres are in Dar es Salaam. To some extent, SDP achievements were undermined by political interference from different power centres of the government. In some cases, proposals agreed by working groups or the DCC were reversed by power centres outside city council before they were implemented.

Frequent changes of upper-level management personnel in the city council contributed to the slow implementation of various action plans and integration of the EPM process in the DCC.

LESSONS OF EXPERIENCE

These lessons of experience have been drawn from the achievements, constraints and the mistakes made by SDP when it was "learning by doing". The activities and approaches leading to achievements should be carefully analyzed and discussed before they are emulated. Care and caution must be taken so that mistakes are not repeated.

Sensitization and Creation of Awareness: It is very important, as a first step, to make the urban authorities' staffmembers and all the stakeholders aware of the concept, benefits and corresponding costs (in terms of finance, staff, time, etc.) of applying the EPM process. This will enable the urban authorities to understand, accept, and commit themselves to the process and ensure the project is integrated with their work.

Political Support: The political will of the relevant politicians, leaders and prominent personalities within the urban authority must be sought to support the smooth establishment and operation of the project. This will eliminate political interference and enhance trust and recognition among the residents of the urban centre.

Budgets for EPM: Adequate financing is a prerequisite for the successful implementation of the EPM process. Funds will be needed for local contribution to the start-up donor funds (counterpart funding) and to cover overhead costs which include vehicles, office equipment and maintenance, implementation of demonstration projects and motivating the working groups which are the mainstay of the EPM process. It is important for the urban authorities to deliberately set aside funds (a percentage of the total urban authority budget) for these expenses.

Local Capacity Building: In order to sustain the project, the capacities of the urban authority should be strengthened by making sure that the staff are posted/seconded to the project right from its inception, i.e. from the preparation of Environmental Profiles onwards. Great care should be taken when choosing the staff, as professional skills are needed to propagate the EPM process. The staff should have the charisma, drive and dependability necessary to mobilize the key stakeholders to work together on the problems confronting their urban centre.

Seconded staff should remain with the project for long periods of time and not be frequently changed. Training is required whenever there is turnover, and the project loses some of the experience already gained by the "old" staff.

Number of environmental issues to be tackled: It is recommended that the urban centres tackle only a limited number of environmental issues with a limited number of working groups. The issues can be incrementally increased, depending on the progress and resource capabilities of the centres.

Institutionalization: To avoid project alienation and difficulties in integration, it is very important that the project management be located within the urban centre's administrative machinery and be under direct control of the local authority, with external agencies only providing the necessary technical assistance.

Participation of stakeholders: Continuous and effective participation of key urban authorities' staff (i.e., department heads, director, mayor and councillors), individuals and institutions is very essential to the success of the EPM process. The process functions on the principle of contribution according to expertise and institutional roles and responsibilities.

Transparency and Democracy: The EPM process needs transparency, an open-door policy and a high degree of democracy. Bureaucracy is the biggest enemy of this process, because it is contrary to the concept of building partnership among stakeholders.

Demarcation of Responsibilities: To avoid conflicts and overlapping activities, demarcation of roles and responsibilities is essential among the various institutions and departments in the urban authority.

CONCLUSION

The Strategic Urban Development Plan (SUDP) can be the answer to the Master Plan which failed to guide the city's development and growth. The SUDP has been prepared in partnership with the different stakeholders through a consultative process, and brings with it a sense of ownership, commitment and responsibility for implementation. The proposed action plans and strategies have a greater chance of being implemented as they are based on the stakeholders' needs and implementation abilities – unlike the Master Plan which said, "Let there be roads, water and electricity!" The SUDP approach ensures that the stakeholders themselves have the resources for implementation and the city council's responsibility is to create a facilitating environment for all stakeholders to participate in the management of the city.

REFERENCES

Environmental Profile for the Metropolitan Area: *Managing the Sustainable Growth and Development of Dar es Salaam*. 1992 Report.

Grigg, N.S. 1988: *Urban Water Infrastructure: Planning, Management and Operations*. New York: John Wiley & Sons.

Summary of the Proceedings of the Workshop on Environmental Issues held at the Kilimanjaro Hotel in August 1992 for the Sustainable Dar es Salaam Project. 1993 Report.

United Republic of Tanzania. 1968: Dar es Salaam Master Plan.

United Republic of Tanzania. 1979: Dar es Salaam Master Plan.

Chapter 9

FISHERIES MANAGEMENT, SUSTAINABLE PRODUCTION AND COASTAL ZONE MANAGEMENT

by Shaibu Mapila

NATIONAL DEVELOPMENT

Mozambique's development strategy expresses the need for reducing poverty, ignorance and disease, through rapid and sustained economic growth, improved income distribution and increased stability of welfare for both the individual and the nation. The policy recognizes that if Mozambique's welfare is to be improved, economic growth will have to exceed population growth. The performance of the agriculture sector will be critical and other natural resources will, where viable, need to be exploited.

Development should not be at the expense of the natural environment and the government has stressed that it will do its best to ensure that environmental degradation is prevented. This is explicitly set out in the National Environmental Programme (NEMP). The basic NEMP strategy is to define a clear national environmental policy, establish a supportive legal basis for policy formulation and implementation, and provide for the enforcement of laws and regulations. The NEMP ultimately aims at sustainable development.

ARTISANAL FISHERIES DEVELOPMENT

Lake Niassa, Africa's third largest lake, is known for the diversity of its fish species, its clear waters and beauty, and the local communities' control over its resources. Mozambique shares the lake with Malawi and Tanzania. Lake Niassa is a natural habitat to an as yet unknown number of fish species. It is believed that between 250 and 500 species of fish exist there, but some sources put the figure at between 500 and 1000. The most important of these is the *cichlid* family. Tilapia, a *cichlid* genus, is an important source of food and income for the people living along the lake. Some of the lake's fish species are heavily prized in the international fresh water aquarium trade.

With the cessation of hostilities in the country, there has been a growing interest in the area's fishing, tourism and agricultural sectors. Independent operators and donors are securing funds to develop and promote various business interests in the area and look into conservation issues. All this points to the area's importance to the development and economy of Mozambique.

TOURIST POTENTIAL

Lake Niassa's clear waters and scenic beauty are important resources in their own right, attracting domestic and international tourists. On the Mozambican side, the lakeshore is not developed, but has a lot of potential; entrepreneurs wish to increase the number of cottages and hotels in the area. But it is important that lessons be learned from the Malawian side, where lakeshore cottage and hotel development is widespread and poses serious concerns to both the lake's ecology and the survival of the fishing communities.

THE AQUATIC RESOURCE

There are a number of problems associated with open-access fisheries. Economic need stimulates effort, leading to overfishing which puts excess pressure on the fish stocks. Open-access fishing can result in excessive capital, in the form of equipment and manpower, to be employed in the fishery; this is called overcapitalization.

Open-access equilibrium commonly represents fishing beyond Maximum Sustained Yield (MSY) in response to the demand and price stimulus. The output achieved at these levels of effort could be achieved at a lower average cost. There is then an incentive to manage exploitation in such a way as to achieve the same output at lower cost. Shifting the excess effort – that is, capital and labour resources – to other areas of the economy would not only generate surplus income from the fishery, but could also be an important contribution to the overall national economy by increasing output in other sectors. Potential benefits of management may bring even greater benefits as effort may continue to enter the fishery beyond the open-access level. A further benefit is likely to be a larger fish population that may be more resilient to environmental fluctuations (Cunningham *et. al.*, 1985). There are, however, associated costs. There is the cost of management itself which must be compared with the benefits obtainable, and there would be a short-term sacrifice before achievement of long-term gains.

Even if open access does not exceed MSY and the resource is not depleted, it may still represent economic inefficiency because resource rent is dissipated. An open-access fishery will always operate at a point where marginal cost exceeds price, because no individual can control the others fishing. The only way to prevent this is to manage exploitation of the resource.

A further argument for management is the need to maintain a minimum viable population, that is, a minimum level from which a stock can rejuvenate. Thus far the model has been encouraging; when effort is curtailed, the stock does replenish itself. Once it is forced below this minimum level, the population would be unable to recuperate, even if effort ceased entirely.

A final argument for fisheries management is it prevents overcapitalization, which ties up too many resources in the exploitation of the fish resource. A possible solution to overcapitalization would be to permit or mandate sole ownership of the fishery in question by allocating property rights. A sole owner would attempt to balance the marginal cost with the marginal revenue. In most countries, however, it has been thought politically or administratively impossible to implement sole ownership approaches. Subsequently, in much of the world, attempts to reduce effective effort have focused on various ways to regulate fishers as a group, but these efforts have only produced a few successes in temperate single-species fisheries, despite years of application and refinement (Pearse, 1974). The fact that most tropical fisheries are small-scale, dispersed and mobile exacerbates the problem.

Development has often followed a process of expanding the fishery from an unexploited or under-exploited state to a state of overexploitation or stock collapse. Many of the world's fisheries are now exploited at a level greater than the optimum level required to achieve stated objectives. Without some form of regulation, the full benefits of development may not be realized. The development of an unexploited stock leads to the generation of consumer surplus only and no producer surplus; further development will lead to a reduction in the consumer surplus. Thus, the development of a fishery may not increase social welfare, but could, perversely, reduce it. Without some regulation of effort, fisheries-related assistance sooner or later proves futile as far as the socio-economic conditions of the fishers and the society's long-term interests are concerned (Panayotou, 1989).

Lieberman (1986) notes that it is unclear what conditions would develop in the absence of intervention, and he asks whether acceptable situations would ultimately prevail and if scarce resources used for management could be better utilized elsewhere. The lack of accuracy and precision in measuring the effects of management hinders our ability to evaluate management actions. Measuring both costs and benefits necessitates the use of multiple proxies or surrogates and a certain degree of subjectivity will consequently persist.

It is generally concluded that, without some form of regulation of effort, there is little chance of achieving sustainable development through the fisheries sector. If we accept this, it becomes important to specify the techniques of management.

REGULATION

Effective action must deal with the problem of allocating scarce resources among competing groups of fishers and finding practical methods of enforcing that allocation. Any such technique must recognize the inherent physical, economic and social difficulties in enforcing restrictions where economic incentives invite violation. The choice of management technique depends on the features and circumstances of the fishery. For a regulation to be politically acceptable and administratively feasible, it should have the support of a majority of fishers.

However, it is unlikely that fishers will be in favour of regulatory measures, as these will generally propose a reduction of effort, which will mean retirement of fishing units and labour. Measures are needed to get fishers to voluntarily advance the collective interests at the expense of their private ones. Unless attractive alternatives are proposed, for example, in the form of alternative employment, such measures are unlikely to find favour with the fishers. Even where alternatives are offered they may not be accepted, as the fishers are often emotionally linked to their traditional way of life and see any change as a threat to their traditions. The extent to which fishers believe the regulations are in their own best interest and are appropriate will affect their willingness to accept and adhere to such regulations. Management must take account of the distributional consequences of the regulation.

TECHNIQUES OF REGULATION

The majority of regulatory techniques have been developed to address problems associated with commercial fisheries. It is important to understand the limitations of these techniques when applying them to small-scale fisheries.

Regulations which do not restrict access have been, and continue to be, commonly used in fisheries resource management. However, as they do not deal with the problem of open-access, they are unable to improve the fishery's long-term economic position.

Catch limits or quotas are an established way of regulating fishing effort in developed countries. However, catch limits in isolation are, even if successful, only capable of solving problems of resource conservation. The problems of overcapitalization and economic overfishing remain. Catch limits are commonly used in conjunction with closed seasons, the fishery being closed once a Total Allowable Catch (TAC) has been achieved. There are no controls on the amount of effort attracted into the fishery and increased effort leads to quota realization in a shorter time. Information requirements are high and quotas are difficult to police, as it is to the fishers' advantage to under-report and the problems of spatial distribution and fluidity make it particularly difficult to track artisanal fisheries.

Restriction of gear type, usually the more efficient gear, has the effect of raising the average cost of fishing and reducing the overall cost-effectiveness of the operation. Gear restrictions of this type are inefficient and inequitable on both economic and socio-cultural grounds. They penalize the more efficient gear types, forcing their operators to use alternative methods. Restricting gear on the grounds of biological damage tend to place the poorer fishing folk at a comparative disadvantage. A restriction on these methods should be accompanied by measures to allow adoption of alternative sources of income or subsistence.

Species size restrictions are a common indirect way of limiting catch. They may be used to lower either growth or recruitment overfishing. Information requirements are high and enforcement costs are also likely to be high.

Closed seasons and areas lend themselves to management strategies and are widely used among tropical fisheries in both marine and freshwater environments. They have been shown to have a degree of acceptability among fishers, which enhances their legitimacy. As a substitute for imposed gear restrictions, they impose less of a penalty on poor fishers. Finally, but importantly, they are comparatively easy to enforce as infringement is usually highly visible to someone in a position to report infractions.

The techniques discussed above do not address the problems of open access. They may serve to protect stocks biologically, but do nothing to improve economic efficiency.

Resource rent charges of taxes are able to correct the problems of open-access exploitation, without disrupting what are seen as desirable effects of competition and, as such, have often been proposed by fisheries economists. A charge is levied to reduce profitability and thus discourage fishing, so that open-access effort moves toward a more optimum level. In developing countries with often poorly functioning tax collection systems and with a dispersed small-scale fisheries sector where fishers earn relatively low incomes, taxes are inappropriate in both economic and political terms. With the heterogeneity and distribution of the sector, variability in production and prices, the determination of the appropriate charge and its collection would be prohibitively difficult.

Licensing is perhaps the most widely used form of limiting entry and effort in a fishery. It seeks to control the amount of effort by directly regulating those who can and cannot fish. The licensing of gear (boats or nets) has proved to be a reasonably effective mechanism in accessible fisheries. As decentralizing control to district level increases accessibility, gear licenses should still have a role to play. The effectiveness of such a technique can be improved by linking credit and other benefits to license holders. Public finance research in other sectors has suggested that taxpayers are more willing to pay locally imposed taxes (or license fees) because they have greater ability to ensure that the funds raised are spent on local programmes of direct interest to them.

MANAGING ARTISANAL FISHERIES

The fundamental problem of small-scale fishers throughout the developing world is their persisting absolute and relative poverty, despite decades of remarkable overall fisheries development and national economic growth. Spatial distribution and large numbers all have a serious effect on the data collection system and make administration a formidable task. Registration is a way of enumerating fishing units, either for information purposes or to ensure they meet certain criteria. Virtually all management approaches require, or would be facilitated by, such registration.

Fishers are often locked into what has been termed a short-term survival strategy and are unable to curtail effort to preserve stocks or increase economic efficiency, for to do so would mean going without food or income. The fishers' mobility into and out of the fishing industry is an important consideration when formulating a management strategy. In general, there is asymmetry between entry and exit of capital and labour. Small-scale fishers are often occupationally and geographically immobile. Entry into a fishery is often easier than exit. Fishing assets are not easily liquidated, as they have few, if any, alternative uses. Alternative employment opportunities are often scarce or the fishers are ignorant of alternatives, because fishing communities are isolated. An effective management strategy must recognize these points. For example, fishers cannot be asked to leave a fishery without compensation if there are no alternative sources of income or food.

PLANNING FOR FISHERIES MANAGEMENT: LESSONS FROM EXPERIENCE

Government regulatory activities in Mozambique and Malawi have provided several key lessons:

- Lack of effective extension services has created a barrier between the fishing communities and the Fisheries Department. There has been little communication between the two sides, and the Fisheries Department has given low priority to development and dissemination of extension messages. The extension staff are poorly trained in communication skills and do not have adequate transportion to carry out their duties effectively.

- The enforcement section of the Fisheries Department has been insufficient. The staff lacked training, equipment and sufficient and suitable transport on land or water. Poor communication channels made assistance from other departments, like the police, hard to come by. Due to financial and structural problems of the Fisheries Department and the government as a whole, the enforcement team became weak and ineffective. Failure to create awareness and consult with the fishing communities on the formulation of regulations made it impossible for regulations to be effective.

- All natural water bodies in Malawi are state-owned; the Fisheries Department has the mandate to manage them. Management strategies and regulations were developed entirely on the basis of scientific research findings and passed on to the fishing communities without their consultation. Different regulations were tailored to suit each particular fishery. The regulations were enforced by the Fisheries Department's enforcement section, which has staff at each district station.

- Although a licensing system was introduced in Malawi to control new workers entering the fishery, it has been impossible to fully implement the system in the artisanal fishery sector. The traditional fishermen are widely spread along the lake, making it impossible for the licensing teams to fully cover the area. The licensing teams, who happen to be part of the enforcement team, do not have the support of appropriate institutional structures that could do the licensing.

With these experiences in mind, and with increased awareness of the socio-cultural constraints on fisheries management, it was recognized that a new approach was needed which could both increase the effectiveness of management and reduce the long-term costs. Thorough reviews have paved the way for implementing such a new approach.

PARTICIPATORY AQUATIC RESOURCE MANAGEMENT

Communities dependent on common property resources have adopted a variety of arrangements by which the resource may be managed. Several forms of traditional management based on property rights have evolved. Such community-based approaches apportion property or rights to the community, to the fishers within a community or to an organization of fishers, allowing a degree of self-control rather than attempting to control the fishery directly. Members are able to reap the benefits of their own restraint, as long as they are able to exclude others from the resource.

Community-based regulation is sensitive to a number of stresses which lead to the loss of community control. High population growth, technology-led development and commercialization have all contributed to the demise of community-based regulations that were once viable. Nonetheless, there has been increasing interest in using such traditional forms of aquatic resource ownership as models for fisheries management that offer an alternative to open-access.

It is the responsibility of governments to implement general policies which benefit artisanal fisheries and, more specifically, to formulate, institutionalize, encourage and support new management policies that link limited access with local participation at either the community or district level. There is a need for international organizations to stress, especially through training programmes and pilot projects, the need to pay more attention to management strategies that link limited access and local participation.

A revival of community-based systems must include the removal of the stresses which caused their downfall. The resource must be explicitly allocated to the artisanal fishers: encroachment and dualistic conflict must be prevented by strong legal measures. The resources should then be allocated to the communities, enabling entry to be regulated and exit gradually encouraged by the provision of alternative employment opportunities. However, as fisheries administrators search for alternative strategies to rehabilitate or complement ineffective government regulatory mechanisms, there is a very real danger that too much will be expected of such traditional management practices. Management strategies which are still both strong and relevant must be fitted into a more comprehensive strategy which includes strong external support.

The establishment of sole ownership by a group can lead to a number of benefits. The group may be more sensitive to the consequences of resource misuse, with all stakeholders having a vested interest in keeping the resource viable. Conflict among fishers may be reduced, and a more flexible adjustment to changes in technology, markets, resource characteristics and the socio-economic structure of the fishing community may be permitted.

Combining limited access with local participation and control requires local organizations which command the loyalty of the fishing communities, are economically viable and are capable of managing multi-species fisheries over the long term with proper external assistance. Unless such organizations give fishing communities a major economic stake in managing fish stocks in a socially compatible way, they will fail as a management mechanism.

In many countries, fishing communities are poor, with low social status. Organizations such as district councils rarely represent the fishers' interests. It has been concluded that the poor need to set up their own separate participatory organizations, either at their own initiative or with external assistance as needed. In either case, some external support is needed, either in terms of legally sanctioned and upheld policies or more direct assistance in establishing and running an effective organizational structure.

A community approach should stimulate local initiative to undertake management and development activities and should lead to more rational use of the resource. Government agencies should support the local community through education and technical assistance to help its residents collaborate on problem solving.

Community-based management will face many of the problems experienced by state management strategies. Fisheries problems cannot be solved with reference to fisheries alone. Whether managed by the community or the government, control and reduction of fishing effort will be easier where there is a broad spectrum of employment opportunities. In communities without employment alternatives, any restrictive strategy is likely to be difficult to implement and enforce. Efforts to improve incomes and living standards of people in fishing communities need to include development of alternative economic opportunities.

An integrated development approach has been widely advocated since the early 1980s. This kind of approach must address the problems of rapid population growth, which is seen as a fundamental threat to the sustained exploitation of fisheries resources and a major constraint to effective management. If the communities enjoying exclusive use rights grow without limiting entry into the fishery, a common-property situation will re-emerge.

Such an integrated approach is being incorporated within the Participatory Fisheries Management Programme (PFMP) for Lake Malombe and the Upper Shire River. The PFMP is divided into seven components:

- Policy and legislation
- Research, monitoring and extension messages
- Community participation
- Public relations and extension
- Licensing
- Compensation and Income Generating Activities
- Law enforcement

The PFMP involves both existing and newly established structures. The new structures include a Participatory Fisheries Management Unit (PFMU), which is headed by the Principal Fisheries Officer in Mangochi District. A Fisheries Management Policy Committee (FMPC) will carry out regular reviews of management policy with the Fisheries Research Unit, Planning, Monitoring and Evaluation Unit, Management Staff and Fishing Communities.

The Fisheries Research Unit (FRU) will continue to monitor fisheries and feed information, in the form of extension messages, to Fisheries Department Headquarters, other branches of government, PFMU and fishing communities. The Planning, Monitoring and Evaluation Unit will monitor the socio-economic status of fishing communities and feed this information to the PFMU.

Two levels of user community groups will be formed, the Beach Village Committees (BVC), and a lake-wide coordinating body, referred to as the Lake Malombe Fishermen's Association (LMFA).

The implementation of the PFMP requires periodic review of Fisheries Department policy and legislation, particularly subsidiary legislation in the form of regulations. This is necessary because the fishery's status is likely to change with time, depending on the programme's impact. It is hoped that user community institutions will develop in the direction of sustainable fishery management, in which case policy and regulation alterations will lead towards the gradual transfer of management authority to community institutions.

The activities of the FRU are central to the implementation of the PFMP. It will investigate and monitor the status of the fish populations and the fishery. The FRU will convert research results into extension messages accessible to community leaders and users, Fisheries Department staff, other branches of the Malawi government and other extension channels.

Research and monitoring will be covered by three activities:

- Current **data collection and analysis systems** will be continued;
- **A study of the aquatic ecology of Lake Malombe and Upper Shire River** will be key to accurately monitoring the effect of management initiatives;
- **Socio-economic studies around Lake Malombe and the Upper Shire River** will shed light on the social dynamics and consequences of changes made to resource access rights under management programmes. Such studies can identify, evaluate and suggest adjustments for the ways such programmes may depart from the expectations of managers and users. Findings will be transmitted to user communities on a regular basis.

Extension messages will be based on the data from these activities. The FRUs will prepare the materials and messages, and will incorporate feedback from communities when revisions are made. This will be an ongoing and interactive process, with regular updates in relation to responses and current circumstances.

The heart of the PFMP is the establishment of community-level institutions to ensure two-way communication between the fishing communities and Fisheries Department, to progressively assume responsibility for management and form the basis for a communal – as opposed to open – access fishery. This required the formation of a Community Liaison Unit (CLU), a sub-unit of the PFMU. The principal goals of the CLU are summarized as follows:

- **Initiate a dialogue with the fishing communities of Lake Malombe and Upper Shire River, to facilitate the formation of community-**

level institutions to promote community management of the fishery. Ultimately, it is expected that this will involve Beach Village Committees (BVCs) and later, a body through which to coordinate the area's BVCs, the Lake Malombe Fishermen's Association.

▶ **Work with community-level institutions to promote and develop dialogue between the Fisheries Department and fishing communities**, to facilitate the identification of fishing community problems, formulation of solutions, monitoring of community implementation of those solutions, and evaluation and adjustment of solutions.

▶ **Work with community-level institutions to spread extension messages in the fishing communities** and feed community responses back to the Fisheries Department.

The CLU priority is to develop relations with key members of the fishing communities and its primary task will be to facilitate the formation of community-level institutions. The objectives of forming Beach Village Groups (BVGs) and BVCs are as follows:

▶ Provide channels for dialogue between user communities, traditional leaders and Fisheries Department;

▶ Provide a forum in which users may identify their problems, formulate solutions, organize implementation of solutions, evaluate progress and adjust solutions;

▶ Provide the basis for community control over access to the fishery;

▶ Provide the basis for representation of users at a higher level forum;

▶ Provide a channel for transmission of extension messages to users and feedback the messages to Fisheries Department.

The BVCs are the link between the Fisheries Department Technical Assistants and the group as a whole. The user community is overwhelmingly male; the Fisheries Department facilitators will encourage the involvement of women in BVCs.

Licensing is fundamental to the PFMP, since it provides the legal mechanism for converting an open-access fishery to a communal-access fishery. It also provides the legal basis for removing unapproved gear from the fishery. Licenses will be restricted to registered gear owners only.

Strong enforcement is an acceptable, and sometimes necessary, supplement to community-based management. For smooth implementation of the programme, and to ease any tension that develops between the Fisheries Department and the fishing communities, it is important that:

▶ **The regulations are fully agreed and understood** by the majority of the user community;

▶ **The enforcement personnel avoid any form of abuse of human rights,** (i.e. illegal entry, arrest, beating, damage of property etc.);

▶ When requested to do so, **the enforcement personnel treat as strictly confidential the source of information leading to enforcement action;**

▶ **Enforcement personnel remain impartial** and avoid favouring the interests of particular individuals or groups.

The new strategy is a combination of both the biological and social science approach in fishery management. It makes use of the results of scientific research, and disseminates information in the fishing communities as extension messages.

Although successful implementation of such programmes requires a lot of time and dedication on the part of the government, it also requires devolution of power from the government to the community, a situation which many administrators do not always favour. Allowing the community to fully participate in the decision-making process will establish a "bottom-up" approach to management. This calls for institutional development which caters to the needs of the fishers. Training is important throughout such a programme, to ensure that the fishers fully understand the need to manage the fish resources and to ensure that the Fisheries extension staff know how to effectively disseminate extension material.

CONCLUDING REMARKS

Traditional management forms are not likely to solve all the problems of small-scale fisheries management, and it is important not to expect too much of them. However, considering the problems facing the Fisheries Department, any alternative approach that increases the legitimacy of the regulations and has the potential to reduce enforcement costs is worth considering. A community-based management approach may offer such an alternative. The fishers must be actively involved at all stages, should be part of the decision-making process, and must clearly understand what decisions are made and why. The decentralization of authority will not come easily to either government or community.

Regulation is costly for both the regulators and the regulated. Planning also involves costs. Saving short-term costs by leaving the fishers out of the planning process may cost more in the long term if regulations turn out to be ineffective or unenforceable. Sharing the planning process should enhance local acceptance, thereby reducing enforcement costs. Delegating a portion of the planning process to a group of fishers will help determine what actions they will find acceptable.

Whether the practicalities of re-establishing community regulation can be solved remains to be seen, but once governments are convinced of the potential benefits of such dialogue, they may be more receptive to the principles of regulatory devolution, where local circumstances warrant an attempt at community-based management regimes.

REFERENCES

Cunninghum, S., Dunn, M.R. and Whitmarsh, D. 1985: *Fisheries Economics. An Introduction*. London: Mansell Publishing Limited.

Lieberman, W.H. 1986: Towards improving fishery management systems. *Marine Policy*, 10 (1).

Panayotou, T. 1986: *Management concepts for small-scale fisheries — economic and social aspects*. FAO Fish. Tech. Paper 228.

Pearse, P.H. 1974: Property rights and regulation of commercial fisheries. *J. Bus. Admin.*, 36 (7).

Chapter 10

AGRICULTURAL PRODUCTION AND LAND USE POLICY IN MALAWI (1875-1997)

by Urgessa Biru

INTRODUCTION

H istorically, the people of what is now Malawi grew crops for subsistence and trade, based on traditional patterns of agriculture and husbandry. This was of little concern to colonial governments until the late 1800s, when Europeans introduced estate farming of cash crops to Malawi. From 1910, the central colonial administration intervened in agricultural production, marketing and pricing generally to benefit Europeans and encourage estate-led economic growth. The colonial government used land tenure, production, marketing and price regulations as instruments of their policies. Even after independence in 1964, Malawi inherited the agricultural policy of the colonial administration and continued to focus on estate-led growth, often to the detriment of smallholders.

In this chapter, we begin by looking into the agricultural policies in the early years of the colonial era, and continue with other policies in both the colonial and post-colonial periods.

THE EARLY YEARS (1875-1944)

Estate-led agricultural policy

Before European agriculture began in the late 1870s, Africans in Malawi grew crops both for subsistence and for sale. Maize, cassava, millet, groundnuts and bananas were major food crops. Local tobacco (*Nicotiana rustica*, a species distinct from one later popularized by Europeans) and cotton were extensively grown as cash crops (Moorhouse, 1973, quoted by Phiri, 1991).

In the 1870s, Europeans introduced coffee, a new species of tobacco (*Nicotiana tabacum*), tea, and Egyptian and American long-stapled cotton varieties. Coffee was first planted by Jonathan Duncan in 1878, and commercial cultivation began in 1881. By 1895, coffee cultivation exceeded 2500 hectares on over 100 plantations (Pachai, 1973, p. 162).

Success on these early plantations convinced the government that economic growth could be based on European agriculture in general, and coffee plantations in particular (*ibid.*, p. 153). Thus, colonial land use and agricultural production policy before 1945 was geared towards expansion of estates. Commercial production of cotton, tobacco, tea and long-stapled cotton began around the turn of the century (Mwakasungura, 1986).

By 1904, tobacco production was over 27 tonnes (Pachai, 1973). It was increased to 1,818 tonnes in 1912 and 5,000 tonnes in 1926. About 50% of the total production was exported and the rest was absorbed by the local market. By 1910 and 1919, tea production was nearly 16 tonnes and 322 tonnes, respectively (Pachai, 1973). In the case of cotton, progress was slow until 1902, when the British Cotton Growing Association (BCGA) was formed to encourage cotton cultivation in Britain's colonies to end dependence on the USA (Mwakasungura, 1986; Pachai, 1973).

Government support to estates/European settlers

After coffee production fell from 975 tonnes to 317 tonnes in 1901-1902, direct state intervention in agricultural production was much more pronounced. One of the first steps the colonial government made was to provide financial support to Europeans to produce exportable commodities. Between 1902 and 1909, the government provided subsidies to European cotton producers because Britain needed cotton, but such financial support was not provided to Africans (Pachai, 1973, Phiri, 1991).

In 1909, subsidies to European cotton producers ended, as European farmers preferred growing tobacco because it was more profitable, even without a subsidy. The Department of Agriculture was instituted to provide extension services to promote African cotton production to replace the supply from Europeans who had shifted to tobacco production. However, no subsidies were provided to African farmers (Pachai, 1973; Mwakasungura, 1986).

Exclusion of Africans from highly valued cash crop production

The colonial government production policy evolved to reserve high-value cash crops exclusively for Europeans. Africans were not allowed to grow these crops, based on the notion that they could not manage tobacco, coffee and tea without European tutelage. This was proved wrong by indigenous cotton and tobacco production (Ngo'ong'ola, 1986; Pachai, 1973 and 1978; Phiri, 1991).

While the government was attempting to prohibit Africans from producing tobacco, they were successfully growing the crop. Some even began to raise their own seedlings, and were able to freely sell tobacco to estates of their choice (Dean, 1966). As Dean (1966, p. 20) put it, "between 1922 and 1926 alone, the smallholder tobacco production increased 200 times." These plants were provided to smallholders by Europeans in central Malawi, on the condition that the tobacco would be sold back to the Europeans. Because Europeans in the central region paid more for smallholder tobacco than Europeans in the southern region paid their tenants, the response was spectacular.

In 1926, the "somewhat bewildered" government responded to the great expansion of a smallholder tobacco industry by establishing the Native Tobacco Board (NTB) (Dean, 1966, p. 20). Initially, the NTB was charged with supervising and assisting smallholder tobacco growers. In 1929, the Board's functions were extended to include control and regulation of smallholder tobacco purchases (Dean, 1966; Pachai, 1978). Under the pretext of "ensuring the best possible quality of tobacco", settlers voted through their representatives on the NTB to support 1929 legislation that restricted the number of registered smallholder growers (Ng'ong'ola, 1986, p. 249; Pachai, 1973). The smallholders were not represented on the board. (Ng'ong'ola, 1986, p. 248).

All tobacco was inspected before it was marketed and low-quality tobacco was refused. In 1936, the Board published rules authorizing destruction of tobacco plants "in smallholder gardens which were deemed excessively large" (Tobacco 'Uprooting' Rules, 1936, Government Notice No. 3/1935 quoted by Ng'ong'ola, 1986, p. 249). But these rules were repealed by the British Colonial Office, on grounds that they were excessively repressive (Ng'ong'ola, 1986, p. 249). However, tobacco remained the reserve of European producers. At this point, the European monopoly came not from legislation, but from control over tobacco seed and seedlings. The Europeans would allow Africans to grow tobacco as tenants on European estates, but not to compete with European planters.

Cotton production fell throughout the late 1920s and 1930s due to the low prices offered by the British Cotton Growing Association (BCGA) (ibid.). After the BCGA lost its monopoly over smallholder cotton in 1931, the administration controlled production, particularly via the Cotton Ordinance of 1934, which authorized the Governor to control "the method, time and place of growing and harvesting cotton" (Cotton Ordinance, No. 16 of 1934 quoted by Phiri, 1991, p. 30).

POST-WORLD WAR II AGRICULTURAL POLICY (1945-1960)

Policy direction

After 1945, the administration indicated that it wanted to develop African agriculture. Accordingly, government policy emphasized the formulation of sound farming systems, more domestic food production and land husbandry, in addition to its policy of development of a cash economy (Kettlewell, 1965, p. 239).

Phiri (1991) claims that three events influenced this change of policy. First, the Abrahams Commission recommended in 1946 that "land occupied by tenants or unused by estates be purchased by the Government and distributed to Africans" (Abrahams, 1946 cited by Phiri, 1991, p. 30). Second, "[Geoffrey Colby], who favoured development of African agriculture, took office in 1948" (Kettlewell, 1965, quoted by Phiri, 1991, p. 30). Third, there was unprecedented "drought and famine in 1948-49 which revealed the vulnerability of the economy" to adverse weather (*ibid.*, p. 31).

To achieve these policy objectives, the government emphasized:

▶ agricultural research, extension and early cultivation;
▶ credit and subsidies;
▶ soil conservation techniques;
▶ land development schemes; and
▶ control and regulation of marketing (Kettlewell, 1965; Nankumba, 1981).

The remainder of this chapter will focus on the first four of these policy objectives.

Agricultural extension was targeted to more responsive individual farmers and cooperative communities, in the hope that others would follow. Three farm institutes, Thuchila in 1954, Colby in 1956, and Mbawa in 1956, were opened to provide tuition in agricultural subjects to selected farmers and community leaders. The selected "progressive" farmers formed a Master Farmer Scheme. The Department of Agriculture gave preferential treatment to Master Farmers, such as a brief "training course at a farm institute", access to extension services ordinarily reserved for European farmers, "a subsidy per hectare", and "priority for sales to marketing boards" (Kettlewell, 1965, p. 275; Mwakasungura, 1986, p. 24).

Agricultural research was considered essential and research stations were opened at Lisasadzi (1947), Mbawa (1949), Chitedze (1950), Thuchila (1951), Makanga (1956) and Chitala (1956). These stations were to generate the knowledge on which to base advice to Master Farmers and European estate owners. Early cultivation was advocated, "based on research showing that early planting of almost all crops reduced unfavourable weather effects" (Kettlewell, 1965, p. 241).

However, the impact of these efforts to enhance the Africans' production capacity was marginal (*ibid.*). The Master Farmer Scheme attracted only a few farmers. By 1960, after six years, the Scheme had "only 745 Master Farmers (15 so-called first class and 730 second class)" (Kettlewell, 1965, p. 276). This was approximately one-tenth of one percent of the estimated rural farming community in 1960. Phiri (1991) argues that the failure of the Master Farmer Scheme and extension work can be attributed to nationalist opposition and smallholder suspicion of the colonial government, and the government's record of prejudice against smallholder farming.

Agricultural credit and subsidy schemes were also introduced to boost agricultural production. Two-tiered agricultural loan boards, one for Europeans and another for Master Farmers, were introduced in 1955 and 1958. From 1952, the Government sold farm implements (ox-drawn farm carts, ploughs and riggers) and fertilizer to Master Farmers at subsidized prices (Kettlewell, 1965). However, the uptake of inputs was small, and lack of cash was blamed for the poor response (*ibid.*). Moreover, like the subsidy scheme, the loan scheme lacked universality and its success was as limited as the Master Farmers Scheme (Kettlewell, 1965; Phiri, 1991).

Land husbandry and soil conservation became a priority for the new government. According to Mwendera (1989) and Pachai (1973), the problem of soil erosion in Malawi was not a serious threat to agriculture before the advent of Europeans at the end of the nineteenth century. Shifting grazing and cultivation were practised; tribal groups, except for the Ngonis, did not own large flocks and herds; human population was low; and the level of mechanization did not involve heavy machines.

With the arrival of Europeans in the late 1890s, however, the lives of the natives changed. Native Reserves were set aside in 1902, resulting in overgrazing and mismanagement in many areas. Heavy machines used on European farms, bush fires, monoculture agriculture and persistent overgrazing conspired to bring about soil erosion on a large and ever-increasing scale (Pachai, 1973).

In the search for solutions to the soil erosion problems, soil conservation became a policy issue, especially after World War II. Although the first soil conservation officer was appointed in 1936, it was only in 1946 that the first Natural Resources Ordinance was enacted (Pachai, 1973). In the 1950s, a variety of special schemes was implemented with the objective of promoting good land use (Pachai, 1973).

One such programme was included in the Master Farmer Scheme. Master Farmers were to set examples of soil conservation in their native areas. Later on, the same scheme with a reduced minimum land-holding requirement was renamed and introduced as the Smallholder Scheme (Pachai, 1973).

The Village Land Improvement Scheme was also introduced, reorganizing villages into large population units for better implementation of soil and water conservation and land use practices. In 1955, the Mechanical Soil Conservation Unit was established to plan, design and construct physical soil and water conservation structures (Pachai, 1978; Mwendera, 1989).

The prevention of soil erosion was the centrepiece of the soil conservation and land husbandry campaign during the colonial era, especially after the 1948-49 famine. Farmers were encouraged to grow on ridges between contour bunds (Nankumba, 1981; Phiri, 1991). Use of force in these campaigns was deemed necessary, apparently to overcome the sluggishness induced by the 1948-49 famine. The intention was to minimize the risk of re-occurrence, and rigid offenders were fined or given jail sentences (Kettlewell, 1965, p. 240).

However, the campaign did not produce positive results. The construction of ridges and other soil conservation activities were quite labour-intensive compared to the traditional system, which involved simply tilling and planting on non-ridged soil; smallholders disliked "the hard work involved in these activities". Moreover, the administration's use of "force" annoyed the smallholders (Nankumba, 1981, p. 12; Pachai, 1973; Phiri, 1991).

Land development and crop husbandry were the fourth pillar of the new agricultural policy. The government thought there was little good, unused land; so policy emphasized improvement of "crop husbandry" on cultivated land, rather than development of virgin areas (Kettlewell, 1965, p. 251).

Some development schemes were planned in selected areas. One of these was a drainage and irrigation scheme proposed for the Elephant Marsh in the Shire Valley to encourage crop production, particularly cotton and sugar. Another was a tung oil plantation, planned for the Limphasa Valley in northern Malawi. Due to lack of funds, neither of these projects were implemented (Kettlewell, 1965).

Toward the end of colonial rule, the administration was still examining less ambitious variants of the original schemes. The administration, with the assistance of the Colonial Development Corporation (CDC, renamed Commonwealth Development Corporation), later established a smallholder flue-cured tobacco industry in Kasungu. However, the land development scheme did not improve the production capacity of the Africans, nor did it enhance their trust towards the colonial government (Kettlewell, 1965; Phiri, 1991).

Synthesis of post-war agricultural production policy

Colonial agricultural production policies between 1945 and 1960 were geared to encourage smallholder agriculture. The focus on developing food self-sufficiency through extension and research, soil and water conservation and crop husbandry schemes, and the provision of agricultural credits to smallholder farmers were all positive attempts by the colonial government to develop African agriculture. This leads to the question: why did the Africans resist these policies?

The government did not make any attempt to correct the unpopular land and agricultural production policies that had clearly favoured the Europeans. These unpopular policies had awakened nationalist sentiments, especially after the imposition of the Federation with Northern and Southern Rhodesia. Disaffected Africans frustrated the successful implementation of most policies, even those which seemed well-intended. Coercion worsened the situation, and concentration on a few yeomen intensified popular suspicions against the government (Kettlewell, 1965; Pachai, 1978; Phiri, 1991).

THE TRANSITIONAL AGRICULTURAL POLICY (1960-1964)

In the early 1960s, African politics focused on colonial agricultural policies. Farmers wanted to frustrate the government by ignoring agricultural production recommendations and resorting to their pre-1945 cultivation practices (Pachai, 1973). General elections on August 15, 1961 produced an African majority in the Nyasaland Legislative Council (LEGCO). Since then, agricultural policy has depended on African leadership (Pachai, 1973).

The transitional government passed the Land Use and Protection Act in May 1962, which outlawed the use of force to make people comply with agricultural regulations. To broaden agricultural development beyond European estates and Master Farmers, the government advanced the first-ever Development Plan (for the period 1962-1965) which, *inter alia*, stated:

> ... *production in agriculture must increase at a phenomenal rate so that reliance on it as a source of income has meaningful content not only for the few, but also for the masses. It will do so only if there is a sustained and effective campaign to encourage and to assist the masses to take cash crop farming. (Nyasaland Government, 1962, p. 46 quoted by Phiri, 1991, p. 35)*

However, as Nankumba (1981, p. 22) put it, although "greater smallholder involvement in agricultural development was implicit in the plan, the means by which the masses would take up cash cropping were not as clearly defined as prevailing national sentiments might have preferred." The masses were apparently annoyed that Europeans still monopolized production of tea and flue-cured and burley tobacco (Pachai, 1973).

Phiri (1991) further writes that the colonial government's development strategy received renewed impetus by the transitional government. A Malawi Young Pioneers (MYP) Movement was formed in August 1963 to "spearhead" agricultural development (Young Pioneers Act No. 23, 1965 quoted by Phiri, 1991, p. 34). The MYP was a paramilitary youth wing of the Malawi Congress Party. Members were resettled in designated development schemes to act as examples to smallholders in and around the schemes (Phiri, 1991). But only one of the proposed schemes (the Smallholder Tea Authority, aimed at promoting development of a smallholder tea industry in Mulanje and Thyolo districts) was operational by 1963 (MG9 1977, quoted by Phiri, 1991, p. 35).

POST-INDEPENDENCE AGRICULTURAL PRODUCTION POLICY (1964-1997)

Emphasis on estate-led growth

Independent Malawi inherited a system where tea and flue-cured and burley tobacco were grown almost exclusively on European estates, and maize, groundnuts, cotton, rice, fire-cured and sun-air-cured tobacco were grown by smallholders (Phiri, 1991). There were few changes in the immediate post-independence period. In its 1965-69 development plan, the government thought that the development of estates would lead to stimulation of exports and high economic growth rates. The latter would automatically lead to poverty reduction and, therefore, rising national living standards (Pachai, 1973; Phiri, 1991, p. 36).

Accordingly, flue-cured and burley tobacco, tea and, later, sugar were retained by law exclusively within the estate sector. The main reason, apparently, was that these crops were "most suitably cultivated on large estates" (MG, 16 December 1966 quoted by Phiri, 1991, p. 37), repeating a long-standing colonial prejudice.

In 1964, the value of estate exports was one-fifth less than smallholder exports. The subsequent growth of the estate sector was such that by 1972, estate tobacco output, hitherto lower than that of the smallholder sector, surpassed smallholder output (Phiri, 1991). Between 1964 and 1972, estate tobacco area rose by 139%, but smallholder tobacco area fell by 5%. (ibid.)

During the same period, estate exports had increased nearly sixteen-fold compared to a three-fold increase in smallholder agricultural exports (ibid.). According to a 1980 World Bank report, the total value of estate exports was four times that of smallholder exports (World Bank, 1982). According to the same report, annual growth of output in the 1964-80 period was 21% for flue-cured tobacco, 13.7% for burley tobacco, 6.3% for tea, and 20% for sugar (1972-80) (ibid.).

However, the alienation of customary land to estates did not enhance the land use efficiency or intensification of agriculture as originally anticipated. The land rent system seems to have encouraged under-utilization of estate land. In 1981, leasehold land rent was at a flat rate of K2.45 (Nankumba, 1987, p. 32), with no reflection of the quality or location of the land. As there was no legal land market, rentals based on commercial market values could not be calculated, and so it was impossible to assess the extent to which nominal rents subsidized the estate sector (ibid.; Phiri, 1991).

Moreover, rent collection was inefficient. The Department of Lands and Valuation did not have the capacity nor the will to collect rents and penalize defaulters (World Bank, 1987, pp. 5-6). For example, only 20% of the rent was collected in 1984 (Ranade, 1986, p. 19) and no legal action was taken against defaulters.

Extension and research

The Master Farmer Scheme was christened the Achikumbi Program. Farmers who had developed their land, achieved a given level of yields and maintained good performance for at least five years were awarded certificates by the President – himself a Mchikumbi No. 1 (Mwakasungura, 1986).

Achikumbi means "progressive" farmers, and Mchikumbi No. 1 means first-class farmer. The Achikumbi program was "Africanization of a European system" (Mwakasungura, 1986, p. 21), much like the Mailo system in the Buganda Kingdom in the aftermath of Johnston's notorious issuance of certificates of land ownership (see also Phiri, 1991).

Land husbandry and soil conservation

The soil conservation regulations were re-introduced, but persuasion other than force was used, in accordance with the 1962 Land Use and Protection Act (Phiri, 1991). The World Bank, the lender for Malawi's first integrated development project (Lilongwe), supported Malawi's land reform program, as it did in other countries (e.g., Nigeria, Kenya).

Alienable land title was considered important to attract investment in smallholder agriculture (Ng'ong'ola, 1986, p. 106; Levi & Haviden, 1982, p. 84). Accordingly, physical conservation measures and conservation planning on estate farms and research stations were emphasized after independence in 1964. The Lilongwe Land Development Programme, launched in 1968, involved massive construction of physical conservation structures on smallholder farms (Ng'ong'ola, 1986; Levi & Haviden, 1982; Pachai, 1978).

In 1968, the Land Husbandry Branch, previously known as the Land Use Section, was created in the Ministry of Agriculture and Natural Resources to provide services in land use planning, land capability assessment, and design and construction of soil and water conservation works. Other developments after independence included the inclusion of certain conservation aspects of the Land Act and establishment of a Land Husbandry Training Centre in Zomba.

There was also a change in conservation policy, including a shift from mechanical to agronomic conservation, based on the conviction that recommended conservation practices can be adopted by educating and persuading farmers rather than by coercing them and punishing non-compliance. The introduction of the

NRDP marked a relative shift of land husbandry services from estate to smallholder farms. This was in line with the government objectives of achieving and maintaining self-sufficiency in food and improving rural incomes.

Nevertheless, soil erosion continued to be a major threat to agriculture on the estates, because recommended land use and conservation practices were not followed. At present, the government is advocating an integrated approach to soil conservation, rather than treating soil conservation separately from general land-use systems. Here, each soil erosion solution is planned by considering the environmental, social, cultural and economic conditions under which the land user operates. The other development in the conservation philosophy has been an emphasis on translating soil loss into crop yields reductions, and soil conservation into increases in crop yield. In the past, this was ignored, making it difficult to sell soil conservation practices to farmers.

Soil and water conservation research

There was no research on soil and water conservation prior to the advent of Europeans in Malawi. When Europeans came and established farms in the country, they set up a few experimental stations where soil and water conservation research was conducted. Most of the research was, however, geared to estate farming, and paid very little attention to soil erosion problems on smallholder African farms (Mwendera, 1989).

After independence, uncoordinated research trials were conducted in the field of soil and water conservation. These included:

▶ runoff plots at Hora in Mzimba and Zude in Chikwawa in the late 1960s and 1970s;

▶ strip cropping trial plots at Nathenje in Lilongwe in the late 1970s;

▶ similar trials at Bunda College of Agriculture in the early 1980s;

▶ similar trials at Hitedze Agricultural Research Station; and

▶ alley cropping trials at Nkhande in Ntcheu district.

Most of these research activities did not make headway, due to lack of equipment, financial support and coordination, among other things (Mwendera, 1989).

The most recent development in this area is the formation of Soil and Water Conservation Research Coordination Committee, which was formally approved by the Agricultural Research Council in early 1988 (Mwendera, 1989).

DISCUSSION

This chapter focused on three main questions:

▶ What were the effects of the macro-level policies, primarily land tenure reforms and agricultural production policy during the colonial and post-colonial period on smallholders production capacity?

▶ Did such policies strengthen the local tenure institutions or institutional security of the smallholders?

▶ What are the effects of such macro-level policies on the sustainability of rural communities?

The following paragraphs summarize the answers to these questions.

Per Capita Land Reduction: Before European settlement in Nyasaland, all land was under customary control and there was no government to intervene in land tenure reform or agriculture. But during the immediate period of "British protection", the administration expropriated 15% of Malawi's land for Europeans, upon whom, it was thought, economic growth would depend. This had two effects on Africans: reduction of per-capita agricultural land available to smallholder African farmers, and the conversion of customary land to public and private (freehold and leasehold) tenure. A combination of customary land alienation and population growth caused a reduction in cultivated land per farmer, from 1.54 ha/farmer in 1968 to 1.17 ha/farmer in the 1980s and 1990s. Arable customary land decreased by 270,000 hectares (15%) in the 1968-80 period alone.

Institutional Insecurity: The land tenure institutional changes which took place during the colonial and post-colonial periods rather weakened the local institutions. Traditional authorities were stripped of their traditional political authority, including the overall trusteeship of land, and were used by the central administration as civil servants to administer land issues at the local/village level on behalf of the administration. As "civil servants", the chiefs are "duty-bound to support the policies of the central administration for the fear of political ostracisation" (Mkandawire and Phiri, 1987, p. 23). This has an effect on the security of local institutions.

Limitation of Use Rights: In addition to reducing the smallholders' access to more agricultural land, the agricultural production and land-use policies further limited the use of their own gardens.

Direct state intervention in agricultural production began in 1902, when the government subsidized European cotton growers to encourage them to grow more of the crop to meet demand from the United Kingdom. However, Europeans shifted from cotton to more profitable tobacco. This led to the creation of the first Department of Agriculture in 1909, this time to encourage Africans to grow cotton. Smallholder cotton exports subsequently increased five-fold between 1909 and 1916.

Smallholder success with cotton was apparently not sufficient to convince the colonial administration of the viability of small-scale agriculture. The government still thought the economic future of the Protectorate lay with European planters, and so sought to protect their interests. To prevent smallholders' gainful participation in cash crop production, which might effect a labour withdrawal from European estates, the government passed successive pieces of legislation to control production, marketing and prices of smallholder crops. The official justification for the legislation was improvement of markets and protection of small farmers, who were deemed to be too inexperienced to understand market fluctuations and at a bargaining disadvantage when they sold crops to traders.

After 1945, the government instituted production policies designed to improve smallholder agriculture, but unresolved political issues alienated the government from the smallholders for whom the policies were meant. Also, the production policies, although seeming plausible, were not supported by complementary marketing and price policies.

Upon independence, Malawi continued with policies inherited from the colonial government. During the colonial period, estate agriculture had been protected by land, production and marketing policies that, intentionally or not, worked against smallholder agriculture. The new government also adopted policies that favoured estates. The Special Crop Act (which was abolished in 1994) has prohibited cultivation on customary land of burley and flue-cured tobacco as well as tea and sugar. Effectively, this prohibition gave the estates sector a monopoly on these crops.

Limited benefits: While land and agricultural policies have limited the smallholders' access rights, as well as the optimum use of the land to which they have access, the agricultural marketing and pricing policies further limited the benefits accruing to them.

The Farmers Marketing Board (FMB) and the Agricultural Development and Marketing Corporation (ADMARC), successors to the colonial marketing boards, were used as "taxing agents" for the independent government, to a greater extent than under the colonial government. Raising revenue, mostly for transfer to estates, became a prime objective for ADMARC, and that necessitated that ADMARC should monopolize the entire smallholder trade. By 1980, estate intervention in land, agricultural production, marketing and pricing was more prevalent than at any time during the colonial period.

Currently, the effects of market liberalization on smallholders is not encouraging, either. For most smallholder farmers, interest rates and collateral requirements make it impossible to access credit and agricultural inputs like fertilizers are too costly. In the absence of credit and agricultural inputs, market reforms are unlikely to benefit a majority of smallholder farmers, who tend to be cash strapped.

Effects on rural sustainability: The combination of land tenure policy, agricultural production policy, and agricultural marketing and pricing policy have affected all aspects of smallholders' "land ownership".

Land policies have reduced their access and control, agricultural production policies have reduced the optimum use and management of their land, and finally, marketing and price policies have further stripped the benefits that may accrue to the smallholders. In so doing, these policies further affect all four dimensions of sustainability (economic growth, distribution of wealth, environmental/material balance and institutional capacity) of the rural communities in Malawi.

CONCLUSION

Post-colonial versus colonial agricultural production policies

Malawi's colonial and post-colonial agricultural production policies were based on the strategy of estate-led growth. Estates producing exports were reaffirmed as the engine to growth, while the customary or traditional farming sector effectively remained an attendant to growth (see also Sahn, 1991). The latter supplied the former with labour and food. Smallholders were excluded from growing marketable or exportable, high-valued crops during both the colonial and post-colonial eras (until the Special Crop Act was removed in 1994). Malawi thus undertook policies that promoted a dualistic structure in agriculture, promoting the growth of the individually tenured estate sector (see also Mkandawire and Phiri,

1987).

Moreover, the policies of independent Malawi were reversals from the policy directions introduced during the transitional period. For instance, re-emphasis of large estates was a significant departure from the 1962-65 plan. The extension, research, land husbandry and soil conservation policy objectives and implementation strategies were all an extension of colonial policies that had been tried and failed. In the words of Phiri (1991, p. 36), "the colonial policies of 1945 to 1960, were re-entrenched in the hope that the same policies that were resisted because a 'white man' formulated them would be accepted when a 'black man' commandeered them."

Production Policy and Agricultural Growth: In terms of agricultural growth, output grew by about seven percent per annum between 1945 and 1980 (Table 10.1). A comparison of the pre-independence and post-independence periods shows that growth was faster in the 1964-80 period than during the colonial era (see Table 10.1). It was slowest during the transitional period of 1960-64, mostly due to declining estate output. This was probably because almost all estates were European-owned and political uncertainties preceding independence might have caused some Europeans to leave and others to scale down their farming operations.

A comparison of pre-independence and post-independence performance of the smallholder sector shows that growth was faster in the 1945-60 period than 1964-80, in spite of the unpopularity of colonial policies. The deceleration of smallholder output growth, relative to the 1945-60 period, was associated as much with abandonment of (useful) agronomic practices forcibly pursued hitherto, as with a confused policy environment that characterizes transitional periods (Phiri, 1991; Pachai, 1978; Kettlewell, 1965).

The government's promise, in its 1962-65 and 1965-69 plans, to accelerate growth of smallholder output (Nyasaland Government, 1962, MG, 19 January 1965, cited by Phiri, 1991, p. 43) was not attained. Furthermore, emphasis on the estate mode of production led to policy design which, while alluding to improvement of the smallholder sector, complemented the estate sector and worked against the smallholder sector.

Table 10.1 Annual growth rates of agricultural output: 1945-80

Period	Smallholder %	Estate %	All %
1945-60	6.2	4.3	5.8
1960-64	5.1	-3.4	3.3
1964-80	5.0	17.0	8.9
1945-80	5.5	9.0	6.9

Sources: Raw data from: Kettlewell (1965, pp. 279-283 cited by Phiri, 1991, p. 41)

Growth of estate output contributed more to high overall agricultural growth; estate output grew at a rate two-thirds higher than the smallholder output. Highest growth (17% per annum) of estate output was achieved in the post-independence period. A land policy that was complementary to estate expansion, and a Special Crops Act which gave the estates monopoly over highly valued cash crops, assisted the process (Phiri, 1991; Pachai, 1978). Prior to estate expansion, most of which happened after 1968, smallholder output grew by about 12% per annum; but estate expansion was associated with decelerating growth of smallholder output (Phiri, 1991).

REFERENCES

Dean, E. 1966: *The Supply Responses of African Farmers: Theory of Measurement in Malawi*. Amsterdam: North Holland Publishing Company.

Kettlewell, R.W. 1965: Agricultural Change in Nyasaland 1945-1960. *Food Research Institute Studies*, Volume V, No. 3. California: Stanford University.

Levi, J. and Haviden, M. 1982: *Economics of African Agriculture*. London: Longmans.

Mkandawire, R. and Phiri, C.D. 1987: *Land Policy Study: Assessment of Land Transfers from Smallholder to Estates*. Mimeo. Lilongwe: Bunda College of Agriculture.

Mwakasungura, A.K. 1986: *The Rural Economy of Malawi: A Critical Analysis*. DERAP Publication, No. 97. Bergen: Chr. Michelsen Institute.

Mwendera, E.J. 1989: *A Short History and Annotated Bibliography on Soil and Water Conservation in Malawi*. Report No. 2. Maseru: SADCC Soil and Water Conservation and Utilization Sector Coordination Unit.

Nankumba, J.S. 1981: *Evolution of Agricultural Policy in Malawi and the National Rural Development Programme: A Historical Review*. Berystwyth: University of Wales, Department of Agricultural Economics.

Nankumba, J.S. 1987: *Progress in Agrarian Reform and Rural Development in Malawi: Country Report for 1980-85/86*. Lilongwe: Ministry of Agriculture.

Ng'ong'ola, C. 1986: Land Reform and Land Dispute Resolution in Malawi: The Work of the Lilongwe Local Land Board. *The Journal of Eastern African Research and Development*, 16, 105-121.

Pachai, B. 1973: *The History of the Nation, Malawi*. London: Longman Group Ltd.

Pachai, B. 1978: *Land and Politics in Malawi*. Ontario: Limestone Press.

Phiri, C.D. 1991: *Agricultural Policy in Malawi: 1971-1987*. Ph.D. Thesis. Cambridge: Corpus Christi College.

Ranade, C.G. 1986: Growth of Productivity in Indian Agriculture - Some Unfinished Components of Narain, Dhorum work. *Economic and Political Weekly*, 21, 25-26.

Sahn, D.E. 1991: *Development through dualism? Land Tenure, Policy, and Poverty in Malawi*. Washington: CFNPP Publications Department.

World Bank. 1982: *Malawi: Growth and Structural Change. A Basic Economic Report*. Washington: IBRD.

World Bank. 1987: *Malawi: Land Policy Study*. Washington: World Bank.

Chapter 11

SETTLEMENT RELOCATION AND ENERGY SUPPLIES; ISSUES AND LESSONS FROM THE GWEMBE VALLEY, ZAMBIA

by Albert C. Chipeleme

INTRODUCTION

From ancient times until the Zambezi River was dammed and Lake Kariba was formed around 1960, the Valley Tonga people lived and farmed in the Gwembe Valley. They were smallholders and farmers on alluvial lands along the Zambezi and its tributaries. They had developed a system of farming related to the annual flooding of rivers and possessed practically no livestock.

They were moved and found themselves squeezed between the lake and the escarpment zone, and had to make a new living from poor soils on hilly slopes where water was scarce. They converted largely to mixed farming, with sorghum, maize and other crops, and acquired livestock, partly for ploughing, but mainly as a way of saving to survive periods of bad crops. The Valley Tonga gave up their villages and integrity for the Kariba Dam, a hydro-electric power project which created both water and energy resources, from which they have benefitted very little.

Today, the problem in the area is a shortage of water for people, animals and agriculture. Where and when water is available, energy resources are needed to lift it. Energy resources are also needed for lighting, agro-industries and heating. There is evidence of inadequate food production and consumption due to erratic rainfall distribution and/or persistent drought.

The development of energy resources for lifting water from storage dams for domestic use, for watering livestock, and, if possible, for small-scale irrigation has been considered the optimal solution to relieve these hardships.

This chapter examines the relocation of the Valley Tonga and their agricultural adaptations. It also examines how alternative energy sources such as biomass, animal-powered, human-powered, solar-powered and wind-powered technologies could be used to improve ecological agriculture for the smallholders in the Gwembe Valley. A social eco-technological system is offered as a means of developing a better understanding of the potential of these alternative energy sources. It will conclude with a review of the implications for planning in the Gwembe Valley.

THE GWEMBE VALLEY COMMUNITIES

Geographic setting

The communities are located in the Gwembe Valley areas of the districts of Gwembe and Siavonga in Zambia's southern province. Available data indicate that the two districts cover most of the Gwembe Valley, on the northwestern slope of the Zambezi Valley along the length of Lake Kariba.

The Gwembe Valley is about 300 kilometres long with an average width of about 25 kilometres; it covers approximately one percent of Zambia's land surface. The valley's population, estimated at 200,000, is about two percent of Zambia's total population. The population density in the Gwembe is nearly the same as on the neighbouring plateau, 20 to 30 people per square kilometre.

The Gwembe Valley is traversed by numerous rivers of various sizes, of which only a few originate from the plateau. These few have eroded wide valleys in the plateau and breaches in the escarpment zone. The area is largely covered with a vegetation characterized as tree savanna, with small sections of woodland savanna in between.

The people of the Gwembe Valley practise agriculture only on small strips of land, often along the many rivers and streams, and graze their cattle, sheep and goats on the savannas. The community generally lives along the rivers and streams, in small villages spread over the lower part of the Gwembe Valley, mainly in its central and southern sections.

In the wet season, December through March, rainfall averages 712 mm but is very irregular and often insufficient because of rapid run-off and the soil's poor moisture-holding capacity. In the dry season, hardly any water is available and often must be transported over several kilometres in drums or buckets. Wells and boreholes are not a solution, as the water is often brackish and insufficient.

The communities in the Gwembe Valley must also cope with seismic activity caused by the impounding of Lake Kariba. Shocks exceeding a magnitude of 5.0 have been experienced.

Social-economic infrastructure and support services

Drinking water for the Gwembe Valley communities is delivered from boreholes, wells, river beds and the lake. Most drilled wells are either permanent or intermittent and are provided with hand or motor pump units. About 40% of the 100 drilled boreholes in the area are not functional.

Many boreholes were equipped with a well-head, belt-driven by an air-cooled diesel engine. Most of the engines were poorly aligned with the well-head and, due to technical problems and the high cost of diesel, have been abandoned. A few were equipped with windmills and had been running, as were a few equipped with mono pumps and driven by electric motors. Some were equipped with hand pumps, but maintenance at the community level was a problem.

In the past, the Department of Water Affairs of the Ministry of Energy and Water Development made services available. Due to constraints, this service is no longer available. People have resorted to traditional water sources (river beds and the lake). Lately, private and non-governmental organizations have supplied solar panels, do-it-yourself (DIY) kits and photovoltaic (PV) pumps for pumping water, but the demand is high and outstrips supply.

Meaningful development is not possible without a proper road system. Because the Gwembe Valley is remote from trading and commercial centres, no important roads pass through the area and the existing road network is poor. Public and private transport is hardly available.

There was a telephone link via overhead lines, but in many areas it has been replaced by new technology, including solar power. Even so, telecommunications in the area are poor.

Except in a very few areas, the Gwembe Valley is poorly electrified. The area has been on the priority list for rural electrification for a long time, but only two areas have been electrified at this time. Industrial energy demand in the Gwembe is actually near zero level, except for the electricity of the Maamba Coal Mine and at Siavonga's Kariba North Bank pump station.

Small-scale industrial projects are few and mainly involve fishing, but civil electricity demand can be described as obvious and considerable. There are many villages in the area, most of which have brick houses, schools, health centres and social and administration buildings. None of these have electricity or an alternative energy supply.

FIELD INVESTIGATIONS

The findings reported here are mainly based on the field investigation made in the Gwembe Valley of the southern province in 1988, 1990, 1993 and 1995. The surveys and studies conducted dealt with, among other things, the prerequisites, impacts and possibilities for renewable energy supplies, electrification and utilization by the smallholders in the Gwembe Valley who need energy supplies for irrigation, domestic use and for smallholder businesses such as fishing.

The studies have considered electricity, coal, biomass/biogas, wind power, solar power, animal power and human power as sources of energy for development and smallholder use in the Gwembe Valley. Smallholders were surveyed on needs assessment, envisaged uses of energy and households' and communities' willingness to pay for the energy.

ALTERNATIVE ENERGY TECHNOLOGIES

Alternative technologies were examined using a social eco-technological system, which is defined as the invisible mechanism by which people in a particular ecosystem utilize scarce resources (time, energy, materials, land, environment, etc.) to acquire some perceived benefit by use of methods that are time and site specific[1].

Why distinguish a social eco-technological system from other systems or approaches?

- Firstly, because other systems are essentially based on the principles of monetary exchange; they attempt to quantify non-monetary aspects in terms of monetary equivalents. In the Gwembe Valley, we often work with smallholders in communities who are outside the cash economy. To quantify decision-making processes regarding a commodity such as alternative energy technology, which is not central to smallholders' lives, is not likely to be effective.

- Secondly, through the non-predictive social eco-technological system, we can develop ways to measure effectiveness and identify potential problems of alternative energy technologies for the smallholders. The social eco-technological system offers a more realistic approach, as it focuses on people

— the smallholders — and enables us to learn from mistakes more readily than most approaches.

At this point, it is important to give a brief description of the alternative energy technologies considered for the smallholders in the Gwembe Valley.

It is also important to stress that consideration of promotion and development and choice of utilization can not be separated from other aspects of alternative energy technologies. Too often, in the past and at present in Zambia, the promoted alternative energy technologies have concentrated on an ideal, without giving due thought to how it would be received by consumers. These technologies have often been over-engineered to squeeze out the extra percentage of efficiency, and this has led to capital-intensive, high-cost production, putting technology such as solar power, biomass fuel and wind mills beyond the means of poor smallholders, the people who need it most.

Better application of energy, especially more accessible forms of alternative energy, can improve the agricultural conditions and sustainability in the Gwembe Valley With alternative energy sources to make water more accessible to the communities, their health, agriculture and infrastructure can be improved.

Some possible sources of alternative energy include:

- **Human-power**: This is mainly the use of hand pumps as lifting devices for domestic and irrigation water supplies. This is suitable when the depth to the ground water is not more than 5 m.

  For heating and cooking, wood fuels have long been the main energy source, supplied by human-powered cutting of trees. But the viability of wood as a reliable resource is threatened by deforestation, drought and erosion, which are serious problems in the Gwembe Valley. Local forests are being lost at a fast rate and the distance to forests is increasing, which eventually increases the burden of women and girls, who gather the wood.

- **Animal-power**: Based on the experience of Asian countries, devices could be developed which use animals to draw water from depths of over 10 metres.

- **Biomass**: Living plants containing chlorophyll store solar energy. Green plants receive sunlight and, in combination with water, atmospheric carbon dioxide and soil nutrients, convert the light energy to chemical energy in the process of photosynthesis.

  Sorghum (sweet variety) can provide grain from its ear heads, alcohol and bagasse from its stocks. It is a short duration crop, maturing in 100 to 120 days, and it is cheap to grow as it requires little water. Animals fed bagasse from the stalks can provide animal power for agriculture and for water lifting, and cow dung can be used to provide biogas for cooking.

▶ **Solar power:** Solar photovoltaic generation of electricity requires a generating part (array), comprising one or more modules with solar cells which convert sunlight into direct current (DC); an inverter which transforms the direct current into alternating current (AC); a storage unit, comprising one or more batteries which store energy to be released when sunshine is insufficient; and control equipment. In the Gwembe Valley, solar levels are quite high and the potential for solar power for lighting, radio, refrigeration and telecommunications is very high.

▶ **Wind power:** The wind along the lakeshore can power water-lifting windmills for both domestic and irrigation use. The size of the windmill and the area which can be irrigated depend on the wind velocity. For the Gwembe Valley, a design wind speed of 3-4 m/s can be adopted. During less windy months, however, windmill irrigation is not practical, so a wind system is only practical during the end of the season, in August and September.

IMPLICATIONS FOR PLANNERS AND IMPLEMENTERS

The government of Zambia, non-governmental organizations (mainly church organizations) and the private sector have been the main promoters of alternative energy technologies and electrification in the Gwembe Valley. The government has been working in conjunction with bilateral donor agencies, mainly in the area of irrigation planning and development in the Gwembe Valley.

Their planning has been based on energy for water pumping purposes and their perspective has been that network electrification is superior to alternative methods of energy supply. But Gwembe Valley does not have such a network. It would have to be constructed at enormous financial and environmental costs.

Long ago, movable diesel pump systems in drawdown areas of Lake Kariba and stationary pumps on the shore were used for pumping lake water. Both the government and non-governmental organizations have compared alternative energy technologies for water lifting, after taking into account local conditions. They have promoted and developed lifting of ground water from wells by animal draught power, solar pumps, windmills and electric borehole pumps for the smallholders in the Gwembe Valley.

Private sector initiatives have promoted liquid product of cellulose (LPC) as a rural domestic cooking and lighting biomass fuel. It has been promoted because it is a renewable energy source which uses abundant agricultural residues, reduces fossil fuel consumption, stabilizes ecological imbalances and enhances the standard of living of every rural smallholder by providing clean, convenient and economical fuel.

Solar power has also enjoyed significant private sector promotion. Combinations of components are supplied, ranging from do-it-yourself (DIY) solar radio kits, basic non-governmental organization kits and DIY solar business start-up kits used mainly for radios, television and lighting.

However, these initiatives do not take into account the way smallholders in the informal sector make decisions. It is assumed that a smallholder will be willing to invest capital, has access to credit and is motivated by profit maximization – none of which apply in the communities of the Gwembe Valley.

An accurate appraisal of decision-making processes and realistic options requires a close working relationship with the smallholders themselves. Localized, low-cost, low-investment technology is more likely to succeed in the long-term because it is more likely to be appropriate.

It is also important to understand what the smallholders are capable of doing or producing, and what their felt problems and constraints are, at both individual and household levels. Planners must solicit their views on what they envisage as possible ways and means to improve their currently unsatisfactory social and economic conditions. This knowledge is vital if an alternative energy technology is to build on existing social and economic conditions.

Of course, in the short-term, the learning process and the risks involved in promoting and developing the technology in the communities will push investment levels up. But by working with the smallholders, one can estimate what each technology costs them in time and money and a minimum price can then be determined. With that information, one can determine a long-term minimum investment level. This may vary substantially from smallholder to smallholder, household to household and community to community.

THE SMALLHOLDERS' PERSPECTIVE

The work and numerous surveys done in the Gwembe Valley communities have provided insights into the opinions, intentions, choices or preferences at both individual and household levels. Nearly 90% of the households expressed that their challenges are basic living conditions, limited availability of water and agricultural problems or constraints.

As far as their basic living conditions, 70% of the Gwembe Valley households complain about inadequate food or, more simply, hunger. The same number mention the limited availability or lack of water. Quite frequently, water and food are mentioned together, stressing the close relationship of the two.

The people want improved basic living conditions, improved access to availability of water, development or fostering of irrigated agriculture and development of alternative energy resources.

However, fewer than 50% of the consulted household heads have ideas as to what development of alternative energy technologies could mean to them. It is interesting to note that most of these centre on use of alternative energy sources for the home, primarily for lighting and radios. About 40% refer to pumping water, either without specifying the purpose, or referring particularly to irrigation.

To ensure that alternative energy technology offers potential and brighter prospects for utilization by the smallholders, it must be made certain that their choices and voices are heard during planning, development, monitoring and evaluation.

ISSUES AND LESSONS

Let us be clear about the fundamental premise of the 'social eco-technological system' as it applies to the alternative energy crisis in the Gwembe Valley. Using wood for cooking does not cause deforestation, drought and erosion. They are caused by bad policies, greed and poverty – the greed of the rich, who over-exploit forest resources, and the poverty of the masses, who are forced onto forest lands to survive and burn wood for cooking because they have no choice.

The ultimate solution lies in rural social and economic development. Any new technology or innovation which does not address the needs of poorer groups/smallholders, for whom the choices are most restricted, must fail. And any technology or initiative that does not provide some stimulus, however small, to the smallholder fails in its obligation to be concerned with wider social and economic realities.

We therefore need to develop means of quantifying the potential, effectiveness and success of alternative technologies for both promoters and end users, the smallholders and different social groups within communities.

CONCLUSION

The Gwembe Valley has good conditions for alternative energy technologies such as solar power, wind power and biomass fuel, and these would most benefit the smallholders if developed. The potential of alternative energy has to be harnessed if ecological agriculture and sustainable development are to become a reality.

Zambia still has a long way to go in its use of alternative energy for smallholders, although there has been much greater awareness of its potential in the last few years, especially in the Gwembe Valley of the southern province. Solar power is no longer just an option, but a necessity, without which rural communities will have to go without light and heating for a long time to come.

In the promotion of alternative energy, sustainable development and ecological agriculture, it has become clear that top-down interventions that suit only suppliers and promoters cannot work. Planning for improvements in infrastructure, water supply and electrification must be done in concert with the residents of the Gwembe Valley, and closely in tune with their needs and perceived problems.

ENDNOTES

1. This definition was adapted by the author from a definition for social eco-technological system in the article "Stoves, the social economics of stove production and distribution" which appeared in *AT (Alternative Technology) Source*, June 1989, 17, 2 (pg. 12). The article was taken from an Intermediate Technology Group report "Stoves for People", on an international conference in Guatemala organized by the Foundation for Woodstove Dissemination.

REFERENCES

Agrindco Int. Ltd. and Agrar-und hydrotechnik GMB. 1985: *Gwembe small scale irrigation project. Design Report, Vol. 1, 2 & 3*. Government of Zambia/The Netherlands Government publication.

Chipeleme, A.C. 1991: Land, water and energy resources potential for irrigation development in Zambia. In *Proceedings of International Seminar on Irrigation in Zambia, Sep. 91, Livingstone, Zambia, (Vol. 2)*. Netherlands Water and Land Use Services publication.

Haskoning, B.V. 1992: *Kariba Northern Catchment Area Project. Design Report, Vol. 1, 2 & 3*. GRZ/Kingdom of the Netherlands publication.

Muralidar, J.S. 1991: *Biomass fuel for cooking*. Technical paper for Seminar on Perspectives in Biomass Development and Utilisation for Industry, Madras. Gangothri Fuel (P) Ltd. publication.

Rushmere, M. 1995: *In search of the sun*. Report on the International Solar Energy Society Congress, Harare, Zimbabwe.

Chapter 12

Technology Choice, Environmental and Socio-Economic Issues in Small-Scale Mining in Uganda: A Survey of Selected Mining Sites

by Wilfred Monte Kaliisa, Joseph Kakooza, George Kakande, Eugene Muramira and Hillary Bakamwesiga

Introduction

Aggregate mining is now one of the most vibrant small-scale mining activities in Uganda. This is largely due to the expanding construction sub-sector in the liberalizing and fast-growing Ugandan economy. In order to meet the increasing market demand, most aggregate miners have begun using explosives in the mining process. Although this is more efficient from a technical and economic point of view, its environmental soundness is questionable. This chapter reviews the impact of aggregate small-scale mining on the natural and social environment in Uganda.

Context

Uganda is a land-locked country in the heart of Africa, covering an area of about 90,000 square miles (236,000 sq km). It lies astride the equator, bounded on the east by Kenya, on the north by Sudan, on the west by the Democratic Republic of Congo and on the south by Tanzania and Rwanda.

The population of Uganda is estimated at 21 million, with an annual growth rate of 2.5%. About 49% are male and 51% are female. The level of urbanization is still low at around 13% (World Bank, 1999), but with an annual urban growth rate of 11%. Administratively, Uganda is now divided into 45 districts.

The country's economy is predominantly based on agriculture, which contributes over 80% to the Gross Domestic Product (GDP) and about 90% to livelihood, especially in rural areas. The industrial sector, which stagnated in the

1970s and early 1980s, has begun to grow more rapidly with a 14% share of GDP since 1986.

The mining sector is an important source of tax revenues and foreign exchange, which are essential for Africa's recovery. This is very true in Uganda, where the momentum of growth is increasing under a liberalizing economy and vigorous investment promotion.

Uganda has a rich mineral potential, with many types of useful minerals, the quantity and quality of which are not yet fully established. In the past, mineral exports accounted for one third of total foreign earnings. Today, following the political turmoil and erratic economic management of the 1970s and early 1980s, mining and mineral exploration plays a small part in the national economy.

By international standards, mining in Uganda is on a small scale. Kilembe Mines, the biggest mine in Uganda, only produced 17,000 tonnes of blister copper at its peak. In the Ugandan context, however, Kilembe Mines constitutes large-scale mining. This also applies to Hima and Tororo Limestone Mining for the production of cement.

In addition to these commercial operations, there are numerous scattered and largely unregistered small-scale enterprises which extract industrial and construction minerals such as clay, sand and stone aggregates. Clay mining is widespread and prolific, while stone quarrying depends on demand. Economic activities in small-scale mining were low in Uganda in the first two decades following independence. However, the mid-1980s and the 1990s have seen considerable activity in this sub-sector. This can be attributed to the relatively stable political climate, and the population expansion which has crystallized the need to raise subsistence levels.

The concept of small-scale mining (SSM) seems to be a new term in Uganda's mining vocabulary. This is largely attributed to the fact that the Mining Act, the only Ugandan law regulating minerals other than petroleum, did not make reference to it (Ampeirwe, 1995). The current Uganda Draft Mining Act, has defined the concept as follows:

Small-scale mining means exploration and mining operations by methods not involving substantial expenditure and the use of specialised technology.

Another perspective (see Bwobi, 1993) describes small-scale mining in Uganda as ranging from use of a pick, shovel, mortar and pestle, a pan and muscle power, to one incorporating a small jaw crusher, motorized jig, shaking table, magnetic separators and pulverizers. Bwobi says that labour varies from one-man operations up to more than 20 workers. The mining method is, by and large, open cast but sometimes includes a few adits and stapes on the reefs.

The present study focused on small-scale mining activities involving clay for brick-making and quarrying for stone aggregates and granite.

SIGNIFICANCE OF THE STUDY

The importance of sustainable development was highlighted at the 1992 Earth Summit in Rio De Janeiro and the major environmental issues facing countries around the world were summarized in Agenda 21, the summit's action plan. The urgent need for action by governments and international organizations was stressed, calling on more initiatives for cleaner production methods, technology transfer, local capacity building and training. The role of business and industry in addressing environmental problems was also highlighted.

The point of departure in this research was the perceived role of low-impact mining in promoting environmental sustainability in the mining industry.

All mining methods involve some disturbance of the surface and underlying strata, including aquifers (World Bank, 1991). But much of the damaging impact on the immediate environment can be minimized through the choice of appropriate mining technologies and procedures for low-impact mining. This would lead to an environmentally sound mining industry, which has been defined as one which exploits mineral resources with maximum economic efficiency without harming human health, damaging local communities or biological diversity, while maintaining ecological stability (World Bank, 1991).

Uganda's mining activities are mainly small-scale surface mining (ODA, 1994). Surface mines include quarries, open pits, strip and contour lines and mountain-top removal; they cover a few hectares to several square kilometres. These operations totally disrupt the landscape in the project area with large open pits, quarries and extensive overburden piles. Sometimes such operations interfere with fragile ecosystems and cultural property.

A wide range of environmental concerns arise out of these operations. These may include, but are not limited to, airborne particulates from road traffic, blasting, excavation and transport, emissions, noise, vibrations from earth-moving equipment and blasting, discharges of contaminated mine water, disruption of ground water aquifers and removal of soil and vegetation (World Bank, 1991).

Thus, there is a need to safeguard the environment by providing important information for management to act on. As a matter of fact, a general agreement now exists on the need to be pro-active and incorporate environmental concerns into investment planning and decision making, rather than simply reacting to environmental problems after they occur.

ENVIRONMENTAL MANAGEMENT

The Ministry of Natural Resources in Uganda is responsible for coordinating environmental affairs to ensure the safety and proper use of natural resources. It is charged with the responsibility of monitoring and evaluating the country's environmental status.

Uganda's environmental legislation includes over 60 statutes governing various aspects of natural resource management and environmental protection, and various local authorities have enacted a further 60 statutory instruments (i.e. by-laws). The legislation is mainly sectoral in nature, relating to forest resources, fisheries and other specified areas. A more recent law, the Uganda Wetland Statute (UWS) is focused on management of wetlands in both protected and unprotected areas. The Water Bill is due for enactment by parliament. The basis of all these laws is enshrined in the national constitution.

The Constitution of the Republic of Uganda (1995) specifically provides for environmental management. Under the Constitution, the entire property and control of all minerals and mineral ores, in or upon any land or waters in the country, belong to the Government of Uganda. Significantly for small-scale mining, however, clay, murram, sand or any stone commonly used for building purposes are not considered minerals.

Clearer guidance is provided in the National Environment Law (1995), which makes environmental planning mandatory for all development interventions that will potentially affect the environment. In the third schedule of the bill, mining – including quarrying and open-cast extraction of aggregates, sand, gravel, clay and others materials – was stipulated as one of the projects to be considered for Environmental Impact Assessment.

National Environment Management Authority

The National Environment Management Authority (NEMA) is an umbrella organization responsible for all issues of environment and development in Uganda.

It is a semi-autonomous body charged with coordinating and supervising all aspects of natural resource management. These include:

▶ improving environmental legislation and policies;
▶ improving environmental education and public awareness;
▶ provision of environmental information;
▶ research in the field of environment;
▶ enhancing the role of environmental non-government organizations;
▶ a range of specific actions such as environmental impact assessment, establishment of environmental standards, and creation of disaster-preparedness plans.

The development of strong links between resource users and NEMA is considered crucial for effective implementation of National Environment Action Plan (NEAP).

Mining legislation

In Uganda, mining has been largely governed by two laws, namely the Mining Act, 1964, and the Petroleum (Exploitation and Production) Act, 1985, and subsidiary legislation derived therefrom (Ampeirwe, 1995). The Mining Act was first enacted in 1949 by the colonial government. This Act defined "minerals" to exclude mineral oils, clay murram, sand or any stone (except limestone) commonly used for building or similar purposes. This meant that small-scale mining activities involving industrial and construction minerals were outside the scope of inspection by the Inspectorate of Mines.

Initiatives at the quarry mining sites

All aggregate quarry operators are members of the Uganda Quarry Operators Association, which brings together all operators involved in open cast quarrying. One of the association's purposes is to assist members in all their efforts to improve on the environmental hazards created by quarrying operations. Thus, its members claim that the association undertakes self-monitoring for environmental concerns.

The operators follow a principle of co-existence. Blasting sessions at Muyenga quarries and Mbalala are adjusted according to the situation. For example, if there are important visitors within the local area, blasting is rescheduled.

Other efforts are made to minimize the effects of mining. Prior to blasting, an alarm is sounded and a red flag is hoisted. Water that tends to settle in the open pits is regularly piped out. Noise, dust and particulates are technologically controlled, according to the quarry managements. In Muyenga a wire mesh which acts as a stone barrier has been erected. Workers within the quarry are provided with protective clothing. However, in personal interviews with some workers at Mbalala, it was reported that protective gear is normally provided in anticipation of visits by important government officials.

Initiatives at the clay mining and brick-making sites

Common clay extraction and brick-making in Mukono is largely carried out by squatters. Squatters acquire the site from landlords through their agents, after paying land rent. It is not as organized as quarrying. There is no elaborate environmental management procedure or responsibility for environmental planning. However, in Kajjansi, clay digging and brick-making is also done by more established companies, using slightly more sophisticated technology. Even so, the large pits left by companies are slowly undergoing natural recolonization, with no specific or deliberate policy for reclaiming or rehabilitating the area.

DESCRIPTION OF ENVIRONMENTAL IMPACTS

Small-scale mining has several environmental impacts:

- Direct impacts change the physical structure of the area being mined.
- Pollution impacts affect human neighbours and the environment.
- The occupational health and safety of workers are affected.
- Mining affects social and cultural aspects of the community.

Landscape

All the small-scale mining activities studied have a physical impact on the landscape. Each month in Mukono and Kajjansi, an enormous volume of clay is extracted to supply the brick-making industry for the fast-growing housing sector in the neighbouring city of Kampala. This massive removal of clay, and similarly quarrying of granite rock in Muyenga and Mbalala, have left large open pits.

Destruction of natural habitats

In both Kajjansi and Mukono, clay is dug in wetlands, causing significant destruction of the natural wetland habitat. In Mukono alone, it is estimated that 5.75 km^2 of wetland (i.e 23 x 0.25) is now used for brick-making, and approximately 0.085 km^2 is cleared each year (MONR, 1996).

Quarry operations only destroy sparse vegetation over relatively hilly areas that do not appear to contain any biological particularities. According to known information, the species growing in and around Muyenga and Mbalala quarries are not rare in the region. Identical environments are found in the vicinity, so there is no risk of local species disappearing.

Quarry operations may affect fauna directly and indirectly. Direct effects include the destruction of microfauna (mainly invertebrates) living in the ground, as well as the nests and burrows of larger species, particularly young animals incapable of fleeing or escaping fast enough. Indirect effects include changes in the behaviour pattern of fauna living on or near the sites, modification of the trails animals follow in their search for food, and the cutting off of feeding areas, resulting in population fluctuations, especially in birds. This is apparently not the case at the Muyenga quarry, where whole flocks of cranes are seen daily.

Such effects must be considered in relative terms, in view of the small size of the operation on a regional scale and the fact that both the quarry and the industrial platform are in areas that can no longer be considered as natural environments in the light of earlier industrial activity.

Land instability

There is no significant problem of land instability at the two clay digging sites studied. However, in the Mbalala and Muyenga quarry pits, the instability of hanging rocks poses a possible danger, especially during blasting sessions.

Abandoned equipment

No equipment is abandoned in clay digging. In Muyenga, the oldest quarry in Uganda, some abandoned plants and buildings were found.

Destruction of habitats as a result of emissions

Dust emissions at the Mbalala study site were reported to contaminate plants and crops throughout the neighbourhood. Respondents indicated that the dust now makes it impossible to eat or even to grow leafy vegetables in the area.

POLLUTION IMPACTS

Dust emissions from sites near living areas and habitats

Dust emissions from the quarrying operations are significant during the crushing of the rock to produce aggregates. In Mbalala, it was found that dust emissions had affected people and vegetation in areas near the quarry plant. Home gardening has been adversely affected. In 1995, five hybrid Friesian cows were lost as a result of grazing in dust-infested pastures and breathing the dust. One owner of the lost livestock is a female head of household; at the time of interview, she expressed extreme bitterness at the way the authorities handled the offense.

All residents living around the crushing plant complained of respiratory problems, eye infections and chest infections. In addition, Mbalala Quarry is adjacent to the Kampala-Mombasa highway; it was reported that dust emissions create dangerous visibility problems for motorists and could cause fatal road accidents.

Oil and fuel spills

Both quarrying operations use motorized equipment for transport, drilling and crushing. At the Mbalala Quarry workshop, a lot of oil spills occur during the processing of what they refer to as "pre-mix", a material used for up-grading roads.

Air emissions from mineral processing operations

In Muyenga, the old trucks used for haulage produce a lot of gaseous emissions.

OCCUPATIONAL HEALTH IMPACTS

Dust inhalation

Quarry workers were heavily exposed to dust inhalation. All those interviewed complained of poor health, especially respiratory problems and chest pain. In Muyenga, workers are provided with some modest protective gear. But in Mbalala, workers reported that such gear is only provided when a government representative is expected to visit. It was reported to the study team that at least four former employees of Mbalala Stirling Company died in 1996 as a result of complications related to dust inhalation.

Noise

There were no significant noise problems reported or observed in clay digging and brick-making, but at both quarrying sites, respondents reported a significant problem of noise caused by blasting explosives, drilling with motorized compressors, trucks and the crushing process. Blasting noise is of short duration and occasional, as blasting is scheduled two or three times a week. The companies use some ameliorative measures, such as sounding an alarm and hoisting a red flag before blasting, to give advance people advance warning. In contrast, noise from trucks and crushing machines may be more prolonged and unbearable. It is estimated that in Kampala, noise from engineering works and related processes such as aggregate crushing is in the range of 90-115dBA. Noise is a serious hazard for those who work directly in the mines, very few or none of whom wear ear protection gear while operating jackhammers and other equipment.

Vibration

Vibration is a significant problem during blasting. In Mbalala, it was found that vibration damaged living quarters in adjacent areas. Some houses cracked during blasts, causing serious safety risks. An earthquake or subsequent blasting can bring down the whole structure. It was estimated that at least 20% of the 200 houses in Kasenge Village are also affected.

Physical risk at the site

Physical risks at the clay digging sites are negligible, but there are serious physical risks at quarrying sites. Common injuries include cuts and burns. In Mbalala, one key informant reported that he fell off the crusher and sustained serious injuries in 1997. He was compensated by the National Insurance Corporation.

Unsanitary conditions

In all sites studied, a reasonable level of faecal disposal facilities was available. However, in Muyenga, there is stagnant water that may undermine the sanitary and health conditions at the site. The team observed workers using such water to clean themselves after work. It was reported that a pipe moves this water out to nearby Lake Victoria, raising concerns about the effect of this water on aquatic life. This issue requires further research.

SOCIAL AND CULTURAL IMPACTS

Demographic impact

The study team found no displacement or re-location problems at any of the four study sites, except for one female respondent in Mbalala, who had lost 3 cows and expressed intentions to relocate her family.

The team did not observe any overall changes in population composition; there has been limited population and labour movement into the four mining areas studied. Brick-making is largely carried out by local residents. Quarrying in Mbalala employs over 90% of the local residents. The few who are not local residents work in clerical and managerial positions.

Socio-economic impact

The availability of regular and higher incomes has had an important socio-economic impact on the area, particularly at the Mukono and Mbalala sites. The average labourer in Mbalala Quarry earns US $600-900 per annum. To put this in perspective, a primary school teacher, with a general Certificate of Education and two years of training, earns US $720 per annum. Per capita GDP in Uganda is estimated at US $220.

Brick-makers in Mukono and quarry workers in Mbalala are largely school drop-outs who had no employment or regular income before working there. While the quarry has brought some negative consequences to the area, the respondents in Mbalala perceived it as having absorbed the youth who were redundant and engaged in various vices and crimes.

Community factors

As there has been no significant population movement, social networks and social cohesion have been only minimally affected. There was no change observed in the division of household labour between genders. Clay and quarry work has remained an almost exclusively male domain. Women have kept their traditional household responsibilities and subsistence activities. In Kajjansi, some women are involved in brick-making, but this is done within the home compound. It does not represent a significant departure from the private/public dichotomy of female/male roles of the patriarchal ideology still predominant in Uganda.

Institutional impacts

There were no reports of increased pressure on local health and education facilities. It was noted that small-scale mining investments have not invested in social facilities such as health units.

Demands on local administrative services may have increased in response to the complaints stemming from the negative results of mining, particularly dust, vibration and noise. Mbalala management was dragged into dispute resolution arising out of the dust problems in 1995.

Crime statistics

There were no crime statistics available in the study areas, but many informants in Mbalala reported that crimes such as petty theft had significantly diminished as the former perpetrators are now earning a steady income at the quarry.

Cultural resources

No historic buildings or archaeological sites were reported at any of the study sites. However, the Kasenge quarry in Mbalala was said to have destroyed a Ryabareema religious shrine.

Land-use conflicts

One case of land-use conflict was reported, involving the Kame Brick factory on Kyetume Road and the neighbouring landlords. This is primarily a land boundary dispute.

RESULTS

Impact assessment

The objective of this research project was to establish the impact of selected small-scale mining activities on the environment. Environmental impacts were understood to mean any negative effect on people, animals, plants and their environment as a result of small-scale mining activities. Environmental impacts were placed in three categories: direct environmental impacts (including ecological, physical and biological impacts), pollution related impacts and impacts related to occupational health. This section presents an assessment of the study findings regarding the identified impacts in the above categories, as well as socio-cultural and economic impacts.

Aggregate extraction

Both of the aggregate mining sites studied use explosives, which are necessary to break hard rock. Picks and concrete breakers are used to break big boulders after blasting. There are several types of explosives on the market today, but the types used at the two sites studied were not established. According to management, information on their explosives is restricted or classified.

The impact of explosives may or may not be harmful to the environment. There is a constant danger of accidental or unplanned detonation, posing serious threat to life, property and the environment. The blasting process creates vibration, noise and flying stones, causing serious problems in the surrounding living areas. Vibration and flying stones were found to have caused significant damage to dwellings in the neighbouring areas. However, the noise was of a short duration.

Use of fire to break rock was still practised, particularly by illegal miners in pits abandoned by the mining companies. This is a traditional indigenous technology used in stone quarrying. Fire is used to heat rock, which is then doused with water. The sudden reduction of the temperature causes the rock to break. This method does not create the problems of vibration, noise and flying stones, but it consumes a lot of firewood and may lead to deforestation if practised on a large scale.

The extracted rock is largely hauled out by lorries and tractors. Most of the lorries are old and tend to emit oils, fuels and gases. However, this was not found to be an important environmental factor.

The most significant environmental effects result from the processing of the rock into aggregates (sizing), using an electrically powered crusher. The process produces large quantities of dust and noise which affect the workers. The wind carries the dust to neighbouring living areas and habitats, with serious consequences to the health of humans, livestock, flora and fauna.

Clay digging and brick-making

Brick-making has long been a socio-economic activity in Uganda, and is on the increase today. Approximately 0.085 km^2 of swamp are cleared for brick-making each year (MONR, 1996). According to the SADC (1994) classification of SSM, clay digging and brick-making in Uganda falls into Group A micro-scale mining – manual work, using simple tools.

The Ministry of Natural Resources estimated that clay extracted from a plot measuring 5x5 metres, dug to a depth of 4 metres, can yield 20,000 bricks

(MONR, 1996). Three types of clay are recognized:

- **Pure clay** is fine and grey in colour. It is fragile and is used in ceramic production. Its firing requires a lot of firewood.
- **Brown clay** is compact and elastic, and is mainly used in brick, tile and stove making. Its firing requires a medium amount of firewood.
- **Dark clay** is naturally mixed with sand at the ration of 1:4. It requires the least amount of firewood.

On average, one lorry load of firewood is required to fire 8,000-10,000 bricks. It takes about 3 months to pile a kiln of about 30,000 bricks. While the demand for fuelwood for brick-making is on the rise, it was not found to be causing significant deforestation.

CONCLUSION

Environmental impacts

Overall assessment indicates that the environmental impacts associated with the small-scale mining activities studied are largely physical in nature, rather than chemical, and affect the local area. The most important impact found is on the physical properties of air quality (i.e., dust particulates). Some effects of dust inhalation on health may not be realized in the short term. Most of the effects are primary or first-order, affecting physical changes in the environment. Higher order effects were observed in livestock, plants and human beings.

Choice of methods and technology

In brick-making, largely rudimentary methods and technologies are used, including picks, shovels, pangas, hoes and wooden boxes, which can be said to be low-impact. But clay extraction has an important impact on fragile wetland ecosystems. In the case of aggregate mining, explosives technology may be the most efficient, given the nature of the rock, but this study concludes that it is not low-impact, because of its significant effects on the people and the environment.

Measures of environmental management

The environmental laws and institutions which have been put in place to regulate environmental management are considered adequate. However, if regulation is to be effective, it must be supported by vigilance, capacity for inspection and demand for compliance, which are lacking. Small-scale miners have initiated self-inspection mechanisms – a good example of community participation in environmental management – through the Uganda Quarry Operators Association. It was therefore not found necessary to develop a separate environmental management model for mainstreaming environmental concerns in the small-scale mining sector.

Compliance with environmental regulations

There is no indication of critical awareness of environmental concerns in clay-digging and brick-making; compliance with environmental regulations is not considered important. This can be attributed to the fact that the licencing is managed by the urban or district authorities, whose overriding interest is revenue. The Mining Act does not include clay in its definition of minerals, so clay mining falls outside the Inspectorate of Mines. Thus, even though there is an Environmental Liaison Unit in the Ministry of Mines, it is not within their jurisdiction to inspect clay mining.

In the case of aggregate mining, compliance with environmental regulations is on the rise. This may be a result of increased levels of inspection by the National Environmental Management Authority (NEMA) and Inspectorate of Mines. However, in Mbalala, the workers complained that they are only issued protective gear when a government bureaucrat is expected.

Mining companies and environmental objectives

Brick-making is largely done by individuals or small groups who do not own the land on which they extract clay. These individuals (squatters) pay rent to overseers in order to acquire land-use rights from landlords. The rents vary from place to place. In some places, squatters pay the landlord 30% or more of the revenue earned from the sale of the bricks. This study concludes that, in the context of such socio-economic dynamics which seem to emphasize accumulation, environmental concerns remain a remote priority.

On the other hand, aggregate mining is well organized and institutionalized at the community level, within the framework of the Uganda Quarry Operators Association.

RECOMMENDATIONS

Production methods

▶ Brick making is a longstanding socio-economic activity in Uganda. It is largely done with rudimentary tools which require great strength and can harm the health of workers. There is an urgent need to identify technologies that will reduce human drudgery in clay digging. This will also pave the way for women to be employed in brick-making.

▶ Granite quarrying must comply with environmental regulations, given the dangerous nature of explosives.

Socio-cultural

▶ In order to create community-based channels for environmental education, brickmakers need to be organized in production and marketing associations. The Ministry of Gender and Community Development in Uganda could be encouraged to include small-scale mining among its social mobilization activities. Non-governmental organizations can also play an effective role in this effort.

▶ Given the level of unemployment in Uganda, most industrial workers operate as if they have no human rights. In this context workers, especially in stone quarries, will not complain even when their health is at stake. Workers in small-scale mines should, by law, be unionized, so they can raise their grievances.

Environmental management

▶ **Environmental Liaison Unit in the Ministry of Natural Resources.** The National Environmental Management Authority should step up the monitoring requirements of the MONR Environmental Liaison Unit to include more elaborate reporting on small-scale mining.

▶ **Inspectorate of Mines.** Construction minerals such as clay and stones should be included in the jurisdiction of the Inspectorate of Mines, even if this entails amending the statutes.

▶ **Environmental Education.** A quality programme of environmental education should be established to inform small-scale miners of the need to preserve the environment.

REFERENCES

Ampeirwe, I. 1995: *Assessment of the Mining Law in Uganda from the Perspective of Environmental Protection. The case of small-scale mining.* LL.B Dissertation. Kampala: Makerere University.

Bwobi, Watuwa. 1993: An Overview of Environment Aspects of Mining in Uganda. Paper presented at the *United Nations International Workshop on Environmental Management at Mining Sites in Developing Countries, Kitwe, Zambia.* Unpublished.

King, B.C. and Deswardt, A.M.J. 1970: *Problems of Structure in the Pre-Cambrian System of Central and Western Uganda* Memoir No. XI. Kampala: Geological Survey of Uganda.

Lands and Surveys Department. Uganda. 1956: *Geological Survey of Uganda Sheet*, North A36/U-1V Kampala, 1:100,000. Kampala.

Lands and Surveys Department, Uganda. 1961: *Kampala Vegetation Map*, NA-36-14, 1:250,000, edition 1-USD. Kampala.

Malango, V. 1997: Use of Explosives and their Handling: Environmental and Safety Aspects. Presentation at the ECEP *Workshop and Roundtable on Small-Scale Mining and the Environment, 16-30 November, Windhoek, Namibia.*

Ministry of Natural Resources (MONR). 1996: *Initial Environmental Assessment of Brick-Making.* Kampala: MONR.

Mundia, P.L. 1997: Small-Scale Mining: Challenges faced by a woman in Zambia. Presentation at the *ECEP Workshop and Roundtable on Small-Scale Mining and the Environment, 16-30 November, 1997, Windhoek, Namibia.*

National Environment Management Authority (NEMA), Mpigi District. 1997: *State of Environment Report.* Unpublished. Kampala.

Overseas Development Administration (ODA). 1994: *An Overview of the Mining Industry in Uganda.* Report of a Project Identification Mission (unpublished). Kampala.

Southern African Development Community (SADC). 1994: *Small-Scale Mining Technologies for SADC Member States.* Lusaka.

Uganda. 1991: *Population and Housing Census, 1991: District Summary Series-Mpigi, Kampala and Mukono.* Kampala: Government Printers.

Uganda. 1995: *Constitution.*

Uganda. 1995: *National Environment Statute.*

World Bank. 1991: *Environmental Assessment Source Book, Volume III: Guidelines for*

Environmental Assessment of Energy and Industry Projects. Washington: World Bank.

World Bank. 1995: *Uganda: The Challenge of Growth and Development.* Washington: World Bank.

World Bank. 1999: *Uganda at a Glance (1997).* On-line. Internet. 13 March, 1999. <http://www.worldbank.org/data/countrydata/aag/uga-aag.pdf>

Chapter 13

South Africa's Informal Mining Industry

by Andrea Hammel, Christopher White, Susan Pfeiffer, Nikolaas J. van der Merwe, Pauline Mitchell and Duncan Miller

Background

The mining industry has changed dramatically since its beginnings: the number of minerals mined has risen, demand has grown exponentially, the scale of activity (the number of mines and their output) has expanded significantly, and more sophisticated methods are used to locate, mine, and process the deposits. Although these new methods have largely replaced physical human labour, there are still miners in Southern Africa who use methods analogous to those used in antiquity. Southern Africa has mined for at least 1500 years, with the exploitation of iron and copper in the first millennium AD and gold and tin in the second.

This report documents four case studies covering the range of sophistication of modern small-scale mining in South Africa, explores the connections between the past and the present in informal mining, and examines whether or not there may still be a niche for the informal miner in South Africa's future. The four case studies are presented in order of increasing organizational complexity, based on levels of skill, technology, and decision-making entailed in an operation, as well as the social organization (hierarchical structure/bureaucracy entailed) and the financial base.

The first involves diamond mining as a subsistence activity using the simplest of equipment, and the last involves a fairly capital-intensive, mechanized small-scale operation. These examples provide insight into some of the methods used by modern informal miners, illuminate some of the constraints they face, and form the basis of a discussion on their future in South Africa.

The case studies illustrate that informal miners seem to be functioning at or below their economic subsistence level. Their progress is limited by problems such as ignorance of the mineral laws and the claims process; a lack of training, effective tools, and available land; and inefficient, unsafe, and often environmentally damaging techniques. This leads to the question: "Is there a place for the small-scale informal miner in today's South Africa?". The last section of the chapter explores this issue and the related possibility of reintroducing ancient techniques into communities that are culturally tied to pre-colonial mining.

INTRODUCTION

Increasingly ... artisanal mining has become a controversial activity regarded by some as dirty, destructive, and illegal and by others as productive, profitable, and often the means of survival in times of need (World Bank, 1996, p. 3).

Small-scale mining is a term with no consistent definition: it can incorporate everything from legal, mechanized, and fairly capital-intensive operations to artisanal or informal operators. In spite of engendering a host of unique problems, artisanal (here, used synonymously with informal) mining has too often been considered only within the broader scope of the small mines sector or not considered at all. At a 1995 World Bank conference devoted to the topic, artisanal mining was defined as "the most primitive type of informal, small-scale mining, characterized by individuals or groups of individuals exploiting deposits—usually illegally—with the simplest of equipment"(World Bank, 1996, p. 1). This paper focuses on the current situation for artisanal miners in South Africa.

Two case studies are included in this report as examples of modern, informal operations:

▶ Case study #1 involves the Gong Gong community near Kimberley, which is based on grass-roots level diamond mining.

▶ Case study #2 involves a group of illegally operating gold miners in the Barberton area.

For the purposes of comparison, two case studies have been included in this paper as examples of small-scale, mechanized operations:

▶ Case study #3 involves the Venmag magnesite mine near Messina.

▶ Case study #4 involves the African United Small Miners Association, a diamond-mining operation on Canteen Koppie near Kimberley.

Modern informal operators (one or two-person operations) are generally only interested in mining gold and diamonds, as these have a high market value which justifies the labour and effort. Iron, although important historically, is no longer extracted by these miners. It is far cheaper to buy mass-produced iron products than to create them.

Past and Present in Makushu, Northern Province

Van Warmelo (1940) provides a fairly detailed account of the pre-colonial copper miners of Messina in the northern Transvaal of South Africa. The mining and metalworking skills of these people were well developed and Van Warmelo describes some of their mining and smelting methods. Among the tools they used were hammers, crowbars/gads, candles made from leaves, ladders made of wood and leather, long cords of leather tied to a large basket and used to lower people into the shafts, and carriers made from animal skins (Van Warmelo, 1940, p. 81).

Van Warmelo (1940: 84) also provides a genealogy of the Musina copper miners, and among these is one of Van Warmelo's informants: a man he refers to as "Makushu" and claims is "probably the only surviving person who actually mined copper himself". In 1940, Makushu was living a few miles outside Messina and was "quite active mentally". It appears that the Makushu lineage has continued at this locale since then.

Through liaison with a former professor at the University of Venda, two researchers contacted this group. They visited the Venda community of Makushu near Messina, the present Makushu family almost certainly related to Van Warmelo's informant. From a translated interview with the chief's wife, the chief's son, and the headman, it became clear that the impoverished community has lost all knowledge of mining and metal-working techniques.

The people of pre-colonial South Africa had a tradition of mining which was truncated by the imposition of colonialism (Miller, 1995). Many communities culturally tied to pre-colonial mining have, like Makushu, lost their knowledge of mining and metalworking. However, many informal miners working in South Africa today (who may or may not be the descendents of ancient miners) are using methods analogous in their simplicity to those used more than a thousand years ago (Hammel *et. al.* in prep.).

Case Study 1: Gong Gong, Northern Cape

Near Kimberley, in Northern Cape province, the research team visited the community of Gong Gong (which is comprised of black and coloured families). In this community, located on the Highveld in the northeast corner of the Karoo, grass-roots level diamond mining is a subsistence activity. Most of these one or two-man operations are legal, although highly inefficient. Researchers interviewed an elderly miner (who gave his name only as "Matteus") while he worked an old dump on his employer's claim, as well as an older couple (Mr. and Mrs. Daniels) who own numerous claims in the area.

The landscape of Gong Gong, and neighbouring Longlands, is dotted with countless piles of excavated rock attesting to the numerous small diamond workings. Virtually every accessible piece of earth has been scoured: miners will even dig under their houses, and old dumps are constantly re-worked. Many of the miners in Gong Gong are third or fourth generation diggers. Their techniques are similar to those used by the first prospectors in the area more than a century ago.

When the researchers met Matteus, he was working alone and moving heavy rock and mining spoil without the aid of machinery. It was his fourth week spent re-working an old dump, and his partner had fallen sick. Matteus was using some simple sorting equipment and a petrol pump that provided water for the washings. His employer, Mr. Chabalala, owned both the equipment and the claim. Matteus claimed that the biggest problem for this small operation was a lack of money for better equipment.

Matteus revealed that, although his father was a digger born and buried in the area, he learned his methods from a European couple who hired him to work their claim. His children, like those of so many Gong Gong residents, have never mined and have no interest in doing so. In Matteus' words, it is a "hard life": his wife died last year and Matteus must support his two children—an 18-year-old daughter still in school and 25-year-old son presently unemployed—on a salary of only R40.00 per week, plus R20.00 per diamond found. The biggest diamond he has ever found was 20 carats, he revealed with pride, and the most recent was a carat diamond one month earlier.

In this same community, Mr. and Mrs. Daniels hold 24 claims. Mr. Daniels is 80 years old. Apart from the time he spent in North Africa and Italy during World War II, he has lived in the community all his life. His father, grandfather, and great-grandfather were diamond miners before him. Mr. Daniels is proud to be a digger: "It's a life that you make." It's not an easy life, however, as this couple – with thirteen children – see themselves as unable to work any of their claims because they lack the finances to acquire transport to and from the sites.

Through discussion, it became apparent that the Daniels do not fully understand the laws and politics surrounding the modern claims process. When trying to explain how he had acquired his own claims, Mr. Daniels brought out numerous pieces of paper that he said he received at the claims office, but he had no idea what they meant or how to explain them. Many of them were written in English which he could not read, and, if they were related to the process at all, were certainly not self-explanatory. Furthermore, Mr. Daniels was confident that the land on which his house was built was his own, but the research assistants ascertained (through a representative of the Land Affairs Department) that the Daniels' home was actually situated on state land. Mr. Daniels said he planned to build and move into a new home someday, and when he did, he would prospect under his present home to "see if there are any diamonds".

Mr. Daniels showed the researchers three diamonds, the largest of which he found while sorting through somebody else's claim, apparently with permission; he hoped that it would fetch R8000.00 from the buyers. This money, he stated, would not be enough to improve his equipment and would be used for subsistence. Although he has left digging at times and tried to work elsewhere, Mr. Daniels explained that he always came back because, in his words, "my thoughts were always on the diamonds".

The miners in this community are certainly not earning much more than they need to sustain their families, and some must find other forms of income to supplement their prospecting activity. Larger, white-owned and relatively capital-intensive operations have opened nearby. With their mechanized equipment, they can dig deeper and exploit previously unmined land. The small diggers, with their simple equipment, are limited by factors such as the water table. They generally only re-work dumps that, as Mr. Daniels asserted, "the whites have mined before". These small diggers need better equipment and fresh land: Mr. Daniels expressed his wish that the large companies would open up some of their holdings to the small diggers, that they might "share".

Case Study 2: Barberton, Mpumalanga

In the province of Mpumalanga, the research team visited the Lowveld town of Barberton, where informal and currently illegal gold mining takes place. The research team first learned of a group of illegal gold miners in the Barberton area through a contact at Mimco Ltd., a relatively large gold-mining operation. The researchers were told that this company was purchasing the land on which these miners were illegally operating, but that it was planning to "work with them" —

specifically, that it would provide skills training and the opportunity for them to work within the company. The sensitivity of this issue became apparent, however, as the contact at the company became increasingly nervous about speaking to the researchers for fear of things "being taken out of context".

The researchers also met with a representative of another fairly large gold-mining company in the area, Eastern Transvaal Consolidated (ETC). He explained that this group of 30 or 40 informal gold miners, who now worked near the Lily Mine, had been illegally mining on land owned by major mining companies in the region for many years. ETC provided some information regarding the "very primitive methods" that these miners use, asserting that their basic tools are shovels and picks. They create small vertical shafts (barely the width of a person) 20 to 30 meters deep and then "follow the seams". The miners mill the ore with hand-made equipment, wash it, and then create an amalgam using mercury. Their practices are both environmentally and personally hazardous. ETC disapproves of Mimco's decision to deal with and attempt to incorporate these miners, saying that it only encourages such illegal operations. ETC's representative explained that "mining shouldn't be that informal", asserting that it needs to be better regulated by the government.

More information on this group of miners was obtained during a visit to the Diamond and Gold Branch of the Barberton Police Department. The police showed the researchers a large store of confiscated items, including some of the improvised equipment used, made, or stolen by these miners. One officer described his feeling of danger when climbing into the shafts created by the illegal miners: he felt that "making a sound might cause the walls to crumble" and said he would "never go in one again". He further attested to the difficulties in apprehending these miners, a situation complicated by the provincial government's intervention on the miners' behalf. Whether these miners should be arrested, incorporated into companies, or given permits seems to be an issue of debate among the police, the government, and the companies involved.

White-owned corporations still control most of the mines in the Barberton region and the work of these miners is still considered illegal, but as a timely CNN report states: "unlike the past, negotiations are under way to make black ownership possible. In areas where corporate miners have stopped looking for gold, the black majority government elected in 1994 now supports miners in their fight to claim mineral rights" (Hanna, 1997).

Case Study 3: Venmag Mine, Northern Province

This small-scale operation, located on the Lowveld south of Messina, mines and processes magnesite, which is used in pulp and paper, fertilizers, animal feeds, and for chemical and pharmaceutical purposes. Although the operation has mechanized sorting and milling equipment, it is also labour-intensive. The work force comprises both women and men (predominantly women) from the surrounding Venda villages.

The research assistants photographed and toured the mine, and interviewed the mine's Area Manager, Mr. Manie Bodenstein, who is white. All other observed workers were blacks from the local Venda community. The mine employed 130 salaried workers, paid by the month, but also offered contract work to those who wanted it. Mr. Bodenstein stated that more than 300 workers operated on a contractual basis, paid according to the amount of magnesite extracted and delivered. Apart from one mechanical excavator, which mainly loosens material, the extraction is done by hand with picks and shovels. The standard of living in this community seemed significantly higher than in other communities visited in this region – for example, the Venda community of Makushu discussed earlier.

Case Study 4: African United Small Miners Association, Northern Cape

Just outside Kimberley, not far from Gong Gong, the research team visited the African United Small Miners Association at their diamond-mining site near Canteen Koppie, an alluvial deposit. The Chairman of the operation, Mr. Allen Ontong, who spoke English fluently, described the methods and machinery used at the site, and provided information regarding the financial and organizational structure of the cooperative. This operation involved approximately fifteen people – most of whom, including the Chairman, would be classed as black or coloured – and depended upon heavy equipment: at least one excavator, one front-end loader, and a variety of washing and sorting machines.

This cooperative is fairly capital-intensive for a small-scale operation, despite some visible inefficiencies. For example, although they use an excavator to drop material onto a coarse sieve during the initial phase of sorting, workers have to physically climb onto the sieve after each load and finish the sorting by hand, as most of the waste rock fails to slide off. This is common practice on such "grizzlies", as these static sieves are known. The operation's dumps did not look unlike their unsorted material, indicating that their sorting efforts were not entirely effective. Diamonds may well sit within the waste heaps and it is likely that the dumps will have to be re-worked several times. In spite of these problems, the operation is secure enough that, as Mr. Ontong explained, 10% of all profits are put "back into the community" and the company subsidizes small, unassociated groups of miners by allowing them to use the equipment (which is leased rather than owned by the cooperative) for a small fee.

In contrast to the informal miners discussed in case studies #1 and #2, this operation seems to have found a profitable and legal niche for itself in the South African mining industry. However, it still faces some major constraints. Mr. Ontong explained that the biggest problems for the cooperative are the lack of finances, technical training, and government support. Allen asserted that, in the future, his operation would like to try and get involved with companies like DeBeers. In Mr. Ontong's words, "It's a hard job but it's a nice job ... I can guarantee that finding a diamond is the nicest feeling you can ever have. Especially if you get a big one. But you have to look hard for it".

Canteen Koppie is significant to South Africa in two different, and potentially conflicting, ways. It has historical significance because it is one of the oldest diamond mining sites in the country and it is the site of far more ancient archaeological materials. The National Monuments Council is striving to preserve the site for its archaeological significance, as the deposits of fluvial gravel contain Early Stone Age and Middle Stone Age implements, as well as some vertebrate fossils (Southern Africa Environment Project, 1998). These are the same deposits being mined for their diamond content. There is ongoing controversy between the African United Small Miners Association and the South African National Monuments Council regarding whether or not further mining should be allowed on Canteen Koppie, which is already riddled with prospecting pits. At the time of the interview, the African United Small Miners Association was mining all around the koppie and was interested in expanding their operations onto the site.

SUMMARY OF CASE STUDIES

The diamond workings in Gong Gong are generally one- or two-man operations requiring very little social organization. Because most activities simply involve the re-working of old dumps, the equipment and techniques used are very basic. Further, as diamonds are immediately sold to buyers, there is no processing involved.

The illegal gold mining operations in Barberton are more complex. These miners work in groups (necessitating social cooperation), use more difficult techniques such as the sinking of shafts, and are involved in the physical and chemical processing of the gold.

In contrast to these informal operations, Venmag and the African United Small Miners Association are small-scale mechanized operations, the latter possessing a more fully mechanized excavation process than the former, which still relies predominantly on excavation by hand. These two operations are essentially equivalent in terms of organizational complexity: both entail mechanical equipment, complex decisions (on issues ranging from mine development and expansion to market assessment), and a more rigid hierarchical/bureaucratic structure.

In all four cases, some technical training is needed. Although both the small-scale mechanized mines and the informal mining operations face constraints, the case studies illustrate that informal operations are problematic and are limited in their ability to grow beyond being a subsistence activity. In contrast to the people involved in the mechanized mines profiled here, the informal operators have not yet found a niche that is both profitable and legal.

Factors limiting the success of these operations include:

▶ **Educational constraints** (e.g. no access to technical training or information regarding the mining laws and claims process);
▶ **Financial constraints** (e.g. a lack of funds and limited access to credit);
▶ **Mechanical constraints** (e.g. a lack of equipment and appropriate technology);
▶ **Physical constraints** (e.g. a lack of land, the inability to mine beyond the water table);
▶ **Bureaucratic constraints** (problems such as inefficiency and understaffing within the Department of Mineral and Energy Affairs, which can be equated with less assistance for and attention to informal miners);
▶ **Legal constraints** (no mineral rights);
▶ **A high degree of health, safety, and environmental risk** (e.g. the improper use of mercury and the unsupported shafts seen among the Barberton mines).

Obviously, these constraints are all interrelated and overlapping. They form a vicious circle that is difficult to break. The next section of this report will explore measures that might enable artisanal mining operations like these to become safe, environmentally sustainable, and economically viable.

POSSIBILITIES FOR THE FUTURE

Many of the communities which formerly had cultural ties to pre-colonial metal working have lost all knowledge of this indigenous technological enterprise. The loss of knowledge has been exacerbated by the fact that the achievements of ancient miners and smelters went unrecognized in modern historical accounts and in formal education. As there is now a growing societal knowledge of pre-colonial technological achievement (eg. Miller, 1995), the possibility of reintroducing – and perhaps even re-implementing – ancient mining and metalworking techniques in communities like Makushu now exists. In order to assess the feasibility of such actions, much research needs to be done. An important aspect of this research must involve furthering our understanding of the situation for current artisanal miners. These workers are the modern-day equivalents of their pre-colonial predecessors. In many cases, they use virtually identical tools and techniques.

In early February 1998, the Department of Minerals and Energy (DME) of the South African government launched the "Green Paper on Minerals and Mining Policy for South Africa". This relatively comprehensive review of minerals and mining policy in South Africa has attempted, as its introduction states, to take "account of the problems and opportunities confronting the mining industry against the backdrop of changes in the country's policy and institutional environment" (DME, 1998, p. 3).

The paper includes a chapter on "small-scale mining" and asserts that it is a relative term with no consistent definition. As was illustrated in this project's four case studies, small-scale mining in South Africa "ranges from very small operations that provide subsistence living (artisanal mining), to the 'junior' companies for which revenue is such that subsistence living is not the prime motivator" (DME, 1998, p. 18). Opportunities for small-scale mining projects in South Africa (which already take place on a sizable scale) are found mainly in gold, diamonds, coal, industrial minerals and in minerals derived from pegmatites. The green paper (DME, 1998, p. 18) acknowledges that these opportunities are often confronted by problems including:

- **Access to mineral rights**. The present South African mineral rights ownership system is seen by many as a major blockage in the development of small-scale mining.
- **Access to finance**. Financiers are seldom willing to participate in small-scale mining ventures which often provide limited security and financial returns.
- **Incoherent structure**. There is a lack of appropriate structures that assist small-scale mining development.
- **Location of operations far from major markets.**
- **Lack of management, marketing, and technical skills**. New small-scale mine operators face technical barriers to participate in mining, including a lack of skills for dealing with complex metallurgical processes, practical mining problems and business transactions.

The green paper provides a list of policy proposals – regarding mineral rights, access to finance and technology, regulation and administration, and environmental management – designed to minimize these constraints. It summarizes the government's intent to "encourage and facilitate the sustainable development of small-scale mining in order to ensure the optimal exploitation of small mineral deposits and to enable this sector to make a positive contribution to the national economy" (DME, 1998). South Africa's mining industry has long been controlled by large corporations, but as Minerals and Energy Deputy Minister Susan Shabangu has asserted, the government will now seek to prevent "hoarding and sterilization" of mineral rights, by applying a "use it or lose it" principle and by aiming, in the long term, to have all mineral rights vested in the state (Hossack, 1998).

While many of the acknowledged constraints, and the policy initiatives proposed to rectify them, are relevant to both small-scale (mechanized) and artisanal miners, the green paper gives no special attention to the unique situation of artisanal miners. Beyond the rather vague assertion that "the deleterious effects of artisanal or subsistence mining on the environment and on safety and health elsewhere in the world dictates the necessity for research in this area" (DME, 1998, p. 19), informal mining is only considered within the broader scope of the small mines sector.

Thus, although much recent attention has been given to the "small-scale" (mechanized) mining industry in South Africa, the plight of artisanal miners has not received nearly as much attention as it has elsewhere in the world. While it is true that informal mining is far less common than in places like Zimbabwe, Bolivia, and Brazil, these operations are nonetheless a reality in South Africa. They are in serious need of further attention and a meaningful development strategy. For this reason, it is important to examine the existing knowledge of artisanal mining from external sources.

The World Bank (1996) asserts that it has an interest in informal mining because part of its mandate is to alleviate poverty and informal mining is largely driven by poverty. In May 1995, the World Bank convened an international roundtable to discuss the problems and potential of the growing number of informal miners worldwide. During the opening remarks of this roundtable, which involved more than 80 delegates from 25 countries (including three from South Africa), it was noted that several million people worldwide depend on artisanal mining for their livelihood. Informal, small-scale miners were said to account for 20% of the gold, 40% of the diamonds, and nearly all the gemstones in Africa. Not long ago, they accounted for 70% of Brazilian gold production. Informal miners also produce copper, gold, silver, tin, and zinc (World Bank, 1996, p. 3).

Although artisanal mining provides a low barrier to entry in terms of skills, capital and infrastructure and it acts as an important source of income (World Bank, 1996), it is constrained by numerous factors and yields a host of problems. Mr. Richard Noetstaller of Leoben University, Austria, provided the roundtable's keynote address. He asserted that the "problem is that both the informal miners and the governments are caught in negative circles of cause and effect"(World Bank, 1996, p. 4). For artisanal miners, Mr. Noetstaller explained, the use of inadequate mining and processing techniques leads to low productivity and recovery, which results in low revenues and the inability to accumulate funds. The lack of funds to improve methods and equipment then traps these miners in crude and inefficient mining and processing (Figure 13.1).

Mr. Noetstaller asserted that mining authorities are caught in a similar cycle: they often lack adequate operational resources to enforce existing regulations – resulting in illegal operations, poor environmental, health, and safety standards and a loss of fiscal revenue. This, in turn, limits the government's ability to perform its regulatory function and perpetuates uncontrolled artisanal mining (Figure 13.2).

Figure 13.1 Negative circle affecting artisanal miners

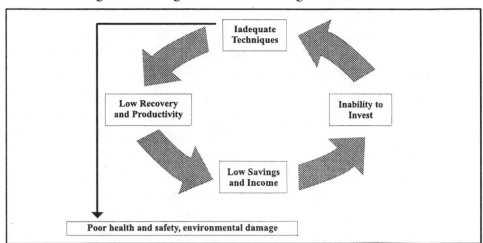

Source: World Bank, 1996

Figure 13.2 Negative circle affecting mining authorities

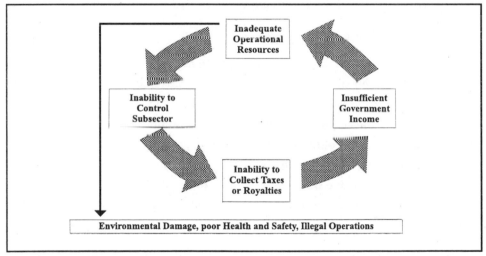

Source: World Bank, 1996

While South African artisanal miners definitely fit within the "negative circle" model, the government is in a unique position, as South Africa is the most developed and wealthy nation in Africa. The model's declaration of "insufficient government income" may not be applied as easily to South Africa as it is to the governments of many developing countries, but many of the other components of this circle still hold true.

A visit to the Department of Mineral and Energy Affairs (Pietersburg office) to gain information about the claims process and laws under the 1991 Minerals Act enabled researchers to experience first-hand the "inadequacy of operational resources". When the researchers telephoned the Department of Minerals and Energy to inquire about the claims process, their inquiry was transferred more than nine times. This made them decide to simply visit the claims office in person. Once there, they spoke to a representative in the rehabilitation department who repeatedly mentioned understaffing problems that make it impossible to help claim applicants through the process and ensure their complete understanding. She further explained that it is impossible to visit every site as often as is suggested in Department guidelines. The information the researchers eventually acquired about the claims process was in contrast to the general understanding expressed by members of the Gong Gong community, who were not even certain what fees they had been required to pay and what rehabilitation of the site entailed. The low level of attention the Department currently provides to each applicant contributes directly to the structural limitations experienced by the informal miners.

CONCLUSIONS AND RECOMMENDATIONS

A central conclusion of the World Bank international roundtable on artisanal mining was that "no real solutions are possible unless artisanal miners are given full legal and transferable mining titles to their claims" (1996, p. 2). It was noted, however, that "the legalization of artisanal mining, although an essential precondition for reform of the sector, can only be considered a start. The problems are so wide ranging that a flexible and integrated approach tackling regulatory, social, environmental, and other issues will be necessary" (1996, p. 2). Table 13.1 presents some of the key recommendations that emerged from the World Bank conference.

Table 13.1 Key Recommendations from the World Bank's International Roundtable on Artisanal Mining

Issues	Related Recommendations
Environmental, Health and Safety (i.e. mercury contamination, destruction of the vegetal cover, land degradation, lack	All mining, including artisanal mining, should be subject to the same environmental, health and safety laws, but the special circumstances of the informal sector should be recognized.
	To bring artisanal miners into the system, regulations and technical

of support in underground workings, etc.	standards need to be realistic and achievable and incentives to comply will be necessary.
	Education and communication of information are the keys in making all interested parties aware of the situation. This can be done through newsletters, comics, seminars, videos, and radio and television campaigns.
	Nongovernmental organizations and private companies can assist the government by playing a role in environmental management.
Organizational and Social (i.e. lack of formal business structure)	Bottom-up initiatives based on participation and cooperation between miners and nongovernmental agencies have worked best in promoting orderly development.
	Voluntary collaborations between miners are more promising than loosely organized companies.
	Artisanal miners need to be encouraged to become entrepreneurs and look upon mining as a business.
	Governments should recognize the significance of women's involvement in artisanal mining and promote it.
Technical and Financial (i.e. lack of equipment and funds, inefficient techniques, etc.)	Introduction of modern mining and processing techniques can increase productivity, mineral recovery and revenues.
	Model mines and training centres could help artisanal miners make the transition to modern mining.
	Financing could be mobilized from entrepreneurs, through no collateral loans, or by creative arrangements such as solidarity groups and third-party guarantees.
Legal and Regulatory (i.e. illegality of operations, legal constraints to formalizing artisanal mining, etc.)	Legalization of artisanal mining is the essential first step towards its transformation into a sustainable activity.
	Discoverers of deposits should be able to establish and transfer title, which will ensure their rights and enhance the creditworthiness of the mining enterprise.
	Regulation of mining activity should protect both the environment and the rights of indigenous miners.

Compiled from: World Bank, 1996

These recommendations can be applied to the South African situation. Policy initiatives such as those outlined in the South African green paper regarding the small-scale mining sector are definitely a beginning. One of the ideas advanced at the World Bank roundtable was the use of model mines (or "self-sustaining mining service centres") to provide long-term help to small-scale miners, an idea now in place in Zimbabwe. South Africa's Department of Minerals and Energy has recently proposed investigating "the establishment of training facilities for small-scale miners" (DME, 1998, p. 20). It would not be difficult to incorporate the special needs of artisanal miners into such a programme.

The solutions to the problems associated with artisanal mining will come from a holistic approach. They must be built on the cooperation of government, non-governmental organizations, international mining companies and the artisanal miners themselves. To improve the situation for informal miners, they must be helped to jump from a subsistence activity to an economically viable small-scale operation (World Bank, 1996). By increasing the funds, improving the equipment, modernizing the techniques, and regulating the operations of these miners, their work will no longer fit the definition of informal or artisanal: the most primitive type of mining, characterized by individuals or groups exploiting deposits with the simplest of equipment. This argument suggests that there is no place for the *informal* miner in today's South Africa, that informal miners need to be promoted to being small-scale miners.

This argument is reinforced by evidence from the four case studies presented in this project. The small-scale mechanized mines function relatively well with a potential for growth (especially in light of the government's proposed policy initiatives), while the informal operators seem to function at or below a subsistence level. In the case of the African United Small Miners Association, the people have formed a legal, licensed cooperative. In the case of Venmag, the Venda people work for the company as salaried employees or as contract workers. Both of these cases involve people being incorporated into mechanized, small-scale corporations and these arrangements seem to be working. In contrast, the Gong Gong and Barberton case studies illustrate the numerous problems that informal miners face.

Although many of the current informal miners are not involved in projects that are economically viable, there may be an alternate strategy. Ms. Hammell and Mr. White discussed this issue with National Parks Board site archaeologist at Thulamela, Mr. Sidney Miller. Mr. Miller suggested the idea of "keeping control of the product". If the mining, smelting, and smithing of a metal could be kept within the community, and a unique craft created (i.e. "traditional" jewelry), this product might prove profitable on the tourist market. Such a project would probably involve mainly gold and copper; the former for its high value and the latter because of the ease with which it can be smelted and worked.

Researchers discussed the pros and cons of such a proposal with Prof. Ralushai, an active member of the Venda community, and the residents of the community of Makushu near Messina. As this community has a history of metal-working and is impoverished, Prof. Ralushai felt they might be interested in a project involving the reintroduction of mining and metal-working techniques for a tourist market. The community expressed an interest, provided that the financing for training and marketing was available from an external source (and hinging, of course, on the chief's approval of the finalized programme). Such a project could possibly be incorporated into existing RDP (Reconstruction and Development Programme) projects.

This strategy – involving the revival of "traditional techniques" for a tourist market – has worked in the case of Venda pottery. Prof. Ralushai and the members of the Makushu community explained that they do not know how to make, nor do they use, traditional Venda pots anymore due to the prevalence of mass-produced commercial products which serve the same purpose more cheaply and efficiently. However, Mr. Miller took the researchers to the Venda community of Mashamba where the women have made a successful of business of selling "traditionally-made" Venda pots on the tourist market. From the mining of the clay and graphite to the creation of the final piece, production is kept within the community. The question of whether such a model could be used for metalworking, and whether this would yield results worth the effort, requires more research.

Renewed knowledge of ancient techniques can be re-introduced for the purposes of re-implementation or, more basically, to educate people about the achievements of the pre-colonial indigenous prospectors. Whether or not re-implementation proves feasible, it is important to draw a connection between the present and the past in informal mining. This connection can both reinforce initiatives to connect Africans with their heritage while supporting the modification of informal practices so that they can be safe and environmentally sustainable. There may or may not prove to be a place for "informal" miners in today's South Africa. They may not be able to avoid transformation into formalized, small-scale (mechanized) operations. Regardless, it is certain that smaller enterprises will play a larger part in the future economy of South Africa. As elucidated by Stear (1990, p. 44): "the architects of South Africa's mining future cannot afford to be complacent about the status of the industry. Circumstances are changing, and there is no doubt that small mining will have a major role to play in times to come".

ACKNOWLEDGMENTS

The completion of this project would have been impossible without the great efforts of Ms. Pauline Mitchell (Department of Archaeology, University of Cape Town) and the guidance provided by Mr. Sidney Miller (National Parks Board site archaeologist at Thulamela). This project also gratefully acknowledges the information provided by Prof. Victor Ralushai (former professor at the University of Venda, Northern Province), Prof. Edwin Hanisch (Anthropology Department, University of Venda), Mr. Kevin Buyskes (Eastern Transvaal Consolidated, Barberton), Ms. Karen Bosman (Palabora Mining Company, Phalaborwa), Mr. Manie Bodenstein (Venmag (Pty) Ltd., Northern Province), Mr. Michael Rautenbach (Dept. of Land Affairs, Kimberley), Mr. Allen Ontong (African United Small Miners Association, Kimberley), Dr. N. Segal (Chamber of Mines, Johannesburg), Inspector P.A. Swart (Diamond and Gold Branch, Barberton Police Department), Mr. Paul Deane-Williams and Mr. Ian Spence (Gold Fields Foundation, Johannesburg), and Mr. John Hollaway (John Hollaway and Associates, Harare, Zimbabwe).

We would also like to thank Gavin Evans, Doreen Carlin, Ted and Sheila Wiseman, Lex and Allen Lyons, Marlise and Johanne Liebenberg, Vanessa Bodenstein, Menno Klapwijk, and Mikki van Zyl for their personal assistance and support.

Financial support from the following agencies is acknowledged gratefully: Environmental Capacity Enhancement Project (funded by the Canadian International Development Agency), Anglo-American De Beers Chairman's Fund Educational Trust, the South African Foundation for Research Development, and the Centre for Science Development. Opinions expressed in this paper and conclusions arrived at are those of the authors and not necessarily to be attributed to any of the supporting agencies.

REFERENCES

Department of Minerals and Energy (DME). 1998: *Green paper on the mineral policy of South Africa*. Government of South Africa. 03 Feb. On-line. Internet. 25 Feb, 1998. <http://www.polity.org.za/govdocs/green_papers/mineral.html>

Hammel, A., White, C., Pfeiffer, S. & Miller, D. (in prep.): *Precolonial Mining in Southern Africa.*

Hanna, M. 1997. *Golden opportunity in South Africa : black miners seek mineral rights held by white firms*. CNN Interactive. 21 July. On-line. Internet. 18 Jan, 1998. <http://cnn.com/WORLD/9707/21/safrica.gold/index.html>

Hossack, C. 1998: *Minerals Green Paper aims to prevent 'hoarding and sterilization' of mineral rights*. Southern Africa Environment Page. 20 Feb. On-line. Internet. 25 Feb, 1998. <http://www.ru.ac.za/departments/law/Saenviro/business/mining.html>

Miller, D. 1995: 2000 years of indigenous mining and metallurgy in southern Africa—a review. *South African Journal of Geology*, 98, 232-238.

Southern Africa Environment Project. 1998: *Diamond mining: exceptional artifacts threatened at Canteen Koppie*. Southern Africa Environment Page. 20 Feb. On-line. Internet. 25 Feb, 1998. <http://www.ru.ac.za/departments/law/Saenviro/business/mining.html>

Stear, W. 1990: Small mining—strategic opportunity in a changing South Africa? *Mining Survey*, 1, 39-44.

Van Warmelo, N.J. 1940: *The Copper Miners of Musina and the Early History of the Zoutpansberg*: 62. Pretoria: Department of Native Affairs. Ethnological Publications 8.

World Bank. 1996: *Regularizing Informal Mining: A Summary of the Proceedings of the International Roundtable on Artisanal Mining*. B. Mamadou (ed.). Washington: World Bank, Industry and Energy Department. Occasional Paper No. 6.

Chapter 14

THE EFFECTS OF SMALL-SCALE GOLD MINING ON THE ENVIRONMENT AT TAFUNA HILL, ZIMBABWE

by Peter van Straaten

INTRODUCTION

Mining has been an important factor in the foundation of our civilization, from the Stone Age, through the Bronze and Iron Ages, to the "Computer Age". Well organized societies, founded on the extraction and use of metals such as copper, iron and tin existed many centuries ago in Asia, Africa, Europe and the Americas. The Industrial Revolution was largely based on the use of steel and metals. Today, our society is based largely on minerals and mineral products. Most machines and appliances are, at least in part, made of minerals and mineral products. Energy is provided from fossil fuels derived from geological resources. Modern agricultural production is largely based on fertilizers made from rocks. Our buildings use large amounts of mineral materials, from concrete floors to gypsum insulation and glass windows. Not only do we require sand and gravel for house and road construction, we use gold for jewellery, as a trading object, and in electronics. Minerals are part of our daily lives.

Minerals are characterized by two geologic factors that make them a challenge to modern civilization. Most of the minerals extracted are *non-renewable* resources. They are formed by slow geological processes and do not "grow" at a rate equal to our consumption. They cannot be "harvested" like fish or maize. Minerals and ores are formed at specific sites dictated by Nature; they have a *place value*. Mineral deposits cannot be shifted to alternative sites.

Mineral deposits are highly concentrated forms of non-renewable resources in a relatively small space. The land used for mineral extraction is usually small in comparison to other land uses like agriculture and forestry. Although mining in Zimbabwe is one of the major industrial activities contributing to 8% of the GDP, it uses only an area of 58.2 km², which is 0.015% of the country's total land use (Svotwa & Mtetwa, 1997, unpublished).

Mineral resource development can contribute considerably to economic growth but, when not extracted responsibly, can also cause environmental damage. The very nature of mining activities involves some degree of environmental disturbance. The physical removal of minerals, by deep underground to surface mining, utilizes different methods which often result in air, water and soil degradation.

In Zimbabwe, 80% of the population live in rural areas and depend mainly on agriculture. After agriculture, mining is the main economic pillar of Zimbabwe's economy, accounting for 45% of the country's exports. Many of the country's mines are conventional medium- to large-scale operations, extracting gold, chromite, coal, copper, etc. But there are thousands of small-scale mines, most of them unregulated, extracting mainly gold from small deposits close to the surface. Large mining operations extract several thousands of tonnes per day, while small-scale miners extract a few tonnes per month in very small "cottage-scale" industries. The people employed in the mining industry vary from relatively few highly skilled labourers in large-scale, mechanized mining operations to large numbers of relatively unskilled small-scale miners.

Small-scale and artisanal mining are manual, low-technology operations, often in remote areas, which extract ore mainly from near-surface deposits. The distinction between small-scale miners and artisanal miners is poorly defined and gradual: small-scale miners use a limited amount of mechanization (e.g. compressors, ball mills), while artisanal miners use only simple tools like crowbars and shovels and they crush and grind the ore manually.

Artisanal and small-scale gold mining are often subsistence activities. In Eastern and Southern Africa, this kind of mining employs several hundred thousand largely unskilled persons (Zimbabwe: approximately 200,000; Tanzania: approximately 200,000 - 300,000; Mozambique: several tens of thousands), contributing to poverty reduction and employment in rural areas.

Two principal types of small-scale/artisanal gold mining activities dominate in this region: alluvial gold mining in and along river beds and mining of primary hard gold bearing rock from solid rock formations. While alluvial mining is largely responsible for river degradation, siltation and destruction of riverine environments, the mining and processing of primary gold quartz veins releases toxic elements such as mercury, arsenic, lead and copper.

The uncontrolled release of mercury during gold ore processing is of particular concern. Mercury is used to capture the fine gold particles and the resulting gold amalgam is finally "burnt" to produce raw gold. Few studies have been carried out in Africa which actually quantify the amounts of mercury and other toxic elements lost to the environment.

Thousands of small-scale gold miners all over the world use mercury for amalgamation, the bonding of elemental mercury to a variety of metals, including gold. Small-scale gold miners use it because it easily and efficiently recovers small amounts and fine gold particles, which would otherwise be lost. In Zimbabwe, amalgamation is mainly used by small-scale/artisanal miners who extract gold from primary gold-bearing ores. It is used in alluvial gold recovery operations at only a few places.

In Zimbabwe, many artisanal and small-scale gold miners work only seasonally. Other small-scale miners, organized in groups, clans and mining villages, mine permanently, extracting gold from officially awarded claim areas. In recent years, the numbers of small-scale and artisanal miners have increased steadily because of the prevailing economic hardships in Zimbabwe caused by economic structural adjustment and unemployment. Small-scale gold and artisanal mining often represents a means of survival in rural areas.

This chapter will discuss the small-scale mining sector and specifically the small-scale gold mining sector in the selected area of Tafuna Hill near Shamva, Central Zimbabwe. This area was selected as it constitutes a well developed small-scale mining camp at a relatively isolated site, where the effects of mining on air, water and land could be studied. At Tafuna Hill, there is no interference with other mining activities or with farming, and the community was willing to share information with the researchers.

Key issues include organizational, social, technical, legal, environmental and human health issues. The environmental and human health concerns centre around occupational health and safety, as well as pollution from the release of toxic elements during mining and processing.

GOLD EXTRACTION AT TAFUNA HILL

Tafuna Hill is located some 8 km southwest of Shamva, approximately 70 km northeast of the capital Harare. The foot of Tafuna Hill (altitude approximately

1,000 m) can be reached by tarmac road, the ascent to the mining community at the top of the 1,300 m hill is by all-weather track. During the rainy season, the community can be reached only by four-wheel-drive vehicles.

The geology of Tafuna Hill was studied extensively; the latest summary of its geology was done by Stidolph (1977). Precambrian greenstones and granites underlie the area around Shamva. The gold extracted at Tafuna Hill occurs mainly in quartz veins and lenses which crosscut the greenstones. Most of the quartz veins strike north-northwest or north-northeast (Figure 14.1) and dip steeply. These gold-bearing quartz veins (reefs) are commonly 20 to 100 cm thick. In 1977, there were 11 active gold mines on Tafuna Hill which had produced approximately 7 tonnes of gold between 1910 and 1965. The average recovered grade from these veins was very high at 12.2 g/t (Stidolph, 1977). A smaller amount of gold is currently extracted from the weathered and gravitationally transported (eluvial) material in the surface environment. These eluvial gold deposits occur at depths of 1-3 m below the current surface. Gold is found mainly at the interface between the weathered country rock and the overlying soils.

Visible left-overs from previous gold mining activities at Tafuna Hill are mine tailings, parts of old machinery and unprotected open shafts.

The small-scale/artisanal gold miners of Tafuna Hill practice exclusively manual mining and processing methods. Obviously, the nature of the mining activities depend on the type of ore body being mined, the location of the mining area (particularly with respect to water), and the technology available to the miners. At Tafuna Hill, two types of gold bearing ores are being mined:

▶ primary gold quartz reefs, a hard rock type, mined underground; and

▶ eluvial gold in near-surface (< 5 m deep) soft environments.

The ore preparation and processing techniques include manual crushing and grinding, wet washing and panning, and recovery of gold, using amalgamation techniques.

Artisanal/small-scale gold mining activities can be divided into separate phases:

▶ The first phase includes activities related to the actual mining of gold deposits, in this case underground mining of primary reef gold and near-surface mining of eluvial gold accumulations. This phase also includes the preparation of the extracted gold-bearing ores, principally crushing and grinding.

▶ The second phase includes all activities associated with the processing of the crushed and ground ores, basically the recovery of heavy concentrates using gravitational separation techniques. The last step carried out in the field is the amalgamation and recovery of unrefined "raw" gold. (The final gold refining is not normally done at the mining sites, but at gold dealers' places in towns and in goldsmiths' shops.)

While the activities of phase one are predominately dry, phase two activities require the use of water.

The different activities have different impacts on the environment and human health:

▶ Phase one activities have a high potential for immediate and direct impacts on human health (accidents due to collapsing pits and underground workings), and the environment (waste rock placement, erosion, dust, noise, etc.).

▶ Phase two activities involve the use of water and mercury, as well as the disposal of wastes contaminated by the process. This phase may cause long-term damage to human health (mercury inhalation) and to the environment (air, water, and soil pollution).

Figure 14.1 Gold reefs on Tafuna Hill

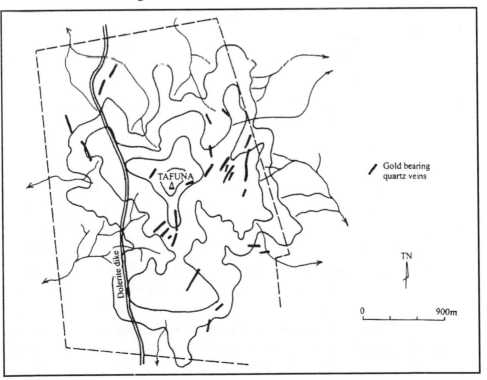

Extracting and crushing the ore

At Tafuna Hill, gold is extracted by completely manual underground mining methods, using hand picks, crowbars, and hammers. Eluvial ore is also mined completely manually, using picks and shovels to break the lateritic weathered zones. Superficial waste material removed during excavations is usually left in the immediate vicinity of the pits, in small mounds scattered throughout the mining area. Only the ore is removed from the mining area for further processing.

The ore grade material is transported from the mining area to local people's homesteads, where crushing and grinding is done by the miners themselves. The ore is usually kept in bags and transported on peoples' backs. At the homesteads, the ore is normally first spread and turned periodically to dry prior to manual crushing.

The dried ore is carried out manually by individuals (often women) hired to crush the ore at a fixed price. The ore is crushed into smaller pieces with small hammers or a small axle bar, and then spread out again for further drying. The workers crushing the ore generally wear no protective devices for their hands or eyes. After manual crushing and drying, the ore is manually ground at the homesteads, using mortars and pestles. The wooden "mortars" are made from local trees and are up to 60 cm high and up to 40 cm in diameter. The "pestle" is usually an old car axle.

The actual grinding produces considerable amounts of dust. After grinding, the fine material is sieved, using locally produced wire mesh sieves, many of which were in disrepair.

Washing and separating the ore

After the ore has been crushed and ground, it is ready for further processing. At Tafuna Hill, the crushed and ground ore is washed, using local wooden washing pans, which are 40 cm in diameter. The water/ore slurry is rotated in a circular fashion. The light fraction at the outer side of the pans is washed into another pan or discarded. Coarse pebbles are removed by hand and discarded. The repeated rotary motion concentrates the heavy fraction concentrate of the ore in the centre of the pan for further processing.

A few individuals at Tafuna Hill use sluice box techniques to recover heavy concentrates from the crushed and ground ore. The sluices are made of local wooden planks, set up at an angle of 20-30°. The sluice is lined with a sisal cloth matting material, which is used to retain the heavy materials washed down the sluice. The finely ground ore and the water form a slurry, which is fed onto the sluice through the use of a simple sluice feedbox on the upper end of the sluice. The sluice boxes are perforated to allow controlled material (slurry) feed from the box to the sluice as water is added. Because water is a valuable commodity at Tafuna Hill, it is used carefully. The wash water that runs off the sluice is normally contained in local sumps for reuse.

With the exception of some crude wooden bars across the sluice, there was no riffle technique in evidence to enhance the separation of gold from the slurries.

Once the ore has been washed, the concentrate captured in the sisal cloth is recovered by rinsing the cloth in a bucket. This heavy concentrate in the cloth contains the gold, which is removed by amalgamation techniques using mercury.

Mercury amalgamation and burning

The handling of mercury and the amalgamation process are generally done in a similar fashion at all the processing sites at Tafuna Hill. Mercury is stored in little glass bottles and covered with water to reduce volatilization.

A few grammes of mercury are mixed with the concentrate in the wooden pan. The workers use their bare hands to rub the mercury into the concentrate to form a paste-like mix. When the gold contained in the concentrate comes into contact with the mercury, the two elements form gold amalgam.

The amalgam mix is then taken into the palm of the unprotected hand, and the thumb of the other hand is pressed firmly onto the amalgam, forcing excess mercury to flow out into the washing pan where it is going to be used again. The metallic mercury is in direct contact with the workers' skin, which, in some cases had little cuts and sores. At a few places, the amalgam was placed in a fine cloth, which was tightened to squeeze out some of the excess mercury.

The next step is to separate the gold from the amalgam by "burning off" the mercury. The few left-over grammes of gold amalgam sponge or bead remain and are wrapped in a small piece of foil paper (usually cigarette foils) for further processing. The amalgam bead (which is approximately 50% mercury and 50% gold) is then heated to evaporate the mercury and produce an impure "raw" gold product. Due to the small amounts of material being heated at any one time (usually less than 10 grammes, often just two or three grammes) the sponge is handled very carefully and special care is taken to heat it properly in an appropriately small fire.

The excess mercury from the bead is evaporated by carefully putting the wrapped amalgam on a spoon or directly onto the bed of smoldering wood or charcoal, and blowing onto the bed to raise the temperature enough to drive off the mercury. The individual heating the amalgam usually gets very close (15-30 cm) to the fire and the amalgam, inhaling the vapours, including mercury vapour released on combustion. The heating of the amalgam bead is sometimes done out in the open air, but many individuals do it at existing fireplaces, most often in the homestead kitchen, especially during the rainy season.

Discarded materials

After the gold from the gravity separate has been recovered by amalgamation methods, the remaining heavy concentrate is discarded. In general, for every bucket of ground ore, approximately one bucket of the light fraction "waste" is commonly discarded around the homestead or added to the light tailings fraction. While the light fraction tailings are usually low in heavy metals, the addition of the heavy fraction make these tailings a hazardous waste, as well as a potential resource for further processing.

Analysis of the discarded materials shows that the recovery techniques are not very efficient, as the post-process tailings still contain a relatively high gold content of up to 50 g/t! At some places, the tailings were worked again to recover the gold lost during the first processing.

The end product

The final product is approximately 90% pure. It is sold to the Reserve Bank of Zimbabwe or to local dealers in the major towns. Although mercury is considered a Group II hazardous substance in Zimbabwe, it is easily obtainable by the miners because there is no effective control of marketing guidelines.

ENVIRONMENTAL EFFECTS OF SMALL-SCALE GOLD MINING ON AIR, WATER, SOIL AND TAILINGS

The use of mercury and other toxic elements released in primary gold processing affect the environment in the following ways:

Effects on air quality

Atmospheric samples were carried out in the open air, but the detection limits of the field instruments were not low enough to get any meaningful results. Measurements were made indoors in kitchens and other sites where the amalgam bead was heated. High concentrations were found in closed buildings where the amalgam was "burned". The concentration of mercury was high enough to make people in the immediate surroundings cough. Up to 5 mg Hg/m^3 were measured in two kitchens at Tafuna Hill. The World Health Organisation (WHO) threshold limit value for mercury vapour exposure is 0.05 mg/m^3, acute intoxication is reached at 10 mg/m^3, chronic intoxication starts at 0.5 mg/m^3.

It is clear that persons directly or indirectly exposed to these high concentrations of mercury vapour are at considerable health risk.

Effects on water quality

Samples of river and stream water, as well as process water, were collected during the field survey (Figures 14.2 and 14.3). The mercury concentration of water bodies, even close to the Tafuna Hill processing sites, were generally low, ranging from 0.02 to 0.65 ppb. Several water samples had elevated arsenic concentrations (up to 76 ppm). This can be explained by the release of arsenic from gold reefs (and possibly from the greenstone country rock) in which arsenopyrite is present. This arsenic is not introduced by humans, except for the fact that its release might be accelerated by grinding of arsenopyrite containing gold ores.

One of the samples with elevated concentrations of arsenic is the drinking water of the population of Tafuna Hill. The arsenic level of the drinking water, which is collected from a drowned mine shaft, was 76 ppm (the WHO limit for drinking water is 10 ppm).

The low dispersion of toxic elements like mercury or other heavy metals in streams draining from Tafuna Hill may possibly be explained by the presence of iron-rich soils and laterites. Mercury is easily adsorbed by goethite and organic matter at low pH ranges. In the project area, lateritic soils and laterite crusts are prevalent and may lower the rate of heavy metal dispersion.

Figure 14.2 Mercury in water

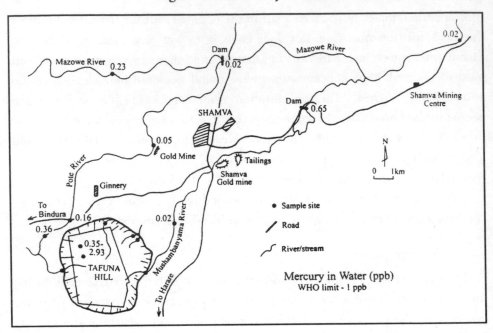

Mazowe River
0.02

Dam
0.02

Mazowe River

Mazowe River
0.23

Dam
0.65

Shamva Mining
Centre

SHAMVA

Pote River

0.05
Gold Mine

Tailings

Shamva
Gold mine

N

0   1km

Ginnery

To
Bindura
0.16

0.36

0.35-
2.93

TAFUNA
HILL

0.02

Mushambanyama River

To Harare

● Sample site

╱ Road

⌇ River/stream

Mercury in Water (ppb)
WHO limit - 1 ppb

Figure 14.3 Arsenic in water

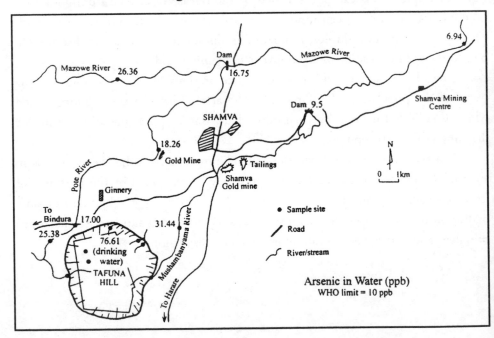

Mazowe River
6.94

Dam
16.75

Mazowe River

Mazowe River
26.36

Dam 9.5

Shamva Mining
Centre

SHAMVA

Pote River

18.26
Gold Mine

Tailings

Shamva
Gold mine

N

0   1km

Ginnery

To
Bindura
17.00

25.38

76.61
(drinking
water)

TAFUNA
HILL

31.44

Mushambanyama River

To Harare

● Sample site

╱ Road

⌇ River/stream

Arsenic in Water (ppb)
WHO limit = 10 ppb

Effects on soils

High concentrations of mercury, arsenic and tungsten were measured in soil samples collected in the immediate surroundings of the gold processing sites. Mercury concentrations up to 25 mg Hg/kg (average soil is 0.098 Hg mg/kg) were measured in soils at Tafuna Hill. The arsenic concentrations reached up to 2106 mg/kg (average soil 11.3 g As/kg). Even gold analyses were high in these soils, some of them ore grade – up to 12.2 mg Au/kg, or g/t.

These contaminated soils are all in homestead environments. People walk barefoot and children play on the contaminated soil.

Effects on chemical composition of stream sediments

Stream sediment samples (silt fraction) were collected at the same sites where water was sampled. Results indicate slightly elevated concentrations of mercury (up to 0.7 mg Hg/kg) at the foot of Tafuna Hill. At a distance of 1 km from these sites, the mercury concentrations are at background levels (0.1 -0.2 mg Hg/kg). Arsenic concentrations were generally high in most samples, ranging from 404 mg As/kg at the foot of Tafuna Hill to 154 mg As/kg some 1 km from the previous site (Figure 14.4).

Figure 14.4 Arsenic in stream sediments

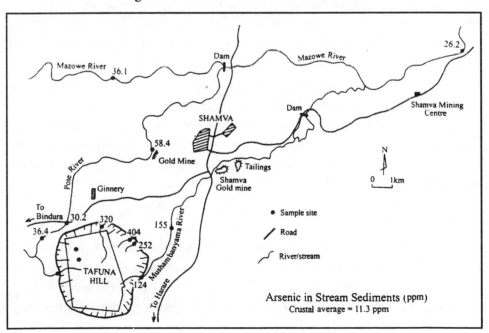

Chemical composition of tailings from small-scale miners

At present, all mine wastes are discarded indiscriminately into the yard around the processing sites. There is no separation of the light fraction tailings and the gravity separate. The latter contains high amounts of toxic elements, as well as high concentrations of still unrecovered gold.

The following concentrations were measured in tailings on Tafuna Hill:

Hg: up to 1 414 mg/kg
As: up to 3 350 mg/kg
Pb: up to 256 mg/kg
Au: up to 54.6 mg/kg (54.6 g/t!)

Children often play in the tailings and chickens use them for dust baths. The tailings in their current form are hazardous, but potentially valuable materials. The hazards could be very much reduced if simple waste separation procedures were followed (for instance, separating the light, relatively uncontaminated fraction from the heavy, contaminated and gold-bearing fraction.

Chemical analyses of mudwalls and 'soot' in selected homesteads

Extremely high concentrations of mercury, arsenic and gold were found in mudwalls and 'soot' inside houses, mainly in kitchens where amalgam was burned. The highest mercury value was analyzed from soot samples. Levels up to 104 mg Hg/kg (average soil is 0.098 mg Hg/kg) were measured in the home of Mr. and Mrs. Banda. The highest arsenic concentrations were found in mudwall materials. Concentrations reached 2 672 mg As/kg (average soil is 11.3 mg As/kg). Gold values of up to 5.04 g/t were analyzed from soot samples.

The high concentrations in mudwalls and soot are a clear reflection of the high mercury losses during amalgam burning. Mercury, arsenic and other elements are volatilized and condense or adsorb onto the organic matter in the soot or the clays walls of the houses.

PATHWAY ANALYSES

The fate of mercury during the processing of gold-bearing ore is followed and measured using a mass balance approach. Every material input and output was recorded and measured gravimetrically, using three different sets of scales (reflecting the range of mass of materials from 0.01 gramme to tens of kilograms).

These detailed measuring procedures were conducted at the processing sites of seven artisanal gold miners at Tafuna Hill.

The general picture emerging from this survey shows large losses of volatile metallic mercury (~ 80%) into the atmosphere during amalgam burning. Approximately 15-20% is released to soil, water and the gravity separate discarded on to the tailings. A typical material flow diagram is shown in Figure 14.5.

Figure 14.5 Pathway analysis of mercury in small-scale gold mining operations in Zimbabwe

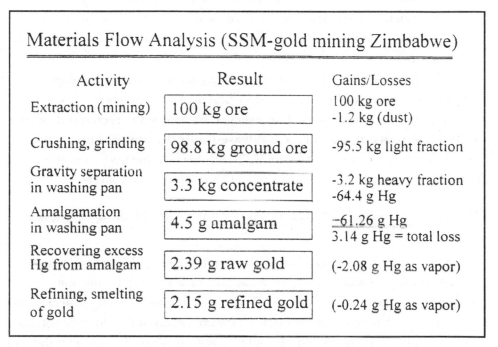

Activity	Result	Gains/Losses
Materials Flow Analysis (SSM-gold mining Zimbabwe)		
Extraction (mining)	100 kg ore	100 kg ore -1.2 kg (dust)
Crushing, grinding	98.8 kg ground ore	-95.5 kg light fraction
Gravity separation in washing pan	3.3 kg concentrate	-3.2 kg heavy fraction -64.4 g Hg
Amalgamation in washing pan	4.5 g amalgam	−61.26 g Hg 3.14 g Hg = total loss
Recovering excess Hg from amalgam	2.39 g raw gold	(-2.08 g Hg as vapor)
Refining, smelting of gold	2.15 g refined gold	(-0.24 g Hg as vapor)

The fate and pathways of the volatile mercury released to the atmosphere is not yet known. Some of this volatile metallic mercury is certainly adsorbed onto organic matter (in and outside the homestead) and into the clay walls of the mud huts (when amalgam is burned inside the houses). To quantify the volatile component released during amalgam burning, more sophisticated equipment is required.

The pathways of mercury in water and soils is probably short. From other studies in similar environments in Tanzania (van Straaten, unpublished), it could be shown that the vertical migration of mercury in soils at the processing site is very low. Usually the mercury is concentrated in the top few centimetres of soil profiles. The reason for this low mobility is the presence of organic matter and goethite-rich complexes onto which mercury is strongly adsorbed. These strong adsorbing mineral and organic materials largely prevent the mercury from dispersion, both vertically and laterally.

The only environmental compartment where mercury could be released (volatilized) is from tailings heaps. There the concentration of mercury is still relatively high and the composition of these tailings, which are rich in quartz sand and lack organic matter, is unfavourable for complexation and adsorption.

The manual nature and limited scale of the activities, the limited use of process additives, and the sparing use of water result in minimal discharges to the environment.

The predominant release pathway of contaminants from mining related activities is through the air. The most critical area of concern is the release of mercury into the environment. **For every 1 unit of gold recovered, about 1.20 - 1.46 units of mercury are released into the atmosphere.** While the most immediate concern is occupational health hazards, the long-term effects are not well understood and represent a potential environmental concern.

HAZARDS AND RISKS CREATED BY ARTISANAL GOLD MINING AT TAFUNA HILL

The predominant hazard and risk associated with artisanal gold mining activities are related to underground mining in areas which, according to the miners, are unsupported. The miners enter old shafts from previous mining activities, the deepest of which is 260 m below surface. However, many of the old mineworks are flooded and access is limited. In most cases, the miners entering the old underground operations do not wear any safety gear. They work in old drifts, many of which are not supported and not safe.

The superficial holes created by eluvial gold mining at the slopes of Tafuna Hill are left unprotected, both during operation and after production activities have ceased. These openings, pits and unsupported holes are generally unmarked, other than by the presence of waste rock, and pose some limited safety hazards to people passing through this area.

From informal interviews and discussion with individual miners at Tafuna Hill, it was found that none who do the amalgamation and amalgam burning have any knowledge of the harmful effects of mercury vapour and they do not use any form of protection for themselves or the environment.

The two most harmful mercurial substances are metallic mercury vapours and methylmercury. The absorption of liquid metallic mercury is low, as are the effects on the skin, as compared to inhaled metallic mercury vapour and ingested methylmercury. Inhalation of mercury vapour can cause acute or chronic effects. Mercury accumulates in the following body parts: thyroid, brain, kidney, pancreas, testes, ovary and prostate, and the highest concentration is in the liver. Approximately 80% of inhaled mercury vapour is retained by the alveoli in the lungs. Typical symptoms in such cases are tremors, gingivitis, sleeplessness and personality changes.

Due to the lack of official statistics, it is difficult to assess the amounts of gold recovered from this one mining camp alone. Preliminary estimates range from 100- 200 kg of gold per year. This would translate into an annual loss of 150-220 kg of mercury from this one source alone. As approximately 80% is released into the atmosphere, the total mercury vapour released to the atmosphere from Tafuna Hill is in the range of 120 170 kg.

POSSIBLE MITIGATION TECHNIQUES

The processing techniques of gold-bearing ores are very basic at Tafuna Hill. Small technical improvements could result in higher gold recovery and profits for the miners, as well as reduced environmental costs.

Adapting appropriate technologies

To increase productivity, some adapted technologies could be introduced. Most of the sluices seen at Tafuna Hill are very inefficient and could be improved by introducing different locally available matting materials, angle iron riffles or expanded metal riffles (Blowers, 1988; Clarkson, 1994). Other methods of gravity separation should be tested for suitability and practicality at Tafuna Hill. These include technologies and equipment designed for industrial processing sites, but could be adapted to central "custom" operations in the field, such as various gravity concentrators and different amalgamation technologies (UNIDO, 1997; Priester & Hentschel, 1992; Blowers, 1988). Application experience could be drawn from other small-scale gold mining regions in Ghana, the Philippines, Papua New Guinea, South America, etc.

It should be stressed that it is technically possible and relatively easy to mitigate the loss of mercury to the atmosphere. However, to substantially reduce the impact on the environment and on human health, the technology must be socially acceptable and provide some economic advantage. The technology must be as transparent as possible to give the owner the feeling that he/she is not cheated – it should be reasonably inexpensive and robust.

Safer methods of burning amalgam

One of the potentially cheapest and easiest steps to significantly reduce environmental and human health impacts would be to control the burning of the amalgam nodule, using well designed mercury recycling equipment which is acceptable to and appropriate for the miners. An effective piece of equipment called a retort is recommended. The retort reduces mercury losses by more than 95%, recycles the mercury and limits the total amount of mercury used in the recovery process.

It is highly probable that adapted, improved, transparent retorts could be jointly developed by miners, local craftsmen and personnel experienced in developing intermediate technologies. Participatory research on this option would be necessary to assure the success of such an intermediate technology approach.

At present, individual miners generally burn the amalgam over very small fires, which do not provide sufficient heat to operate most retorts effectively. One alternative, which should be considered and discussed with the miners, is based on contracting local goldsmiths to do the burning more safely and efficiently, using hand-driven fans for hotter fires. A similar approach would be a central amalgam burning site, set up with a suitable retort plus implements used by local blacksmiths. The "retorter" would provide services to the processors. The retorter would burn the customer's amalgam bead in a transparent retort, in the customer's presence to remove any fear of being cheated.

Central custom milling

Another way to improve productivity and reduce environmental and human health risks is already practiced in parts of Tafuna Hill. This is the collection and transportation of ore to central custom milling sites to handle the ore, the gravity concentrates or tailings from the artisanal miners. (At present, however, the custom milling sites such as Shamva Mining Centre and some local milling operations require more transparency to assure the miners that they are not being cheated.) This sort of centralization improves recovery, reduces losses of heavy metals, contributes to a cleaner environment and reduces worker exposure to hazardous materials.

However, this approach is only practical when large shipments of ore have been accumulated and custom processing sites have been established. Because artisanal miners want immediate returns for their work, this option is only partially practical. However, the processing of tailings and separately stored post-amalgamation concentrates – products which now have only limited value for the miners and contribute to environmental and human health problems – should be encouraged.

Investigating alternatives to mercury

Research should be directed towards eliminating mercury altogether. Mercury-free gold recovery techniques like the one developed in Ghana should be considered. The School of Mines in Tarkwa, Ghana worked with local small-scale gold miners to assess the use of dry separation to recover gold after panning. This method yields gold recovery equal to (or greater than) those using mercury-based recovery techniques. Furthermore, the researchers and small-scale gold miners claim that the gold recovered this way has a higher market value than that processed with mercury (UNIDO, 1997).

A more formal framework should be established to investigate other such initiatives and to facilitate the ongoing exchange of African ideas and experiences in this area.

Improved disposal methods

Another way to minimize and isolate the materials that come in contact with contaminants is to improve the disposal and handling of mine waste. Possible areas for improvement include modification of the handling of sluice concentrate and tailings to minimize the amount of contaminated materials. Proper management and separation of sluice concentrate and tailings can significantly reduce the volumes of material exposed to mercury.

The separation of the gravity concentrate tailings from other non-mercury contaminated tailings could significantly reduce the volume of contaminated materials. It is recommended to encourage the artisanal miners at Tafuna Hill to keep materials that have come in contact with mercury separate from others materials. A mechanism of collection and recycling at a central station should be investigated, which would not only reduce environmental and human health damage, but also provide some economic incentives for the miners.

Conclusions

Artisanal gold miners at Tafuna Hill extract gold from primary, quartz "reef" deposits and from eluvial accumulations near surface. Batches of ore are crushed and ground manually, and then processed using mercury to extract the gold. For every gramme of gold won, some 1.20 to 1.46 grammes of mercury are released into the environment. Eighty percent of the mercury is released into the atmosphere in the form of mercury vapour. The handling of mercury and treatment of the amalgam is very hazardous and dangerous for human health. Inhalation of mercury vapour is considered one of the most harmful and potentially deadly forms of mercury absorption in human bodies.

The dispersion of mercury in air could not be measured in this study. The dispersion of mercury in water and soil is low, as evidenced by the analyses of several selected samples, probably because of the high adsorption of mercury onto lateritic soils and laterite crusts which are widespread in the area overlying the greenstones. Very high mercury concentrations were found only in soils and tailings near the miners' homesteads, as well as in kitchens and at fireplaces where amalgam is burnt in the final extraction phase in the field.

Apart from mercury, high arsenic levels were found in the area's water and stream sediments. Very high concentrations of arsenic were found in soils around processing sites and in human dwellings where amalgam is burnt.

At present, the main concern which needs urgent attention is that of human health, specifically for those directly and indirectly involved in handling and burning of mercury and amalgam.

Mitigation techniques to be tested on small-scale/artisanal mining camps must bring economic advantages as well as environmental improvements. Better recovery techniques, better gravitational separation, the use of mercury recycling equipment (e.g. a retort), as well as mercury-free techniques which have been tested in similar goldfields need to be adapted.

Other improvements towards better management and lower environmental and human health costs are:

- facilitating the availability of appropriate and affordable mining tools;
- providing supportive extension services for small-scale miners;
- promoting partnerships between local small-scale miners and large scale investors to facilitate technology transfer;
- streamlining and simplifying the licensing of artisanal miners;
- enhancing legalization of the artisanal and small-scale miners activities;
- preparing, disseminating and enforcing a code of conduct in mining and mineral processing which takes account of health, safety and environmental concerns;
- providing business opportunities that will encourage financial institutions and NGO s to support the various efforts of the mining sub-sector;
- encouraging the private sector to reprocess tailings from small-scale mining operations, especially the gravity concentrates.

Practical and immediate measures for reducing human health exposure and losses of mercury into the environment include the following:

- **Link economic improvement with better environmental management of small-scale gold mining** by assisting with technical improvements of existing mining and processing equipment and techniques. Appropriate, low-cost, robust equipment should be developed with the small-scale miners.
- **Conduct awareness campaigns** through extension efforts by medical and mining personnel. It is important to make the small-scale mining community aware of the dangers of using mercury during amalgamation and amalgam burning,
- **Participatory research and development on mercury retort** by local miners, craftsmen, engineers, etc. The aim would be to produce a socially acceptable, adapted, effective, low-cost mercury recycling device or to investigate mercury-free recovery techniques.
- **Training** of small-scale miners, trainers, and technical staff on various technical, environmental and health issues. Training courses at the existing Shamva Mining Centre should be supported.
- **Monitoring** of the impacts of mercury release, as well as the changes in mercury dissemination into the air, water and soils close to the processing sites. Emphasis should be put on monitoring the pathways of mercury vapour.
- **Encouraging local entrepreneurs** to collect heavy concentrate wastes

which would otherwise be discarded in tailings, and process these in such a way as to provide some economic return to the entrepreneurs and the community, while reducing environmental pollution.

REFERENCES

Blowers, M. 1988: *Handbook of small scale gold mining for Papua New Guinea.* Christchurch: Pacific Resource Publications.

Clarkson, R. 1994: The use of nuclear tracers to evaluate the gold recovery efficiency of sluiceboxes. *CIM Bulletin,* 87, 29-37.

Priester, M. and Hentschel, T. 1992: *Small-scale gold-mining. Processing techniques in developing countries.* Vieweg: GATE/GTZ.

Stidolph, P.A. 1977: The geology of the country around Shamva. *Rhodesia Geological Survey Bulletin,* 78.

UNIDO. 1997: *Report on 'Expert group meeting on UNIDO high impact programme: Introducing New Technologies for Abatement of Global Mercury Pollution Deriving from Artisanal Gold Mining', Vienna 1-3 July 1997.*

Chapter 15

Diffusion of Science and Technology for Environmental and Natural Resource Management in a Fragile Mountain Ecosystem

by Alex Tindimubona, William Balu-Tabaro and Dezi Ngambeki

Introduction

Uganda is struggling to recover from two decades of economic decline and political chaos which brought, among other ills, severe environmental degradation and mismanagement of its natural resources. Most environment and natural resource management (E/NRM) problems are caused by a lack of appropriate information among more than 90% of the population – the peasant subsistence farmers who exploit natural resources for daily existence.

This chapter investigates the diffusion of science and technology (S&T) information for E/NRM in the fragile mountain ecosystem of the Kigezi Region of southwestern Uganda. The issues in Kigezi are sustainable land use, including soil erosion, loss of fertility, deforestation, energy crisis and wetland/watershed management. The chapter is based on research covering both institutions and grassroots communities, using participatory methods to establish the nature and content of S&T information diffusion, and the factors which enhance or hinder the diffusion process. The results reveal important gaps and structural weaknesses in the diffusion system for the study area, and the study recommends possible policy and technical interventions to improve the system.

It is generally agreed that in Uganda, most of the environmental destruction is carried out by two categories of people (Uganda, 1994): those that do it out of ignorance and/or necessity; and those that do it out of greed, not wanting to use environmentally friendly and sustainable methods of resource utilization. The vast majority of people (about 92%) fall in the first category, being subsistence peasants or urban poor trying to satisfy basic needs of food, shelter, fuelwood, water and sanitation.

At a fundamental level, therefore, environment and natural resource management (E/NRM) boil down to the three factors which have been identified as the main determinants of sustainable development: science, technology and managerial capacity (Museveni, 1986). These must be orchestrated by correct leadership.

. In our recent studies on development of a science culture in Africa (Tindimubona, 1993) and on science and technology indicators (Tindimubona, 1996), we found a strong feeling among Africa's science managers that the time has now come to focus more on the utilization of S&T results in Africa. There is a sense that modern S&T reside in town, while the people are out there in the country-side. It is not clear how (or whether) the S&T conducted in research institutions is actually relevant, used or usable by Africa's peasants. In Ugandan agriculture for example, the performance (using yields as indicators) on farmers' fields were found to be only 13-33% of that achieved in research station fields (Uganda, 1996). Such a large gap must be bridged and better diffusion assured.

It is therefore, very important to understand how (or whether) science and technology are diffusing to the people and how this affects their capacity for environment and natural resource management.

THE RESEARCH PROBLEM

To determine how science and technology diffuse to the people of Kigezi to enable them to sustainably manage their environment and natural resources. Specifically, to determine:

1. The nature of the S&T diffusion system for E/NRM in Uganda and its effectiveness for the Kigezi region. What is the S&T diffusion "network" through which concepts, methods and processes of E/NRM are received, mastered and utilized by the people? Is it centralized or decentralized (BOSTID, 1984)? To what extent is it effective or not; endogenous or exogenous?

2. What is the S&T content that the S&T diffusion system carries? What is the public understanding of S&T (Durant, Evans & Thomas, 1989) and their role in E/NRM?

3. What factors enhance or hinder the S&T diffusion and E/NRM processes and

how can they be encouraged/discouraged? What are the gaps and conflicts in the diffusion system?

RESEARCH TECHNIQUE

The research was conducted in three stages:

▶ The first phase involved a survey of institutions in Kampala, Entebbe and Kabale. This gave an understanding of the top-down S&T diffusion system.

▶ Then, three participatory rural appraisal (PRA) exercises were conducted in the study area, Central Kigezi. This contributed to a Rural Development Seminar in which the preliminary findings were reviewed.

▶ Finally, a two-day Validation Workshop was held in Kabale and attracted 25 residents of the study area, ten scientists and other stakeholders from the district, Kampala, and Canada.

EXISTING NETWORKS FOR SCIENCE AND TECHNOLOGY DIFFUSION FOR E/NRM IN UGANDA

A number of initiatives contribute to the diffusion of technology. However, they tend to be centralized, top-down and weak, with very limited reach, especially in the study area. The existing approaches to S&T include:

The government agriculture cluster

This initiative began in colonial times and was basically set up to assure the efficient production and export of cash crops, mainly timber, coffee, cotton and tea. Later, a number of elements were added to support some indigenous food crops. This cluster now boasts ten agricultural research institutes responsible for commodities under the National Agricultural Research Organisation, plus a few District Farm Institutes for extension under the Ministry of Agriculture. Most of the institutes are performing poorly, with few scientists and much instability caused by constant internal reorganization and retrenchments, apparently related to the World Bank economic structural adjustment programme.

The cluster is still struggling to break away from its colonial past, during which most of the institutes were established in the so-called "Fertile Crescent" around Lake Victoria, where the colonial economy was centered and their priorities were focused. The rest of the country was generally reserved as a labour pool.

The services nearest to the study area are the Kachweekano District Farm Institute, which is near Kabale Town and instructs farmers, and the Kalengyere Highland Research Station, which mainly does research on Irish potatoes. These services are still far from the study area and have a negligible impact on the area. The Ministry of Agriculture has a presence in the District headquarters at Kabale. Their activities hold promise but, despite national policy statements, deployment in the field has been so disrupted by retrenchments that there is not one resident extension agent at the sub-county level in the entire study area.

The area's traditional food crops (sweet potatoes, sorghum and field peas) and cash crops (arabica coffee, bananas and now passion fruit) are not seriously on the national research agenda, and they face major challenges. With the exception of tea, which is being tried in Rutenga sub-county, no new cash crop has been established in the study area.

The NEMA cluster

The National Environment Management Authority (NEMA) is a broad governmental organization, which was established in 1994, in line with the current decentralization movement sweeping through Uganda and encouraged by the World Bank. The aim is to form a Local Environment Committee in all the sub-counties' District Councils and post District Environment Officers with the committees. The committee nearest to Central Kigezi is in Kabale Town.

The international NGO cluster

In recent years, the beautiful Kigezi region has attracted spectacular worldwide attention as the home of the endangered Mountain Gorilla. The area has high potential for developing ecotourism. Several NGOs, notably CARE, ICRAF, Africare and the World Bank-funded Mgahinga Bwindi Impenetrable Forest Conservation Trust, have arrived in force to protect the gorillas. They believe that to prevent people from encroaching and destroying the gorilla habitat, you must work with the local communities to develop alternative sustainable livelihoods. So they are involved in Sustainable Agriculture, Environment and Natural Resource Management (SANREM) and conventional community development activities in the "buffer zones" around the gorilla habitat. Their coverage is not extensive and their effectiveness is limited. They are not present in the study area, except in a small part of Rutenga sub-county.

The Museveni NRM political cluster

Since coming to power in 1986 through his National Resistance Movement, President Yoweri Kaguta Museveni has not been impressed by the processes described above (Museveni, 1997). Museveni says:

> I must talk about the environment. When we came into government, there was a Sunday School song about environmental protection. This song comprised clichés on political rallies, an occasional seminar and one energysaving stove in a biannual exhibition. I denounced this lack of seriousness and demanded an Act of Parliament to protect the environment. I was told that we could not have an Act of Parliament unless we had an environmental plan first. After wasting many years, something called Environmental Action Plan was worked out.

> Then an Act of Parliament was passed in 1995. Little action, however, has been taken ever since. In spite of my appeals, little, if anything, has been done. NEA (National Environment Management Authority) has been set up. I have, however, not been briefed on a comprehensive action plan to protect the rivers, which are brown with soil eroded from the hillsides, the lakes that are silting up with aquatic plants slowly claiming the water bodies back to the terrestrial domain, the endless burning of grasses in the dry seasons, the cutting of most precious trees, the bare hillsides, the crushing of the soil due to compaction, exposure and overstocking of animals. In this coming year, I will demand results through simple action plans that permit us to mobilise like we did against the AIDS epidemic.

> However, to save the environment, one must, first of all, solve the question of fuel wood. In Uganda, 96% of our energy comes from firewood. This means destroying 33 million cubic metres of wood per annum, equivalent to 50,000 hectares of forest. Uganda presently has only 1.3 million hectares of high tropical forest which is equivalent to 6% of the total land mass. In order to stop this destruction of wood, we need to generate 4,800 megawatts of electricity. Of course, in the short run, we could use more deliberately planted fuel wood rather than destroy our wonderful species of trees I saw during my recent trip to Buwekula and Nebbi. We talk of banishing genocide of human beings. We must also stop the genocide of plants. If we destroy the plants, the human race will be at risk.

> In pursuit of this, I expect the Prime Minister and Minister of Natural Resources to move fast not only on the second dam at Jinja, but also on two other privately

built dams at Bujagali and Kalagala. These investors come because of the good will we have created. The people responsible must expeditiously utilize this groundswell of investors' interest we have created (ibid., p. 46).

This election year (1998), Museveni moved in a simple, innocuous way that could revolutionize the way E/NRM is conducted in Uganda in the years to come. He modified the statute governing the elected local village councils, to create within them a post of Secretary for Production and Environmental Protection (PEP). By this stroke, he has mandated some 100,000 persons nationally (about 100 per sub-county) to plan, implement, monitor, regulate, and evaluate E/NRM politically in their locality on a daily basis, accountable to their neighbours who elected them. These Secretaries have been named Museveni's mini-NEMAs by the authors.

This is the single most fundamental institutional innovation to date, which could change the course of S&T diffusion for E/NRM. It puts real bottomup pressure on the technobureaucratic structures to perform and deliver, promotes and implements S&T knowledge and concepts, and integrates E/NRM science and technology culture into everyday cultural practices. Ways to work with and enhance this structure are now being explored in the study area.

SCIENCE AND TECHNOLOGY CONTENT IN THE DIFFUSION PROCESS

It has been found that the main E/NRM problems in the study area are already well understood, both by the topdown S&T structures and by community members themselves. The problems fall into four main categories:
▶ Soil erosion and land fertility decline
▶ Deforestation
▶ Drainage of wetlands
▶ Climate change

The scientists have postulated that the main causes are population pressure, land fragmentation through subdivision to distribute land to new generations, poor land management and poor choices or unavailability of appropriate technology. Peasants in the study area agree that they have contributed to environmental degradation, but claim that they have no other options for livelihood or basic survival. They want to know how to manage their relationships with the environment in a sustainable way.

The necessary and appropriate S&T interventions for better E/NRM in the study area have been catalogued by the scientists (e.g. Mbonye, Ngambeki & Tindimubona, 1997; Kabale District Nutrition Master Plan, 1996; Mutabazi, personal communication). They fall into the following clusters:

- Soil conservation and water management techniques
- Agroforestry and reafforestation
- Sustainable agriculture, increased productivity from crops
- Intensive animal husbandry

GRASSROOTS STRUCTURES FOR DIFFUSION OF SCIENCE AND TECHNOLOGY

The conventional topdown S&T diffusion paradigm in Uganda is linear: produce technologies in the government laboratory or research station and then transfer the technologies through the agricultural and E/NRM extension service or an international NGO. However, in Uganda the extension link is weak and sometimes nonexistent. This leads to complaints that research results from researchers and officials are not used and farmers and community members are neglected. The authors hypothesized that the breakdown could be rooted in the technobureaucratic S&T system's misunderstanding of the social context for information diffusion.

Most of the people in the study area, though very poor, have some schooling and can read and write, especially in the local language. More importantly, we found a great sense of social organization in the form of active local councils, associations and groups, and a culture of disciplined, open discussion which appears to have been encouraged by the present national political system of democratic, participatory, nonsectarian governance. Therefore, the communities are easy to mobilize for good and innovative causes.

We discovered a surprisingly coherent, appropriate and robust structure at the grassroots level which, if correctly approached and utilized, can diffuse S&T information. The structure is nonlinear, extensive and largely informal.

We asked community members, "What is the source of your information on good agriculture, environment and natural resource management?" Indications from analysis of 434 respondents are shown in Tables 15.1-15.4.

Table 15.1 Ranking of people's channels/sources of E/NRM knowledge and information

Rank	Channel/Source	% of Respondents
1.	Neighbours	62
2.	Local Councils	60
3.	Churches	55
4.	Radio	55
5.	Groups/Associations	41
6.	Courses	32
7.	Visits to other regions	30
8.	Extension Agents	22
9.	District Farm Institute	21
10.	NGOs	18
11.	Traders/Companies	16
12.	Experts	15
13.	Returnees	10

This survey shows that residents of the area learn, first and foremost, from local sources. In previous years, Ngambeki found the neighbours, followed by churches to be the top sources (Ngambeki, 1992). The ascendance of the Local Councils shows that the NRM's participatory model of democracy is becoming a formidable tool for sustainable development. This will improve with fine-tuning in the local councils to activate Production and Environment Protection Secretaries. It also points the way to a possible design of an effective S&T diffusion system for Sustainable Agriculture, Environment and Natural Resource Management (SANREM).

Table 15.2 People's awareness and ranking of E/NRM problems, Central Kigezi

Problem	% of Respondents
1. Soil erosion	90
2. Climate change	79
3. Deforestation	73
4. Land fertility	66
5. Drainage of wetlands	36

Table 15.3 People's awareness and ranking of solutions to problems

Solution	% of Respondents
1. Tree planting	84
2. Terracing	79
3. Crop rotation	70
4. Compost/manure	65
5. Mulching	59
6. Hinga-Raaza	57
7. Fertilizers	29
8. Irrigation	17

Table 15.4 People's educational levels

Level	% of Respondents
No education	15
Primary: Class 1-3	10
Primary: Class 4-7	47
Secondary: 8-12	20
Tertiary 13-15	8
Average years of education = 6.2 years	

FACTORS HINDERING DIFFUSION OF SCIENCE AND TECHNOLOGY FOR E/NRM

Reach

It is clear that the principal factors hindering the diffusion of S&T for E/NRM in the study area are access, coverage and fit. The top-town S&T diffusion system is simply not reaching the people it is intended to benefit.

The Validation Workshop highlighted "policy degeneration" as a major constraint which has hindered diffusion of S&T. A heated discussion between scientists and local farmers pitted the desire for colonial-type bylaws to regulate E/NRM against more consensual, participatory procedures based on local needs assessment. They reached a tentative agreement that E/NRM policies need to be revamped and modernized through closer engagement between government and the people.

Content

Most of the available technologies, developed in the national system described earlier, are actually too generic or inappropriate for the region. To be applicable, a technology must be adapted and adopted through participatory testing and even modification by the recipient to fit the actual conditions. This process has not been significantly undertaken for any of the technologies offered (Mutabazi, personal communication). This refutes the idea that there is a shelf full of technologies ready to be implemented by Uganda's subsistence farmers. The shelf is practically empty, and much work is still to be done to make generic technologies applicable to specific situations and regions.

POSSIBILITIES FOR SCIENCE AND TECHNOLOGY DISSEMINATION

Scientists agree that most of the available technologies can be simplified to fit the needs of the people of the study area. These people have enough education and literacy (particularly in the local language) to absorb and understand new S&T concepts, practices and techniques. In the participatory rural appraisals, we even initiated some obvious interventions immediately (e.g. rehabilitation of terrace technology, coffee nurseries and composting). The authors also taught them to lobby government to appoint an extension officer to their sub-counties. The peasants are innovative, receptive and eager to learn new ways of improving their E/NRM, because they want to avoid a major ecological disaster that threatens them with massive food insecurity, migration or starvation.

There is some evidence of attempts to improve the E/NRM in the study area by S&T, but not in any sustained way. New crops and practices have been introduced, then abandoned in mid-cycle, to the detriment of the residents – who begin working on an initiative (e.g, a new disease prevention technique) which collapses when the experts who started the whole project leave. Work undertaken with Irish potatoes, wheat, coffee, passion fruit, donkeys and tree planting shows signs of faltering.

Technologies are still primitive: people use the backbreaking hand hoe and machete, haul materials manually and use fire to clear land. We found little evidence of mechanization, animal traction, irrigation, fertilization or improved seeds. But we learnt that these improvements had been started in the area before Uganda's socio-political breakdown. For example, one part of the area had a coffee processing plant, draught animals and government subsidies for agriculture. Some progressive farmers were on the verge of buying cars. This shows that it is possible to rehabilitate the area, if there is a will to do so.

The smallholders have a lot of good traditional knowledge, attitudes and practices, and they are amenable to modernization. They are hardworking, innovative and willing to try new things. But they need to be updated, through demonstration and practice, on matters such as introducing and handling new seeds as older ones degenerate, soil and water management techniques, land use planning, choice of technology and other activities. The top field scientist in our group (Dr. Ngambeki) indicated that some of these issues are still being taught and debated at university level, and several of the scientists and extension workers in the field were eager to update themselves in these areas! How much more then, is the need of the smallholder farmer?

The residents find it difficult to relate to the government S&T extension agents, based on long experience with repressive government activities. The international NGOs face similar problems, as they are perceived as paternalistic, with money to spend but no practical familiarity with local problems. This perception is exacerbated when the NGOs hire expatriates with expensive lifestyles (4WD vehicles, fancy houses and offices in towns). They also have a tendency to promote foreign S&T solutions. For example, they have not adequately explored the use of indigenous trees in agroforestry and they have neglected research and development on the region's traditional crops, which would support people's food security.

The last constraint — which is fundamental — is the poor infrastructure of the remote study area, making the diffusion of S&T almost impossible. The researchers were unable to reach a PRA site when the alleged road to the village disappeared suddenly. The chagrined residents sent a delegation to Dr. Ngambeki at midnight to plead for a visit. We found a few efforts towards solving infrastructure problems in the study area, mainly undertaken by CARE and a tea company, but the challenge is still daunting. Africare is in nearby areas and could possibly be enticed to cover the study area.

The key factor for S&T diffusion in SANREM is engagement. Engagement can be achieved mainly through committed private volunteer organizations which help the community, not necessarily for permanent salaried jobs, but through facilitation. The communities need catalysts that bring together all the S&T diffusion forces and make the whole system work.

CONCLUSION

The findings indicate a jigsaw puzzle with two pieces which are too far apart and seem unlikely to fit well for S&T diffusion in the study area (Figure 15.1).

Our main strategic recommendation is the design and creation, in the study area, of a complementary set of initiatives and institutional innovations that will bring together top-down and grassroots elements necessary to improve S&T diffusion for E/NRM (Figure 15.2).

Figure 15.1 Existing S&T diffusion system for E/NRM in Central Kigezi

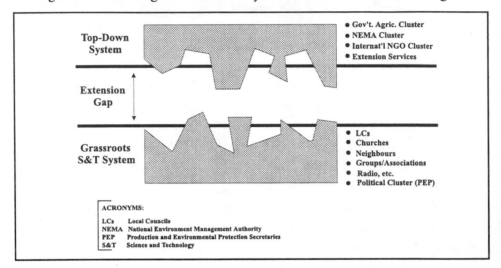

Figure 15.2 Proposed S&T diffusion system with linkage innovations

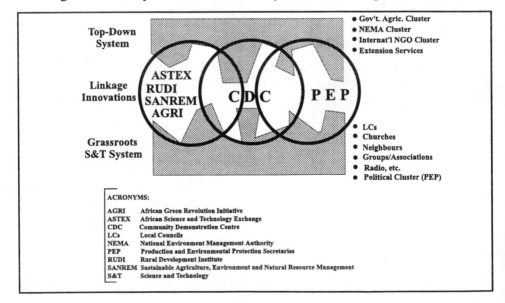

Emerging elements of such a structure include:

- The creation of a Rural Development Institute (RUDI) in the study area with SANREM and AGRI programs as the dynamic catalyst that integrates initiatives in the region. The Institute would bring in new ideas, and combine personnel and activities in a way that keeps the structure fresh and vigorous. The Institute would act as an effective **intermediary agency**, not only in technical and financial matters, but also politically, in the sense of providing an **independent mediator** between the government agencies and the grassroots which are often in an adversarial relationship. This mediation is crucial for enabling consensus to emerge and charting a way forward.

- Community Demonstration Centres to be created by the local communities in each sub-county of the study area. These will operate as local laboratories and showcases for best practices, technologies and innovations, where extension agents, researchers, RUDI Fellows, and model farmers all work and learn together.

- Production and Environmental Protection Secretaries: These local mini-NEMAs, working with RUDI and CDC, will help to plan, prioritize, monitor, lobby and promote S&T expertise and diffuse it to every villager.

- Kigezi Income Generating Association (KIGA), a grassroots association to be set up under the technical assistance and strategic planning of ASTEX, as recommended in the Validation Workshop.

- Rural Planning and Development Initiative: The study area is at once a typical and possibly worst-case example of the problems of a much larger area, the fragile mountain ecosystem of Kigezi. This particular ecosystem needs special attention, as the UNCED itself has noted (UNCED, 1992). In this area, we have proposed a major international Rural Planning and Development (RPD) initiative on the level of world-renowned efforts such as the Tennessee Valley Authority, encompassing all aspects of deliberate and planned science-led rural development. Its main aim is sustainable modernization and rural transformation.

- There are strong hints that a broader, one-day **stakeholder's workshop** should be held in Kampala to disseminate the results of our initiative nationally, with possibility of replication in other regions of Uganda and possibly attracting support towards implementation of interventions already identified. This is in keeping with the current national dynamic atmosphere of wanting to modernize the country as fast as possible.

▶ **Request for government experts in the study area**: Soon after the Validation Workshop, the researchers learned that the Uganda government, in its drive for modernization, is pursuing a new innovation of posting university graduates in agriculture, veterinary science, environment and human medicine at every sub-county. The researchers quickly wrote to the Minister of Public Service, asking that our study area be among the first sub-counties to benefit from this nationwide initiative.

These recommendations were fully discussed and endorsed at the Validation Workshop.

REFERENCES

Board on Science and Technology for International Development (BOSTID). 1984: *Diffusion of Biomass Energy Technologies in Development Countries*. Washington: National Academy Press.

Durant, J.R., Evans, G.A. and Thomas, G.P. 1989: The public understanding of science. *Nature* 340, 11.

Kabale District. 1997: *Kabale District Plan of Action for Nutrition*. Incorporating J.K. Kakitahi and A.N. Kalule Sewali (1997): Kabale District Level Preparation of Action Plans for Nutrition. Technical paper. Food and Agriculture Organization.

Mbonye, A.M., Ngambeki, D.S. and Tindimubona, A.R. 1997: *Fuelwood energy demand and supply in a fragile mountain ecosystem*. ASTEX Working Papers No. 3. Kampala: ASTEX.

Museveni, Y.K. 1986: *Selected Articles on the Uganda Resistance War*. Kampala: NRM Publications.

Museveni, Y.K. 1997: Museveni spells out agenda for parliament. Speech to open the second session of the 6th Parliament of Uganda, Monday April 28 1997. *New Vision*, Thursday May 1, 1997, 446.

Mutabazi, S. 1997: *Annex I. Inventory of Available Technologies from Research*. Personal communication.

Ngambeki, D.S. *et. al.* 1992: *Coffeebased farming systems baseline study in Uganda, 1992*. Report to Farming Systems Support Program, Ministry of Agriculture, Animal Industry and Fisheries, Entebbe, Uganda.

Tindimubona, A.R. 1993: Establishment of a Science Culture in Africa. *Science and Public Policy*, 20, 40, 245.

Tindimubona, A.R. 1996: *A Consolidated Methodology for Assessment of the Quality and Range of Science and Technology Capacity in African Countries.* Consultancy report prepared for the World Bank African Capacity Building Foundation, Harare, Zimbabwe.

Uganda. 1994: *The State of the Environment Report for Uganda, 1994.* Kampala: Ministry of Natural Resources, National Environment Information Centre.

Uganda. 1996: *Draft Medium Term Agricultural Sector Modernization Plan 1996-2001.* Kampala: Ministry of Planning and Economic Development.

Chapter 16

PLANNING WITH NATURE AND MANAGING DROUGHT IN MOZAMBIQUE

by Kevin Head

INTRODUCTION

Drought[1] is a serious problem with many consequences. It causes crops to fail, families to starve and can aggravate tense political situations. Many developing countries have become trapped into relying on emergency relief measures to feed, clothe and house their people when seasonal rains fail. Access to water is even considered to be a potential source of conflict in the coming decade. Furthermore, recurring drought reduces the stability of ecosystems (Ellis, 1994) which affects human development needs.

The adverse effects of drought may become worse in coming years. According to a World Bank Report on sustainable development in sub-Saharan Africa (1995), "Climatic variability appears to be increasing in a number of areas particularly dependent on rain fed agriculture....The production systems and the economies as a whole in these areas are becoming less resistant to this variability."

Mozambique has been exposed to three devastating droughts since the early 1980s, including "the worst drought in living memory" in 1992 (WFP, 1995) and what was commonly called "the drought of the century" in 1982-83. Not only is drought a common occurrence in Mozambique, it has a severe impact on the population. During the drought of 1992, Mozambique received over one hundred million dollars of aid from the World Food Programme (WFP) alone, and "3.9 million Mozambicans...were saved from starvation" (WFP, 1996).

Drought is a recurring feature of Mozambique's climate and has serious impacts which are, in general, much greater and more severe than in other, more developed countries. Drought impacts the economy, the environment and society in Mozambique. A few of these impacts are summarized in Table 16.1:

Table 16.1 Drought's impact on the economy, environment and society

Economy	Environment	Society
▸ Loss from production ▸ Income loss for farmers ▸ Decline in food production and supply (increases in prices and imports) ▸ Revenue loss to government ▸ Cost of water transportation or transfer and new or supplemental water resources	▸ Increased incidence of fire ▸ Damage to plants and animals ▸ Decrease in air quality (dust) ▸ Decreased carrying capacity of grazing lands	▸ Food shortages ▸ Loss of human life ▸ Conflicts of water use ▸ Poorer living conditions, increase in poverty ▸ Population migration to urban centres

(adapted from Wilhite, 1993a)

It is difficult to differentiate between the effects of drought and those of war[2] in Mozambique – and even more difficult to determine how much suffering or loss of life has been caused by each, and how much relief has been provided as a result. It is clear that Mozambique is a poverty-stricken nation with a fragile and vulnerable population. From 1988 to 1996, Mozambique was listed as the world's poorest country, with a GNP per capita ranging from $60 to $100 per year (World Bank, 1996). Other development indicators are equally low.

Mozambique's population has low resistance to high variability, and the country has limited capacity and resources to deal with problems such as drought. This is a result of the country's history of colonialism and the years of war that followed. Today the country is experiencing rapid political and social change. Mozambique needs a drought management strategy which makes the most of scarce capital resources, can be supported by a weak institutional framework and is effective at mitigating the consequences of drought. In other words, what is needed is an adaptive, holistic approach to drought management.

CRISIS MANAGEMENT AND RISK MANAGEMENT OF DROUGHT

Living successfully with risks, such as those associated with drought, involves assessing risk and making decisions about how to live within the risk. In 1983, the US National Academy of Sciences developed a model for assessing and managing risk (Baker, 1996). It defines the components of risk assessment and risk management, and how the two are related (see Figure 16.1). If risks are not managed properly, a crisis situation often develops.

Figure 16.1 Risk assessment and risk management

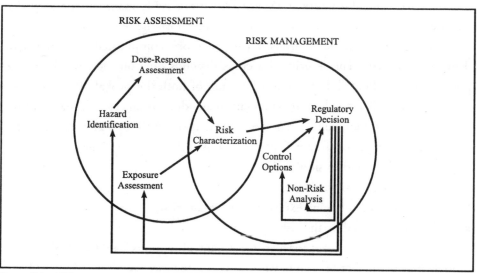

Source: Baker, 1996

Strategies for managing drought can vary, depending on the geographic scale and the number of people affected. Strategies can usually be grouped as:

▶ **Crisis management** strategy deals with the problem once it occurs.

▶ **Risk management** seeks to reduce the exposure to risk faced by people, communities or countries, through anticipatory and preventative measures.

In the eyes of the donor community, crisis management – Mozambique's present drought management strategy – is a fast and easy way of dealing with the impacts of drought. However, it tends to be more expensive, less efficient and less sustainable than risk management strategies. For example, in the United States, California Congressman George E. Brown suggested in 1989 that by diverting 0.1% of US drought relief funds (approximately half a million dollars) to risk management programmes, tens to hundreds of millions of dollars would be saved (Wilhite, 1993b).

While crisis management offers effective and immediate relief, and is sometimes the only option, it can lead to a loss of indigenous knowledge of risk management strategies. During a drought in the 1960s, a tribe in the central highlands of New Guinea was declared to be suffering from drought. They suddenly became eligible for food aid. Traditional ways of coping with recurring drought, developed over generations, were soon lost because they were no longer needed (Comeau, 1996). Thus, a system of crisis management, delivering food aid in times of need, replaced a sustainable risk management system of adapting agricultural practices to drought conditions. In this situation, crisis management helped to "un-develop" a community through short-term, short-sighted assistance.

Managing the risks of drought can be more complicated than managing drought as a crisis. The severity of a crisis depends only on the hazard an event poses to those affected, but risk is a function of both the probability of an event occurring, as well as the hazard. There are many dimensions to risk, such as time, geography, economics, culture, choice, as well as other factors. How these factors are perceived and prioritized will affect the way different groups view similar risks, and how they respond to similar risks.

Risk involves two elements:

▶ the probability of being exposed to a certain risk;
▶ the hazard posed by the risk.

Risk management approaches (or "control options" in the USNAS risk model) may be further broken down into two categories:

▶ those that reduce risk by adapting livelihood strategies to fit into natural variability such as drought;
▶ those that reduce risk by adapting nature to suit human needs.

During periods of extended drought, the latter must resort to crisis management (food aid) while the former need only do so in a worst-case scenario, or when poor choices have been made in selecting livelihood strategies (see Figure

Figure 16.2 Risk management and crisis management of drought

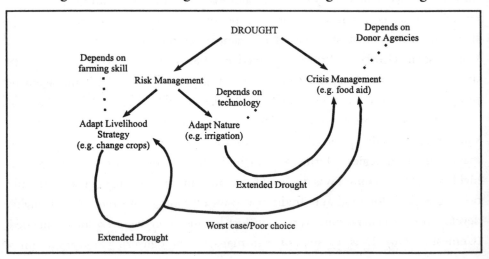

16.2). Risk management is frequently used in farming in industrialized countries. American farmers employ risk management strategies which include diversification, buying insurance, leasing land, spreading sales throughout the year, contract sales and hedging (Harwood, Heifner, Coble & Perry, 1996).

Crisis management is a stop-gap measure, while reducing risk through adapting livelihood strategies is sustainable development. For practical, political and economic reasons — stemming from the almost constant state of war from 1964 to 1992 — drought management in Mozambique has followed the crisis management approach in recent decades.

This is less than satisfactory for a number of reasons. It is not a sustainable way of managing drought, as it ignores environmental factors which have major impacts on society and the economy. Secondly, it is not feasible or, at the very least, not cost-effective to manage drought this way in a country which has very little infrastructure in terms of roads, railways, ports and communications, and has a very dispersed, rural population. Finally, it is not holistic, in that it only looks at the problem from one aspect, for example the shortage of food in a given area during a drought year. Thus, in order to successfully plan for and manage drought in Mozambique, a risk management approach must be adopted.

There is room for improvement in managing the risks of drought in Mozambique in two key areas:

- **Drought prediction**, as evidence suggests that El Niño/southern oscillation (ENSO) teleconnections may be used to make seasonal forecasts.
- **Improved drought management strategy**, based on risk management of drought.

If the government of Mozambique is to use these tools in planning for and managing the effects of drought, functioning institutions are needed, requiring a methodological approach for assessing Mozambique's capacity to manage drought.

Predicting drought

In recent years, there has been significant interest in investigating "linkages over great distances of seemingly disconnected weather anomalies" (Glantz, 1991), otherwise known as climatic teleconnections. Most of this interest centres around the El Niño/southern oscillation (ENSO) phenomenon, which is regarded as the most important representative of climatic teleconnections (Latif, Serl, Maier-Reimer & Jugne, 1992). ENSO teleconnections have been used successfully in agricultural planning, most notably in Peru and Brazil (NOAA, 1994). In these regions, El Niño has become a widely recognized and respected weather event, with newspaper headlines such as "El Niño causa seca, tempestade e destruição" ("El Niño causes drought, storms and destruction", 21 August, 1997, São Paulo, Brazil) published at the onset of an anticipated major El Niño event. The combined cost of flooding, hurricanes, droughts and fires attributed to the 1982-83 El Niño amounted to some US$8 110 000 000 (UCAR, 1994).

While El Niño and the southern oscillation are intimately linked, they are not synonymous. El Niño is distinguished by anomalously warm surface water in the entire tropical Pacific for about one year (Rasmusson & Carpenter, 1982), while the southern oscillation is "a coherent pattern of pressure, temperature and rainfall fluctuations [whose] primary manifestation is a seesaw in atmospheric pressure at sea level between the southeast Pacific subtropical high and the region of low pressure stretching across the Indian Ocean from Africa to northern Australia" (Rasmusson and Wallace, 1983). An ENSO event (associated with El Niño, a positive Sea Surface Temperature (SST) anomaly, a negative Southern Oscillation Index (SOI) and the low index phase of the southern oscillation) can be considered to occur when the following conditions are satisfied:

▶ the SST of the eastern equatorial Pacific is anomalously positive for at least three seasons;
▶ at least one of these seasons has a SST anomaly of $+0.5°C$;
▶ the SOI remains below -1.0 for the same three seasons (Kiladis & Diaz, 1989). La Niña, the name often given to the years when there is no El Niño, generally has the opposite characteristics.

The state of the southern oscillation can be quantified by the southern oscillation index (SOI), which is the standardized difference of surface pressure in Tahiti and Darwin, Australia. The SOI has been recorded since 1876 and is generally deemed to be the most useful way to measure ENSO (Ropelewski & Jones, 1987). A negative SOI is associated with an ENSO event, and signifies a fall in pressure over Tahiti, a rise in pressure over Darwin and a reversal of trade winds from easterlies to westerlies.

It is widely agreed that there is a climatic teleconnection between ENSO and rainfall variability in southern Africa. Specifically, below-average rainfall is found during low-index southern oscillation years, and (perhaps to a lesser extent) above-average rainfall is found during high-index years. Furthermore, temperatures in southern Africa are found to be influenced by ENSO. Higher than normal temperatures are found in low-index years and below average temperatures are found in high-index years. ENSO can be predicted up to one year in advance.

There is significant evidence that precipitation in Mozambique specifically is influenced by ENSO. This evidence comes from both global and regional studies of ENSO teleconnections (Trenberth in Glantz, Katz & Nichols, 1991; Matarira, 1990; Cane, Eshel & Buckland, 1994; Lindesay, 1988; Lindesay & Vogel, 1990; Matarira & Unganai, 1995; Jury, 1995; Jury, Pathack, Rautenbach & VanHeerden, 1996).

At least two seasonal forecast models have been developed for southern Africa, for which results are readily available. One has been developed by Dr. Mark Jury of the University of Zululand (who has developed many such models for different regions of homogeneous rainfall). The other has been developed by the United Nations Development Program (UNDP) and World Meteorology Organization (WMO), and run at the Drought Monitoring Centres in Nairobi, Kenya and Harare, Zimbabwe. Both use skill-tested[3] multi-variate models to provide monthly and seasonal forecasts of factors such as rainfall, temperature, maize yield, sugar cane yield, fish harvests and malaria incidence. However, only one of the models provides forecasts for Mozambique specifically, and only for the southernmost part of the country.

A link between ENSO and rainfall variability in Mozambique was established by comparing the country's historical records of rainfall data and the SOI for a 31-year period. A network of 58 stations was divided into seven different regions, based on climate classification (Atlas Geográfico, 1986) and estimates of the influence of the Inter-Tropical Convergence Zone (ITCZ) on seasonal rainfall (Rojas, 1997). Seasonal totals of rainfall data for the seven regions were then compared to the SOI. A significant relationship was found between ENSO and rainfall in parts of Mozambique. Little or no relationship between ENSO activity and rainfall anomalies was found in the northern part of the country (where the ITCZ plays a major role in seasonal rainfall). However, positive correlations exist between ENSO and rainfall anomalies in the southern part of the country, as well as parts of Tete province. Furthermore, if only years when ENSO is in an extreme state (for the purposes of this research, when the SOI is greater or less than + or - 0.5 SD) are considered (13 cases over 31 years), then the relationship between rainfall variability and the SOI increases significantly, implying an exponential relationship.

While this study did not find a strong enough relationship to accurately predict how much rain would fall in a coming rainy season, it can be said with as high as 85% certainty whether rainfall will be above or below average in certain regions.

Pearson's R was calculated for regions where ENSO teleconnection appeared strongest. Values for the southern part of the country are as high as 0.58, although they tended to be closer to 0.30 to 0.40 in general. This means that ENSO is responsible for, at most, a third of the variation in inter-seasonal rainfall in Mozambique. As population data was used, no confidence levels are needed.

Drought management strategies

The severe droughts of the 1980s and 1990s in southern Africa have sparked interest in better ways to manage recurring drought. There is no way to prevent drought, but there are many strategies for off-setting the impacts associated with drought. While conventional, modern drought management strategies, plans or policies have many benefits, they also have serious drawbacks, such as those described earlier in this chapter. From an agro-ecosystem perspective, it is argued that modern agriculture practices have sacrificed equitability, sustainability and stability in favour of productivity[4], making it more difficult to plan for and manage drought, especially in the context of Mozambique. Thus, in examining the problem of how to improve modern drought management strategies, we must look at improving the stability, sustainability and equitability of agro-ecosystems, while maintaining or even increasing present productivity levels.

Holistic resource management

We must also take into consideration that agro-ecosystems exist in the full context of a social, economic, environmental and political world. Holistic Resource Management (HRM) (Savory, 1988) is an approach which stresses the importance of examining problems in their entire context, and could serve as the basis for developing an adaptive, holistic, risk management strategy for managing drought in Mozambique.

In using Savory's HRM model, a three-part goal must be set by those affected by drought and those involved in drought management (Savory, 1988). The three parts and their definitions in this context are:

▶ **a statement on quality of life**: Quality of life is the ability of a family or community to meet its basic and felt needs.
▶ **a system of production which will achieve the quality of life sought**: The means of production is, in most cases, subsistence farming of livestock and crops, with some supplement from off-farm activities such as hunting, gathering and wage labour.

- **a statement of how the landscape will support the mode of production in the long term**: As the means of production relies heavily on natural ecosystems, it is essential for the natural landscape to maintain a relatively constant level of production. In other words, environmental degradation, or desertification, would be extremely detrimental to subsistence farming, and hence to quality of life.

HRM is centred around four "ecosystem foundation blocks":

- succession
- the water cycle
- the mineral cycle
- energy flow

The state and behaviour of these foundation blocks, along with certain guidelines and available tools, determine how the system in question is to be managed. While very little information was available upon which to base either the direction or feasibility of this type of drought management strategy, some conjectures can be made which may be useful in directing possible further research.

In the context of drought management in Mozambique, the mineral cycle and energy flow are relatively fixed and are not affected by drought as much as the other two blocks. The mineral cycle is linked to succession through the slash-and-burn agriculture widely practised in Mozambique. When a *machamba* (plot of land) loses its fertility, a farmer will abandon it for fresh soil. While there could be improvements in building soil, such as composting, this system seems to meet most farmers' needs, as long as there is enough land. The situation is similar for energy flows.

The water cycle, however, can be extremely variable. For example, given a mean seasonal rainfall of 494.37 mm and a standard deviation of 147.09 (as is the case for much of Inhambane province), it would not be unusual to have a seasonal total in the range of about 200 mm to 800 mm. Such variability is very difficult to manage, given Mozambique's economic, technical and social constraints.

Succession occurs as part of nature. While it is an extremely complex process, certain aspects of succession can be manipulated through human intervention for human benefit. Crop rotation is an example of managed succession. Given that drought may be predicted in certain regions which have highly variable rainfall, succession could take on a new form, using ENSO signals to predict what crop will fare best in an upcoming season. The other "ecosystem blocks", especially the water cycle, should not be discounted as possibilities for drought management. In the future, they may prove to be an effective way of managing the risks of drought in Mozambique, and would compliment succession management.

The HRM model continues by using tools and defining guidelines for achieving the three-part goal. There is little point in discussing these in general terms, as they will vary from community to community, and will depend on factors such as culture and wealth.

A complementary concept to HRM is agro-ecosystem theory, which could be used to assess the success of HRM in drought management. Agro-ecosystem theory is useful in this case because it links the holistic point of view to a manageable and quantifiable level. Agro-ecosystems are also the basis of most livelihoods in Mozambique, especially in rural areas where roughly 80% of the population lives, and most of these people rely on subsistence agriculture. Even in urban areas, most families have a *machamba* (plot of land) to supplement wage earnings. If Savory's HRM model is to be used in managing drought, the agro-ecosystem is the basic unit that farmers or planners will be managing.

Conway (1991), defines agro-ecosystems as "ecological and socio-economic systems, comprising domesticated plants and/or animals and the people who husband them, intended for the purpose of producing food, fibre or other agricultural products". Mozambican agro-ecosystems are variable, but usually have semi-controlled conditions within defined boundaries. Competition from weeds, pests and disease is reduced within the agro-ecosystem, while nutrients, seeds, water and other beneficial components are "subsidized" by human intervention on a variety of scales.

The state of an agro-ecosystem can be measured through four properties (Conway, 1991):

▶ **Productivity** measures "the output of valued product per unit of resource input", and can be quantified in terms of nutritive value, caloric value, market value, yield or some other measure.

▶ **Stability** measures "the constancy of productivity in the face of small disturbing forces arising from the normal fluctuations and cycles surrounding the environment", such as a dry spell or insect infestation.

▶ **Sustainability** measures "the ability of the agro-ecosystem to maintain productivity when subject to a major disturbing force", such as a prolonged drought, and can be measured in terms of inertia, elasticity, amplitude, hysteresis and malleability. Any change as a result of a disturbing force is termed a strain, and can be elastic (e.g. temporary slow growth) or plastic (e.g. stunting or death).

▸ **Equitability** is "the evenness of distribution of the productivity of the agro-ecosystem among the human beneficiaries".

From these definitions, it can be seen that productivity is the main objective of most agro-ecosystem management strategies. This is in agreement with the HRM model, which includes production as one component of the three-part goal. The other three properties of agro-ecosystems are all measured relative to productivity, either in its maintenance or distribution. It has been argued that productivity should be increased as much as possible, as this raises the "social value" of an agro-ecosystem, which is its primary goal (Conway, 1991). However, in altering one property there are trade-offs with the others, as the four properties are linked. Because all properties are desirable, choices must be made as to which to focus on. These choices must take into account external variables such as climate, local economy and human knowledge. This reinforces the idea that agro-ecosystems are indeed ecological systems, albeit modified by humans.

Using these criteria to measure agro-ecosystems using current drought management practices against those using proposed drought management practices, it could be determined which are more suitable for managing drought in Mozambique. It is anticipated that by planning with nature – using a holistic and adaptive drought management strategy – the productivity, stability and sustainability of Mozambique's agro-ecosystems will be increased in the long term, in part through increasing diversity (ie, by managing succession). As a result, equitability may increase as well.

INSTITUTIONAL CAPACITY TO MANAGE DROUGHT

In order to assess and manage the risks of drought – that is, in order to plan for drought – functioning institutions are needed. What is required of institutions will depend on how drought is being assessed and managed, as well as the economic, social, educational, technical and other capacities of the country. This study assumes that managing drought risks – or planning with nature – will allow for more effective drought management and drought impact mitigation.

If drought prediction and a holistic drought management strategy are the tools to be used, then the questions are: how can a country such as Mozambique plan for drought, what institutions will be required and what is required of them?

Effective drought management is an "essential first step toward a reduction of social vulnerability" (Wilhite, 1993b) and has been called "an essential action" (Frederiksen, 1992). Crisis management of drought (and other natural disasters), a common strategy in the era of modern planning, has in many cases proven to be less than effective in reducing social vulnerability to drought (Comeau, 1996).

Drought planning requires input from several disciplines, and the process may face many constraints, including:

▶ institutional, political, budgetary and human resource constraints;
▶ a lack of understanding of drought;
▶ a lack of communication and cooperation between scientists and policy-makers;
▶ financial and technical constraints (Wilhite, 1993b).

This study revealed a variety of constraints hindering Mozambique's ability to plan for and manage drought effectively. Virtually every person interviewed cited insufficient budgets and a lack of resources, most notably transportation and communication, as the main constraints in their respective fields. Other constraints include technological limitations (such as communications technology), insufficient databases, directors (often the only people with advanced degrees) tied down by bureaucracy, and a lack of staff motivation.

After many years of drought and war in Mozambique, there is a very good understanding of drought and its consequences. The institutional capacity to respond to drought emergencies is fairly strong. However, effective management is hampered by the above-mentioned constraints.

Drought response relies heavily on international aid. International aid agencies are increasingly being staffed by Mozambican nationals rather than foreigners, which indicates that the country's institutional capacity for managing an emergency response is increasing.

Mozambique's long history of dealing with drought exclusively as an emergency must be considered in discussing drought management from an institutional perspective. Drought repeatedly exacerbated the war years, when starvation was occasionally used as a tool of mass destruction (Hanlon, 1986). In this situation, crisis management is the only possible response to drought. There is now a marked shift towards preparing for drought, recognizing that it is a recurring feature of the Mozambican climate. However, most current drought alleviation measures, as well as planning for imminent drought, are geared towards being better prepared to combat drought once it arrives – rather than altering agricultural (or other) practices to adapt to the drought cycle or adopting a risk management approach.

Incidentally, this move towards preparedness is mainly driven by a desire to reduce the cost of emergency response measures. It can be categorized as pro-active crisis management of drought rather than risk management, because it reduces only the individual's risk, and not the nation's risk. In a true risk management approach, the risk to both would be reduced.

Mozambique has many barriers to successful drought management. Most stem from the country's many years of war and a general lack of funds. Despite these constraints, there is a working organizational structure to manage drought crises. There are also the beginnings of a structure to deal with drought on a risk management basis. Both structures rely heavily on aid from the international donor community, yet they are still under-staffed, under-equipped and under-funded – and, on their own, would have great difficulty accomplishing what is required.

The benefits of planning for drought will likely outweigh the costs. The cost of being prepared is fixed and constant, while the costs of drought are uncertain and occur at some future date (Wilhite, 1993b). Furthermore, as droughts affect virtually all facets of life – economics, society and the environment – many costs are likely to occur within a short period of time.

The development of a successful drought policy or plan must incorporate all levels of government, with internal support, institutional support and support from high-ranking officials.

To facilitate the development of a drought policy and a drought management plan, Donald Wilhite proposes a "generic ten-step methodology" (Wilhite, 1993b) which can be adapted to different contexts. Wilhite's approach is slightly more comprehensive and uses different terminology, but includes all the basic steps of Frederiksen's (1992) seven-point list of preparing a general drought management plan. Wilhite's approach appears more useful in assessing Mozambique's capacity to manage drought. Wilhite advocates managing drought through the following ten steps:

- Appointment of a National Drought Commission (NDC).
- Statement of drought policy and planning objectives.
- Resolving conflict between environmental and economic sectors.
- Inventory of natural, biological and human resources, and financial and legal constraints.
- Development of the drought plan.
- Identification of research needs and institutional gaps.

- Synthesis of scientific and policy issues.
- Implementation of the drought plan.
- Development of multi-level education and training programs.
- Development of drought plan evaluation procedures (Wilhite, 1993b).

While there are many gaps and barriers to drought management in Mozambique, this study has found that the country has the institutions needed to use Wilhite's approach. Table 16.2 summarizes what institutions exist and are lacking in relation to Wilhite's ten-step approach.

Table 16.2 Summary of institutional capacity to manage drought

Step	What Exists	What is Lacking	Recommendations
1. Drought	Dept. for the Prevention & Control of Natural Disasters (DPCCN) responsible for emergency action; Coordinating Min. for Environmental Action (MICOA) heads body which is responsible for more pro-active planning.	No drought commission *per se*.	The two bodies should be integrated or linked to some degree to ensure full cooperation and collaboration.
2. Statement of drought policy	Policy on natural disasters in the process of being ratified.	At present there is no policy on drought.	Once the policy has been ratified it must be evaluated against certain criteria.
3. Conflicts between environment and economy	There are some advocates of the environment.	No laws protecting the environment; little concept of environmental protection.	At present this is not a pressing issue although since there are no laws it may become one in the future.
4. Inventory of resources and constraints	Preliminary list has been compiled through this research.	Not yet been done comprehensively.	An inventory should be made before drought policies and plans are developed.
5. Development of the drought plan	Various components exist, such as organizations and available resources.	There is no drought plan.	As with step one, organizations should be integrated or linked to some degree to ensure full cooperation, collaboration and the full use of resources.
6. Identification of research needs and institutional gaps	Many research needs, and many of them are known.	Little research being done; many institutional gaps.	Donor agencies should assist in funding research and closing institutional gaps.
7. Synthesis of science and policy issues	Good synthesis of science and policy.	Response by policy makers to new ideas can be slow.	A conscientious effort should be made to maintain a good synthesis. A working group could be established to review new ideas and technology and to make recommendations to policy makers.
8. Implementation of drought plan		No drought plan to implement.	
9. Multilevel education and training programs	Extension programs exist and there are plans for more.	Extension programs severely hindered by shortage of funds.	Donor agencies should help fund extension and education programs.
10. Evaluation procedures	Impacts of drought and response to drought are evaluated.	No evaluation of any other aspect of drought management.	Other aspects of evaluation should be strengthened with the aid of donor agencies or consultants.

While Wilhite's ten-step approach is a useful tool to help a country prepare for drought and analyze its state of preparedness by stating what institutions are needed, it does not question what is required of institutions. The approach seems to make the assumption that the institutions are in place, function normally and have the capacity to fulfill their respective roles. This is not always the case, especially in poorer countries such as Mozambique. This is a serious gap because if institutions cannot provide information or services, or develop, implement and enforce policy, then the approach will fail.

Institutional requirements can be separated into two groups (see Table 16.3): those pertaining to the people working in the institutions, and the mechanisms of the institutions themselves. Some can be placed into both groups.

Table 16.3 Institutional requirements of drought management in Mozambique

People	Mechanisms
▶ interdisciplinary understanding of the problem	▶ communication
▶ technical knowledge	▶ organizational and decision making structures
▶ understanding of policy	▶ linkages to relevant organizations or institutions
▶ understanding of potential solutions	
▶ ability of various institutions to participate	▶ ability of various institutions to participate
▶ conflict resolution skills	▶ funding
▶ impartiality	▶ ability to manage information
▶ ability to conduct research (gather, analyze and disseminate information objectively)	▶ coordination between organizations or institutions
▶ ability to manage information	▶ defined hierarchy
▶ management skills	▶ transportation
▶ understanding of responsibilities and actions required	
▶ extension/training skills	
▶ evaluation skills	

This study has found that in Mozambique, many of the "people requirements" for managing drought are either lacking completely or there are so few people to fill a certain role that institutions cannot function effectively. The key informant interviews revealed that the people requirements most often found lacking are:

▶ an interdisciplinary understanding of the problem;

▶ an understanding of potential solutions;

▶ extension/training skills.

The first two could be addressed through a workshop on the risk management of drought and other facets of drought management. As drought is a problem of great concern in neighbouring countries in southern Africa, the workshop should include these countries. The third could be addressed through training courses or funding to hire more extension workers.

Most "mechanism requirements" were found to be lacking as well, and the existing mechanisms were often over-taxed. Those found to be most lacking are:

▶ communication

▶ funding

▶ coordination between organizations or institutions (ie, defining roles of various departments or institutions).

The first requires investment in communication infrastructure such as telephones, fax machines and the internet, as well as a culture of open communication. The second requires either more efficient institutions or increased funding from the government or the donor community. The third requires a government task force or consultancy team to establish how such coordination should work.

In order for Mozambican institutions to function properly and for seasonal forecasting and drought management to be successful, these shortcomings must be addressed. Much work remains to be done by both Mozambique and the international community. However, the foundations of both crisis management and risk management of drought are in place in Mozambique, and await further development.

AREAS FOR FURTHER RESEARCH

This study has established that seasonal forecasting of precipitation is possible in parts of Mozambique, has explored an adaptive, holistic method of managing the effects of drought and assessed Mozambique's institutional capacity to plan for and manage drought. There is room for improvement in all these areas.

The accuracy of seasonal forecasting in Mozambique could be significantly improved with research in the following areas:

▶ Principal component analysis should be used to regionalize Mozambique's rainfall.

▶ As previously mentioned, a high correlation coefficient was obtained between seasonal precipitation and maize yields in Zimbabwe, and eastern equatorial sea surface temperatures. A study along these lines should be undertaken in Mozambique.

- Climate data at INAM should be re-organized, properly archived and entered into a database.
- To increase the accuracy of long-range forecasting, factors other than ENSO activity must be examined, such as the zonal and meridional strength of the ITCZ, strength of the Atlantic and Indian Ocean anticyclones, and sea surface temperatures of the Mozambique channel. The relationship of these variables to temperature and precipitation should be considered.

Taking an holistic, adaptive approach to drought management presents many research opportunities. First and foremost among these is research into Mozambican subsistence farming systems, including what farmers do, what they want, and how their livelihood systems can be improved. Much information is needed in this area for a successful risk management approach to drought management. Some potential starting points for this research include:

- Researching traditional strategies of coping with drought.
- Researching appropriate farming strategies for specific regions.
- Making an inventory of strategies and resources available in times of drought, how these are affected by drought, and their impact on the environment.
- Establishing permanent test plots at the village level to compare the relative success of traditional practices, current practices and expert advice (ie, that given by the FAO or the Ministry of Agriculture).
- Using seasonal forecasts – provided by INAM (National Institute of Meterology), INIA (National Institute for Agricultural Research), FAO (Food and Agricultural Organization), SADC (Southern African Development Community), the University of Zululand, or others – and test plots in rural extension to help family sector farmers make decisions in how to cope with drought (in other words, how to manage succession) and to live in a sustainable manner in a region of recurring drought.
- Make linkages with Latin American institutions (especially those in Peru and Brazil) which use ENSO to help plan for and manage drought.

The Next Step

Opportunities and challenges for planning with nature in managing drought in Mozambique have been presented here. To take full advantage of the opportunities, the challenges must be addressed in a substantial and meaningful way. Successfully using seasonal forecasts to manage the risks of drought will require action to overcome institutional weaknesses and fill knowledge gaps.

The weakness and gaps addressed in this section have been discussed in detail. Increasing institutional capacities and conducting further research are necessary for achieving this study's goal, which is to develop a risk management approach for managing drought in Mozambique. Thus, the final step of this study must be carried out by the government of Mozambique, its institutions and the NGO community.

To aid in this process, the following action plan has been developed for Mozambique, to be implemented at the national level. The objectives of the action plan are to fill knowledge gaps, improve the institutional capacity to use seasonal forecasting in managing the risks of drought, and ultimately ensure a pro-active local response to drought. With the exception of one step, the time frame is approximately two years.

Activity	Time Frame	Potential Lead Agency	Outcomes
1. Contact major development organization such as UNEP or UNDP to state intention of developing a risk management strategy for drought management.	1 month	MICOA, DPCCN or joint appeal from MICOA and DPCCN.	(a) ensure that all parties have a shared understanding of how to manage drought in Mozambique (b) establish Government of Mozambique as initiator and leader (c) ensure institutional and organizational support (d) have access to funding, information, expert advice and other facilities if required (e) completion of an action plan to improve drought management in Mozambique
2. Hold workshop addressing inter-disciplinary nature of drought and opportunities for reducing risks of drought.	6 months	MICOA, with participants from relevant institutions, including neighbouring countries, foreign experts and Latin American organizations using ENSO forecasts (eg Brazil, Peru).	(a) better understanding of the problem of drought at all levels (b) better understanding of risk management solutions to managing drought at all levels (c) list compiled of opportunities for reducing the risks associated with drought (d) outline of a strategy and time line for further action (e) division of responsibilities between relevant organizations (f) consideration of various recommendations, including those made in this study
3. Research in key areas of drought prediction and drought management.	1 year or more (steps 3 & 4 carried out concurrently)	Various agencies depending on task, including INAM, INIA, Ministry of Agriculture, MICOA and others.	(a) improved seasonal forecasting for Mozambique (b) documentation of traditional coping strategies which existed or are currently used (c) impact of these strategies (d) how traditional strategies could be improved or restored (e) development of improved traditional or new crops (f) development of new coping strategies
4. Infrastructure improvements in some key areas, notably communication.	1 year or more (steps 3 & 4 carried out concurrently)	Various agencies involved in drought management, such as MICOA, INAM, INIA, Ministry of Agriculture, DPCCN and others.	(a) improvements to physical communication links, such as telephone systems, the internet or roads (b) improvements in the capacity of institutions to exchange information in a timely, accurate and open manner both internally and externally (c) outcomes could result in improved monitoring of drought conditions, improved extension services and better communication of forecasts, warnings and advice to rural communities

5. Increase local level capacity to manage drought.	5 to 10 years	MICOA, DPCCN.	(a) ensure that national action will have a local response (b) improved communication between national and local level institutions (c) rebuilding of local institutions and increasing their capacity to implement drought management plans (d) reestablishment of traditional crops, or introduction of improved crops (e) restocking of animal herds where appropriate (f) use of risk management livelihood strategies (g) increased capacity in other areas
6. Workshop to assess advances and progress.	4 months	Agency which has assumed coordination role in 2 (e).	(a) detailed strategy covering all aspects of a risk management approach to drought management in Mozambique at the national and local levels

All of the above steps will involve mobilizing funds and other resources from the government of Mozambique or the international donor community. This will involve writing proposals, lobbying and other approaches. While adequate funding has been identified as a major barrier for most institutions in this study, the idea of a risk management approach to drought management should help to mobilize funding and other resources from the international donor community. However, in the absence of funding, there will remain a need to focus on these issues.

If the above steps (or the steps of some other action plan) are carried out collaboratively between Mozambican institutions and NGOs, experts in the field or consultants, the country's institutional capacity could be improved significantly. Ideally, the collaborative completion of such an action plan would not only result in a successful risk management plan for managing drought in Mozambique, but also strengthen functioning institutions' ability to direct, implement and manage.

CONCLUSIONS

This chapter has demonstrated that a risk management strategy for managing drought in Mozambique is possible. It has also proposed that this will be a more efficient and effective way of managing drought. The scientific basis for such a strategy exists and has been described. The institutional capacity to plan for drought does not exist at present, although this human side to the problem can be developed.

More specifically, the study has developed the exposure assessment and control option components of a drought assessment and management model. It has determined that ENSO teleconnections can be used in predicting drought in certain parts of Mozambique, a poor and fragile country exposed to recurring drought. It has further determined that present drought management strategies are either not sustainable or not feasible in Mozambique, and therefore an adaptive, holistic approach to managing drought has been developed.

This study has also determined that all institutions required to manage drought using this model do not at present exist. Furthermore, of the relevant institutions that do exist, many do not have the capacity to perform their respective functions. However, with further research and action in certain areas institutions can be built and institutional capacity can be increased, meaning that planning with nature in managing drought in Mozambique is not only possible, it is also plausible.

ENDNOTES

1. The definition of drought used in this study is "when precipitation, soil moisture, atmospheric moisture and evaporation and evapotranspiration rates are at levels that reduce crop yields to such an extent as to cause increased hardship on a given population, in particular rural subsistence farmers".

2. Two wars have been fought in Mozambique's recent history. The war of liberation was fought from 1964 to 1974. A second war was fought between governing FRELIMO and RENAMO, a Rhodesian, then South African sponsored, and in later years locally supported guerilla army, from the late 1970s and ended in 1992. This second war was fought throughout the country and caused immense hardship for the rural population.

3. This means that the models are tested against actual climate records not used in the development of the models.

4. Except where noted, the terms sustainability, stability, productivity and equitability are used according to the definitions of Conway (1991), and are discussed later in this chapter.

REFERENCES

Atlas Geográfico. 1986. Maputo: Minesterio da Educação, Republica Popular de Moçambique.

Baker, S.R. 1996: Regulating and Managing Risk: Impact of Subjectivity on Objectivity. In *Handbook for Environmental Risk Decision Making*, chapter 6. CRC Press Inc.

Cane, M.A., Eshel, G. and Buckland, R.W. 1994: Forecasting Zimbabwean maize yields using eastern equatorial pacific sea surface temperature. *Nature* 370, 204-205.

Comeau. 1996: *Bridging the Gap: From Disaster Relief to Long-term Development*. Major Paper. University of Guelph.

Conway, G. 1991: *Sustainability in agricultural development: trade-offs with productivity, stability and equitability*. Paper presented at 11th Annual AFSR/E Symposium, Michigan, Oct. 5-10, 1991.

Ellis, J. 1994: Climate variability and complex ecosystem dynamics: implications for pastoral development. In I. Scoones (ed.), *Living with Uncertainty: New Directions in Pastoral Development in Africa*. New York: Intermediate Technology Publications.

Frederiksen, H.D. 1992: *Drought planning and water efficiency implications in water resource management*. World Bank Technical Paper No 185.

Glantz, M.H. 1991: Introduction. In M.H. Glantz, R.W. Katz and N. Nichols (eds.), *Teleconnections Linking Worldwide Climate Anomalies*. New York: Cambridge University Press.

Hanlon, J. 1986: *Beggar your Neighbours: Apartheid Power in Southern Africa*. Bloomington: Indiana University Press.

Harwood, J., Heifner, D., Coble, K. and Perry, J. 1996: Strategies for a new risk management environment. *Agricultural Outlook*, October 1996, 24-30.

Jury, M.R. 1995: A review of research on ocean-atmosphere interactions and South African climate variability. *South African Journal of Science*, 91, 289-294.

Jury, M.R., Pathack, B., Rautenbach, C. and VanHeerden, J. 1996: Drought over South Africa and Indian Ocean sst: statistical and GCM results. *The Global Atmosphere and Ocean System*, 4, 47-63.

Kiladis, G.N. and Diaz, H.F. 1989: Global climatic anomalies associated with extremes in the southern oscillation. *Journal of Climate*, 2, 1069-1090.

Latif, M., Sterl, A., Maier-Reimer, E., and Junge, M.M. 1992: Structure and predictability of the El Niño/southern oscillation phenomenon in a coupled ocean-atmosphere general circulation model. *Journal of Climate*, 6, 700-708.

Lindesay, J.A. 1988: South African rainfall, the southern oscillation and a southern hemisphere semi-annual cycle. *Journal of Climatology*, 8, 17-30.

Lindesay, J.A. and Vogel, C.H. 1990: Historical evidence for southern oscillation-southern African rainfall relationships. *International Journal of Climatology*, 10, 679-689.

Matarira, C. 1990: Drought over Zimbabwe in a regional and global context. *International Journal of Climatology*, 10, 609-625.

Matarira, C. and Unganai, L. 1995: *A rainfall prediction model for southern Africa based on the southern oscillation phenomena*. SADC/FAO Early Warning System technical handbook. Harare, Zimbabwe.

National Oceanic and Atmospheric Administration (NOAA). 1994.

Rasmusson, E.M. and Carpenter, T.H. 1982: Variations in tropical sea surface temperature and surface wind fields associated with the southern oscillation. *Monthly Weather Review*, 110, 354- 384.

Rasmusson, E.M. and Wallace, J.M. 1983: Meteorological aspects of the El Niño/southern oscillation. *Science*, 222, 1195-1202.

Rojas, O. 1997: Agrometeorologist, Food and Agriculture Organisation (FAO) and Instituto Nacional de Investigação Agronomica (INIA). Personal Communication.

Ropelewski, C.F. and Jones, P.D. 1987: An extension of the Tahiti-Darwin southern oscillation index. *Monthly Weather Review*, 115, 2161-2165.

Savory, A. 1988: *Holistic Resource Management*. Covelo: Island Press.

Trenberth, K.E. 1991: General characteristics of El Niño Southern-Oscillation. In M.H. Glantz, R.W. Katz and N. Nichols (eds.), *Teleconnections Linking Worldwide Climate Anomalies*, Chapter Two. New York: Cambridge University Press.

UCAR. 1994: *Reports to the nation on our changing planet: El Niño and climate prediction*. Boulder: UCAR.

Wilhite, D. 1993a: The enigma of drought. In D. Wilhite (ed.), *Drought Assessment, Management and Planning: Theory and Case Studies*, Chapter One. Boston: Kluwer Academic Publishers.

Wilhite, D. 1993b: Planning for drought: a methodology. In D. Wilhite (ed.), *Drought Assessment, Management and Planning: Theory and Case Studies*, Chapter Six. Boston: Kluwer Academic Publishers.

World Bank. 1995: *Toward environmentally sustainable development in sub-Saharan Africa: a World Bank agenda*. Draft for discussion.

World Bank. 1996: *World Development Report, 1996*. Toronto: Oxford University Press.

World Food Programme (WFP). 1995: *Mozambique in War and Peace*. Rome: World Food Programme.

World Food Programme (WFP). 1996: *WFP Annual Report, 1995: Ending the Inheritance of Hunger*. Rome: World Food Programme.

INDEX

arsenic, 223, 226
artisanal fisheries, 135, 140, 142
artisanal mining, 196, 206, 216
assisted land purchase, 30

Bakiga, 42
Barberton, 199, 200, 203, 210
bean production, 42
belief systems, 94
bio-diversity, 61, 63, 64, 65
biomass, 171, 173
birds, 102, 104
blasting, 181
botanical conservation, 63, 65
botanical surveys, 91, 96
Brachystegia, 66
Braun-Blanquet approach, 65, 68
Braun-Blanquet Scale, 68, 72
brick making, 182, 188, 189, 191
building materials, 128
building standards, 120
canonical correspondence analysis, 69

Canteen Koppie, 202
capacity building, 122, 132
CARE, 238
cash crops, 149, 150
catch limits, 139
central custom milling, 230
centralization, 28
chiefs, 25, 160
Chinamwali, 29, 95
Chirisa Safari Area, 65
CIAT, 41
cichlid, 135

Domasi River, 96, 97
donors, 127
drainage of wetlands, 240
Drama as Technology Transfer Project, 43
drama, 41, 46, 48
drought, 167
drought management strategies, 258
drought management, 251, 255, 261, 262, 263, 264
drought prediction, 255
dry separation, 231
dust emissions, 184
Dzalanyama Forest Reserve, 110

Eastern and Central Africa Bean Research Network, 42
ecogeographic surveys, 63
ecological zones, 63
economic development, 5
economic motive, 9
ecosystems, 235, 258, 259
ecotourism, 238
education of farmers, 111
egenvector technique, 69
Ekikambi, 43, 52
El Nino, 255, 256
electricity supply, 169
elephants, 80
eluvial mining, 228
energy resources, 167
energy supply, 167
ENSO, 255, 256
environment, 16, 120
environmental degradation, 10, 14, 15, 63, 67, 89
environmental effects, 222
environmental impact, 179, 182, 187, 188, 189, 216
environmental issue working groups, 122

freehold tenure, 12, 17, 23

gear restrictions, 139
gender, 92, 95, 186
gender roles, 43
genetic resources, 63, 64
geology, 66, 218
Gokwe, 78
gold mining, 196, 199, 200, 203, 215
Gong Gong, 196, 197, 198, 202, 208, 210
gorillas, 238
grassland, 76
grassroots structures for diffusion of science and technology, 241
Green paper on Minerals and Mining Policy for South Africa, 204
group land acquisition, 31
Gwembe Valley, 167, 168

habitat conservation, 107
habitat loss, 107
handicrafts, 211
hazard land, 118, 128
hierarchical cluster analysis, 69, 72
holistic approach, 267
holistic resource management, 258, 259, 260
household food production, 9
human power, 171
human resource development, 123
human rights, 9, 191
hunger, 174
hunting, 102, 103, 105
Hwange National Park, 65

ICRAF, 41, 238
illegal mining, 200
illiteracy, 111

Ndere Dance Troupe, 41
neighbourhood committees, 31
networks for science and technology diffusion, 237
NGOs, 122, 127, 238, 245, 267
Noetstaller, Richard, 206
noise pollution, 184, 185
non-renewable resources, 215
nurseries, 100

objectives of land reform, 8
occupational health, 184, 219, 223
occupational health and safety, 203
occupational safety, 185, 228
oil spills, 184
open access, 34
open access regime, 35
open-access fisheries, 136, 145
overcapitalization, 136
overcrowding, 14, 27
over-population, 10
Overseas Development Institute, 13

participatory aquatic resource management, 142
participatory democracy, 241
Participatory Fisheries Management Programme (PFMP), 144
paternalism, 17
pathway analyses, 226
physical resources inventory programmes, 62
physiognomic classification, 67, 69
phytosociological classification, 67
planning for drought, 263
planning systems, 1
planning tools, 2
plant associations, 61
plant resource utilization, 91

quarry mining, 181
quarry operations, 183
quotas, 139

racism, 14
rainfall, 259, 266
rainfall variability, 256, 257
Ralushai, Prof, 210
RDP, 210
reafforestation, 112
recycling of waste, 232
redistribution, 6, 7, 8, 10, 12, 14, 15
registration of land, 28, 29
regulation of fishing activity, 138
regulatory techniques, 138
research stations, 153
reserves, 15, 153
resettlement, 11, 15, 167
resettlement schemes, 17
resource-based economy, 1
resource inventories, 62
Resource Management, 110
resource management regimes, 33
resource use, 63
resources utilization, 13
retort, 230
ridging, 154
risk assessment, 252
risk management, 252, 253, 254, 263, 266, 269
Rukuni Commission of Enquiry, 17
rural development, 174
Rural Development Institute, 247
rural employment, 12
rural living standards, 5
Rural Planning and Development Initiative, 267

rural unemployment, 13

savanna woodland, 71
Savory, Allan, 256
science and technology content, 240
science and technology diffusion, 235
science and technology dissemination, 244
SDP, 121
seasonal forecasts, 268
Secretary for Production and Environmental Protection, 240
security of tenure, 7
Sengwa Wildlife Research, 65
settlement relocation, 167
sewer system, 118
Shabangu, Susan, 205
shared ownership, 34
shifting cultivation, 36
Shire Highlands, 23
Shire River, 144, 145
shopping areas, 119
shrubland, 75
siltation, 111
small farmers, 6, 16
small farms, 7, 16
small mining, 211
small-scale fishers, 140, 141
small-scale miners, 210, 216
small-scale mining, 2, 177, 178, 195, 196, 204, 215
smallholder agriculture, 155, 161
smallholder farmers, 162, 163, 173
smallholder farming, 161
smallholder farms, 164
smallholder tobacco, 151
social behaviour, 43, 52
social eco-technological system, 170, 174